"*Scarlett* is both a deeply intimate family history as well as a candid consideration of the history of slavery and racism in the United States. Perhaps more importantly, *Scarlett* demonstrates the ways that these two histories are inextricably bound for American families on all sides of the color line. Much in the tradition of Edward Ball's *Slaves in the Family*, *Scarlett* faces a difficult history head-on, showing how slavery continues to reverberate in the lives of all Americans."

—JASON R. YOUNG, author of *Rituals of Resistance: African Atlantic Religion in Kongo and the Lowcountry South in the Era of Slavery*

"Many of us who came of age in the bruising, suffocating silence of an enslaver family are awakening to how this silence cripples us all and deeply endangers our nation. . . . Leslie Stainton's *Scarlett* awakens us as it issues its summons, both elegant and heartbreaking. While refusing to look away from her Georgia cotton-empire family's many racist sins and their effects on the present, Stainton's exquisite writing and personal transformation shines a sure and steady light for others who would, like her, answer those summonses that our long-stifled grandmothers issued to us in childhood."

—KAREN BRANAN, author of *The Family Tree: A Lynching in Georgia, a Legacy of Secrets, and My Search for the Truth*

"Leslie Stainton 'gets it.' This modern-day Fanny Kemble didn't marry into the slavocracy of coastal Georgia; she inherited its wealth, its mythology, and its 'Scarlett' letters. Her lyrical and rewarding book, rich in historical detail, recounts with candor a brave journey of self-discovery. Stainton's deeply personal odyssey links present to past and dares other privileged Americans with troubling family roots to do the hard emotional and archival work of confronting their real ancestral story. This way lies healing, for self and society."

—PETER H. WOOD, author of *Black Majority: Race, Rice, and Rebellion in South Carolina, 1670–1740*

"With history again being weaponized, it makes perfect timing for the release of Leslie Stainton's vital story."

—JOSEPH MCGILL JR., founder of the Slave Dwelling Project and coauthor, with Herb Frazer, of *Sleeping with the Ancestors: How I Followed the Footprints of Slavery*

"Beautiful, elegiac, and urgent, *Scarlett* resonates with tidal force. Leslie Stainton takes us on a search for the truth about her enslaving Georgia ancestors, the Scarletts, and through a reckoning with the myths and distortions of their painful history, from *Gone with the Wind* to today. In her family as in the American nation, the truth about slavery and segregation lay buried under denial, delusion, and pride. Pulling us all into its depths, this is a memoir that manages to be both bracingly honest and profoundly hopeful."

—WILLIAM G. THOMAS III, author of *A Question Of Freedom: The Families Who Challenged Slavery from the Nation's Founding to the Civil War*

"This timely and powerful book . . . sheds important new light on the evils of historic slavery and its persistent and profound present-day impacts on all Americans. With searing detail, Leslie Stainton traces her ancestors' complicity in the barbarous practices of buying, selling, hunting, and violating enslaved men, women, and children. *Scarlett* exemplifies the kind of candor and courage we so urgently need if we are ever to undo the cruelties and lies of racism and heal as a nation."

—THOMAS NORMAN DEWOLF, author of *Inheriting the Trade* and coauthor of *Gather at the Table*

"An unflinching look at one Southern family's ties to slavery, *Scarlett* is a richly wrought portrait of how the complex legacy of enslavement echoes down to today. Leslie Stainton has given us a remarkable, brave, and beautifully written book."

—SCOTT ELLSWORTH, author of *Midnight on the Potomac: The Last Year of the Civil War, the Lincoln Assassination, and the Rebirth of America*

"Leslie Stainton's beautifully written and heartfelt personal memoir . . . so intertwined with American slavery, should be read by all those interested in the complicated nature of America's racial past. As William Faulkner wrote, the past is neither dead nor truly past."

—JONATHAN DANIEL WELLS, author of *The Kidnapping Club: Wall Street, Slavery, and Resistance on the Eve of the Civil War*

"Stainton is a talented storyteller, gradually revealing how this white Georgia family's history is interwoven with stories of enslaving and what the lives of those enslaved persons were like."

—PHOEBE KILBE, coauthor with Betty Kilby Baldwin, of *Cousins: Connected through Slavery, a Black Woman and a White Woman Discover their Past—and Each Other*

Scarlett

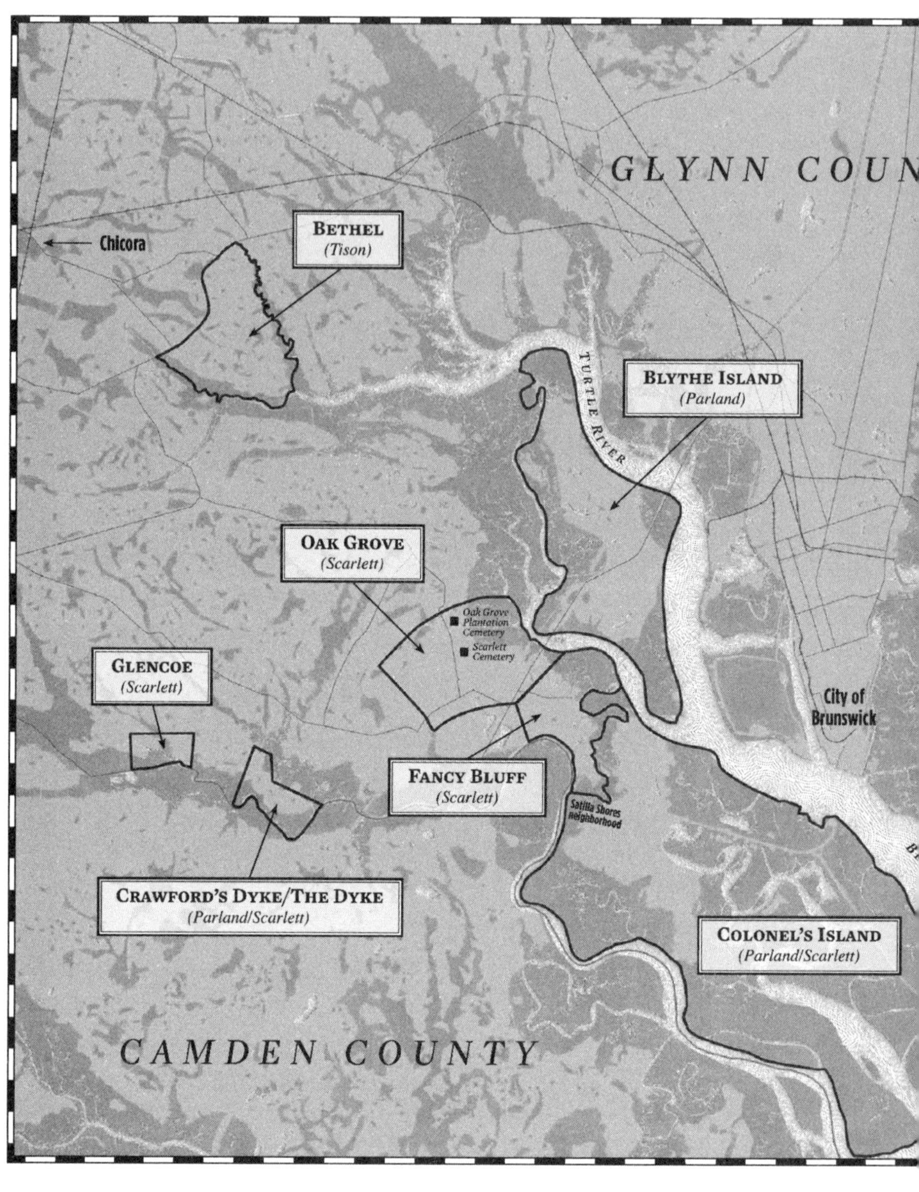

GLYNN COUN
Chicora
BETHEL
(Tison)
TURTLE RIVER
BLYTHE ISLAND
(Parland)
OAK GROVE
(Scarlett)
Oak Grove Plantation Cemetery
Scarlett Cemetery
GLENCOE
(Scarlett)
City of Brunswick
FANCY BLUFF
(Scarlett)
Satilla Shores Neighborhood
CRAWFORD'S DYKE/THE DYKE
(Parland/Scarlett)
COLONEL'S ISLAND
(Parland/Scarlett)
CAMDEN COUNTY

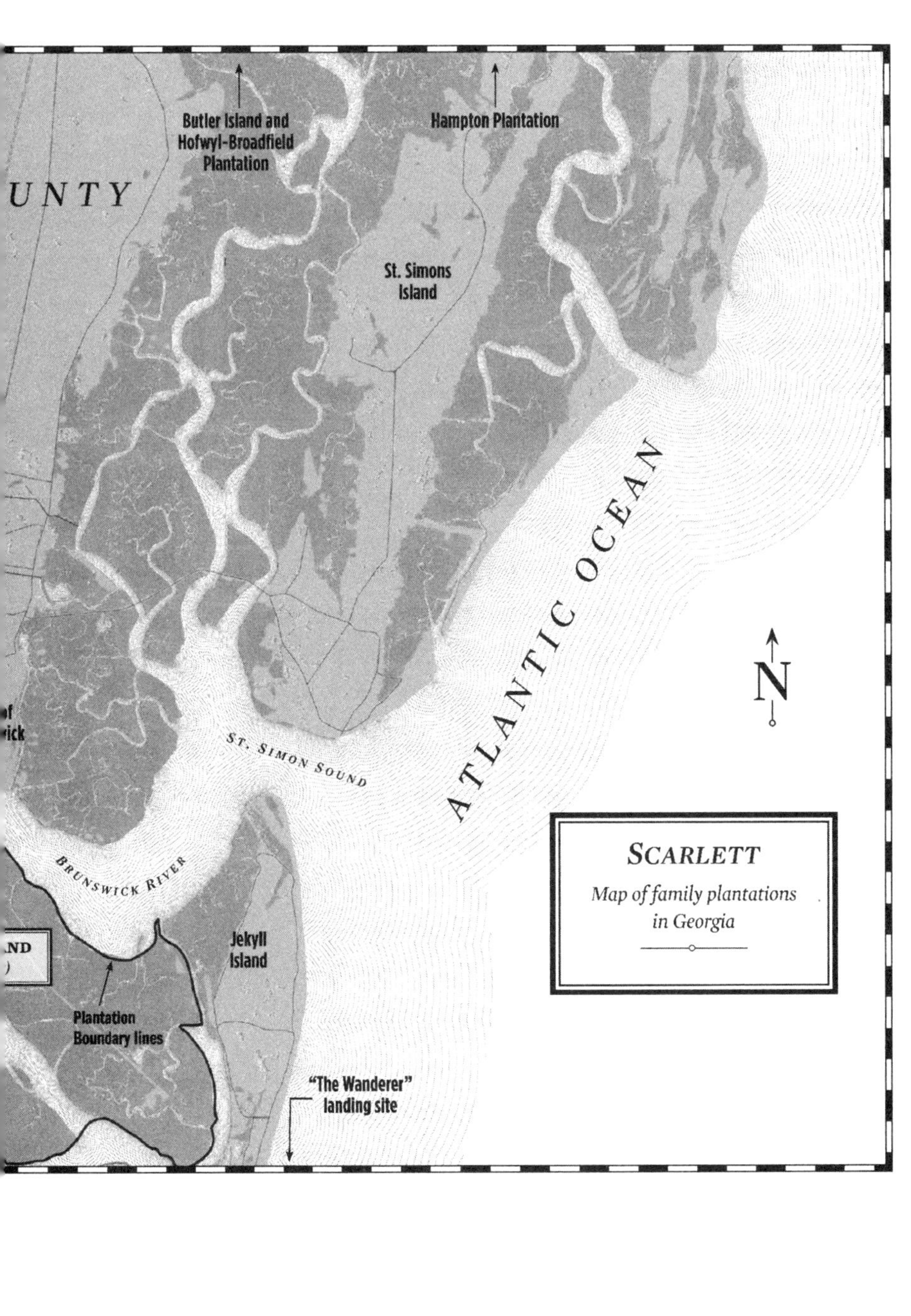
Butler Island and
Hofwyl-Broadfield
Plantation
Hampton Plantation
UNTY
St. Simons
Island
ATLANTIC OCEAN
N
ST. SIMON SOUND
BRUNSWICK RIVER
Jekyll
Island
Plantation
Boundary lines
"The Wanderer"
landing site
SCARLETT
Map of family plantations
in Georgia

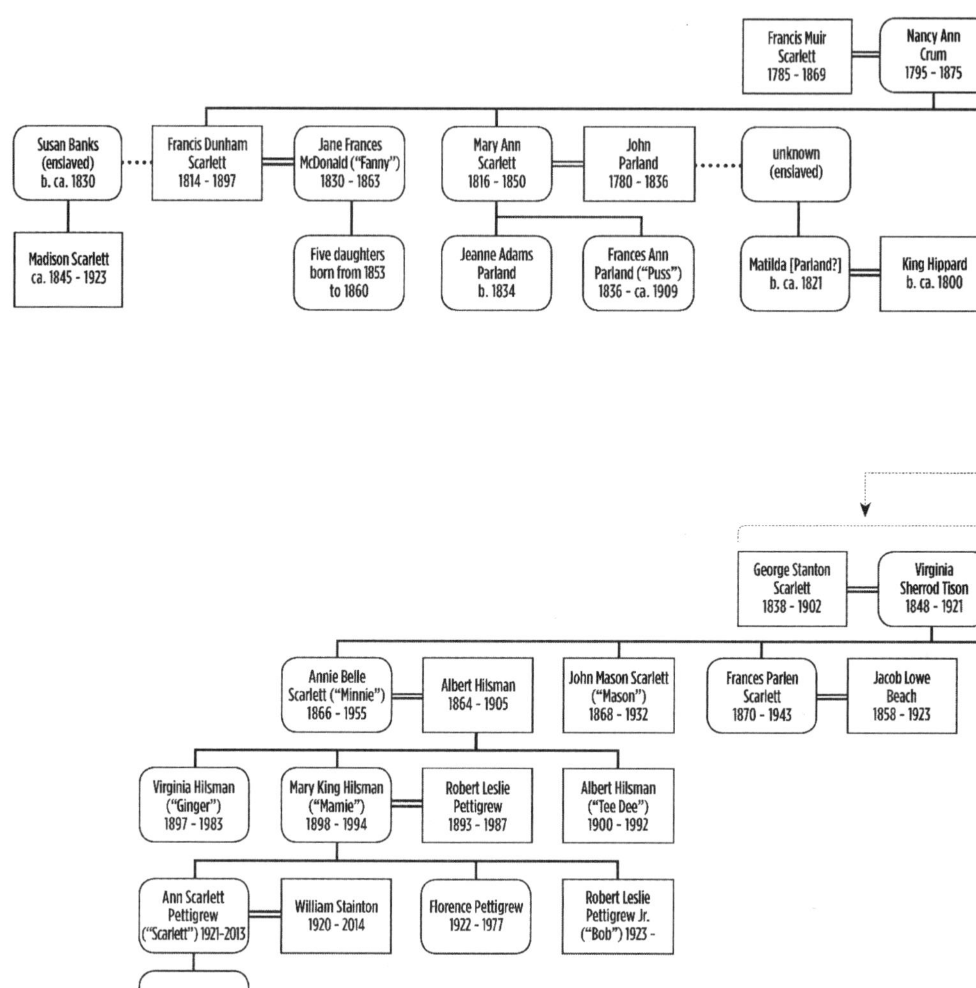

Francis Muir Scarlett 1785 - 1869
Nancy Ann Crum 1795 - 1875
Susan Banks (enslaved) b. ca. 1830
Francis Dunham Scarlett 1814 - 1897
Jane Frances McDonald ("Fanny") 1830 - 1863
Mary Ann Scarlett 1816 - 1850
John Parland 1780 - 1836
unknown (enslaved)
Madison Scarlett ca. 1845 - 1923
Five daughters born from 1853 to 1860
Jeanne Adams Parland b. 1834
Frances Ann Parland ("Puss") 1836 - ca. 1909
Matilda [Parland?] b. ca. 1821
King Hippard b. ca. 1800
George Stanton Scarlett 1838 - 1902
Virginia Sherrod Tison 1848 - 1921
Annie Belle Scarlett ("Minnie") 1866 - 1955
Albert Hilsman 1864 - 1905
John Mason Scarlett ("Mason") 1868 - 1932
Frances Parlen Scarlett 1870 - 1943
Jacob Lowe Beach 1858 - 1923
Virginia Hilsman ("Ginger") 1897 - 1983
Mary King Hilsman ("Mamie") 1898 - 1994
Robert Leslie Pettigrew 1893 - 1987
Albert Hilsman ("Tee Dee") 1900 - 1992
Ann Scarlett Pettigrew ("Scarlett") 1921-2013
William Stainton 1920 - 2014
Florence Pettigrew 1922 - 1977
Robert Leslie Pettigrew Jr. ("Bob") 1923 -
Leslie Stainton 1955 -

SCARLETT FAMILY TREE*

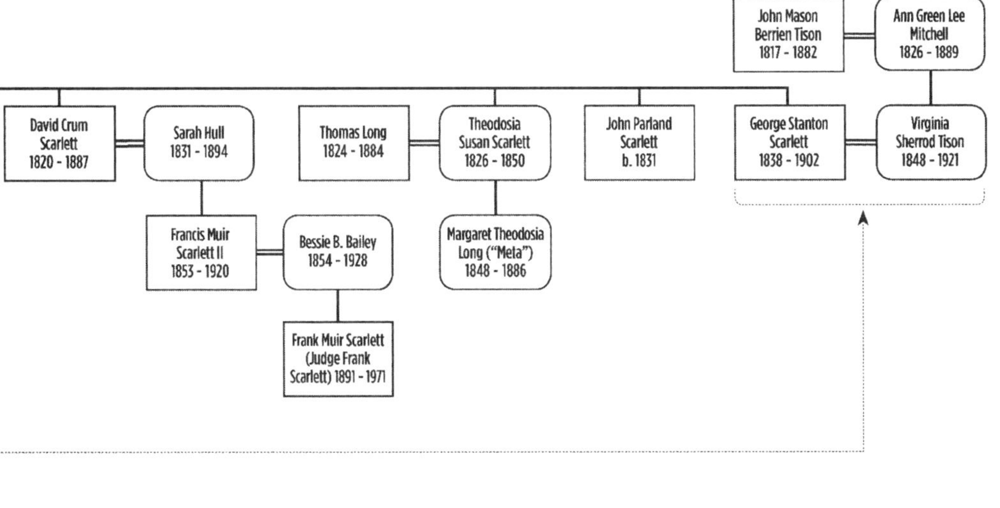

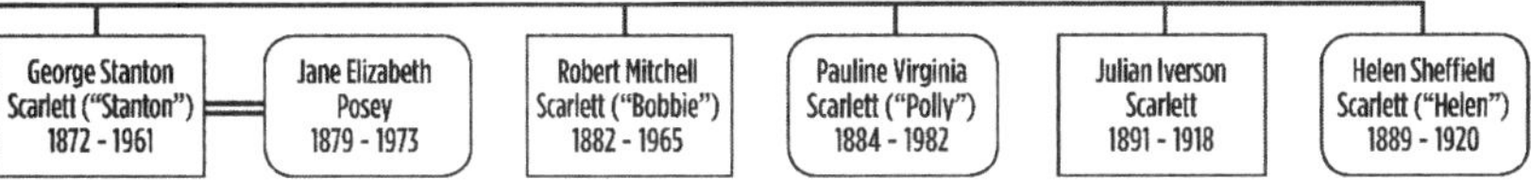

Note: Some family members and descendants have been omitted for clarity.

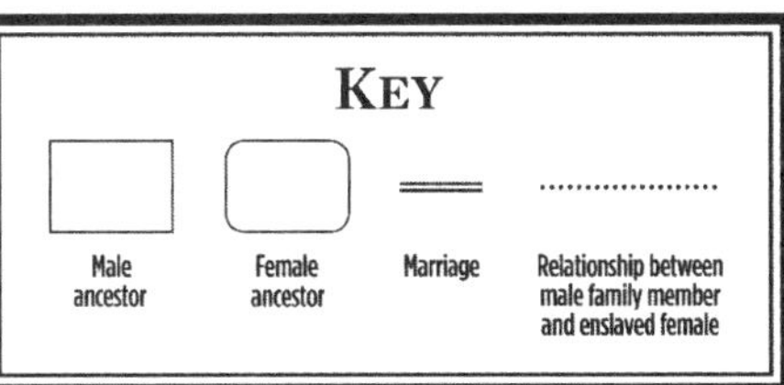

Scarlett

Slavery's Enduring Legacy in an American Family

LESLIE STAINTON

Potomac Books
An imprint of the University of Nebraska Press

Acknowledgments for the use of copyrighted material appear on page xv, which constitutes an extension of the copyright page.

 Potomac Books is an imprint of the University of Nebraska Press.
Manufactured in the United States of America.

Library of Congress Control Number: 2025013228

Designed and set in Minion Pro by A. Shahan.

For

Nancy Hippard Cahoon
Margie Hippard Clinch
the late Avedell Grant
Gertrude Hippard Maxwell
Edward Wood
and their families—
then and now

and in memory of

Ahmaud Arbery and Fricie Griffin

CONTENTS

ILLUSTRATIONS

ACKNOWLEDGMENTS

This book is a long-overdue effort to repair some portion of the damage inflicted on people of color by my family over the course of centuries. I offer it in humility and sorrow, knowing that nothing can repair the atrocities of slavery and racism in the United States, and in the hope that the story I tell here does not inflict further harm. Any missteps, oversights, and errors are mine alone.

I am grateful to those who so graciously shared their histories and experiences with me and whose generosity has been such a blessing. I am grateful, as well, to the countless other people who have contributed in ways I may have overlooked here. I am indebted to all of you.

In particular, I am grateful to the descendants of Matilda and King Hippard, whom I have come to know and love: Gertrude and the late Gilbert Maxwell, Margie Clinch, Nancy Cahoon, Wanda Cahoon, Brenda Bailey, the late Johnny Hippard, the late Avedell Grant, and their extended families. I am indebted to the collective Hippard-Bell-Blue families for so warmly welcoming me to their reunions in 2011 and 2019.

My thanks go to Edward Wood, a descendant of Madison and Julia Tison Scarlett, who so kindly shared documents, stories, and insights into our shared Scarlett ancestry and my family's crimes.

Members of Coming to the Table and the Slave Dwelling Project provided invaluable resources, insights, and support. Special thanks to Joe McGill, Tom DeWolf, and Prinny Anderson and to all members of both organizations for their persistent efforts to confront slavery's ongoing impact on American life and lives. Thanks go to Karen Branan, Kwesi DeGraft-Hanson, Michael McDonald, and the late Dave Pettee for their help in unearthing critical information about the Scarletts. I am equally grateful to Sarah Eisner, Lotte Lieb Dula, Phoebe Kilby, and Josiah "Jazz" Watts for their help in my quest to make tangible reparations to the people and communities harmed by the Scarletts.

Jamie Bracewell and Bracewell Charters allowed me to retrace the probable route by boat that Matilda and King Hippard and their companions took in 1862 as they sailed to freedom from the Scarletts. Carolyn Rock of Brockington Associates took me to visit her firm's archaeological digs on former John Parland land. She shared copious details about their discoveries and Parland's legacy and responded promptly to my every inquiry. Kathleen Marcaccio and her fellow Windies let me join them on their visit to Atlanta and Margaret Mitchell haunts and gave me new insights into Mitchell's complexities.

Without Amy Hedrick and her indispensable research into Glynn County genealogy, her many contacts in the region, and her inexhaustible website, glynngen.com, *Scarlett* would not be the book it is. My debt is beyond measure.

I am grateful to archivists Andrew Marroquin of the Jekyll Island Visitors Center; Don Evans, who helped me navigate the vast holdings of the Georgia Archives; Judy Buchanan and D. Harland Harris of the Bryan-Lang Historical Library in Woodbine, Georgia; and director W. Todd Groce and the staff of the Georgia Historical Society in Savannah.

For their many detailed answers to my questions, I thank historians Eric Calonius, Abigail Cooper, Scott Ellsworth, Lester Monts, William G. Thomas III, Peter H. Wood, and Jason Young. For their editorial insights and ideas, I thank Waverly Fitzgerald, Rachel Howard, Stuart Horwitz, Emma Sedlak, Lynn Stegner, Sara Talpos, and Anne Frances Wysocki. My longtime friend and fellow writer Helen Sheehy has been with this project from the start, and I am, as ever, in her debt. Hank Meijer, Carol Mann, and Natasha Saje were indispensable in getting *Scarlett* into print. Mary Bisbee-Beek, my inveterate book Sherpa, has played a critical and ever-encouraging role in the publication process. Press director Jane Ferreyra and editor Taylor Gilreath, together with the University of Nebraska Press and Potomac Books team, have been a constant and welcome marvel—my deep thanks.

My thanks go to Don Hammond and Beth Hay for their graphic contributions to *Scarlett*, to Kristen Weber for her web expertise, to Jennifer Dix for her genealogical skills, and to Howard Saulles for his technological support and endless patience.

Without the healing ministries of Paul Frolick and Paul MacMahon, I would not have been able to complete this book. My heart is full. I am also grateful to Mike Biddle, Ewa Bienick, Timothy Egan, Taz Faqqouseh, Terri and Alan Mellow, J. P. Purtell, and Jay Winegarden for their care and encouragement in difficult times and to Julie Woodward for her calming presence.

Lastly, love and thanks go to my family: to my cousins Sheron Adicks Miller, James Miller, the late Clarke Adickes, and Lisa and the late George Liounakas for their hospitality in Georgia; and to my cousins Ginger Hamby and the late Scarlett Renze and my brother, Bill, and sister, Mary, for their unflagging belief in the need to expose the truth about our family's history. May they be an example to other Americans wrestling with this history. My stepchildren, Jeremy and Julia Whiting, have been welcome companions on several research trips to Georgia, and I extend my thanks and love to them and their families. Their father, my husband, Steve, has kept me going throughout. To him—my blessing and my love—everything.

ABBREVIATIONS

ARCHIVES

GA	Georgia Archives, Morrow
GHS	Georgia Historical Society, Savannah
Griffin Appeal	*Fricie Griffin v. State*, Georgia Supreme Court Case File A-24559.pdf
Griffin Trial	*The State v. Fricie Griffin*, Brief of Evidence, Testimony Felony Cases, Glynn County Courthouse, 1:72
PP	Parland Estate Papers, Glynn County Probate Court files
SA	Scarlett Archive, in the Scarlett-Tison family collection, Georgia Historical Society

PEOPLE

FAP	Frances Ann Parland
FDS	Francis Dunham (Frank) Scarlett
FMS	Francis Muir Scarlett
GSS	George Stanton Scarlett
JAPK	Jean Adams Parland King
JFMS	Jane Frances (Fanny) McDonald Scarlett
JP	John Parland
MKHP	Mary King Hilsman Pettigrew
RLP	Robert Leslie Pettigrew
RLP Jr.	Robert Leslie Pettigrew Jr.
VTS	Virginia Tison Scarlett

NOTE ON LANGUAGE

When quoting directly, this publication maintains original language that depicts beliefs and perspectives of previous eras (including negative stereotypes of women, persons of color, and ethnic groups) or insulting and offensive language that was once commonplace. Wherever possible, *Scarlett* seeks to avoid the term *slave* to describe persons held in bondage. Except in quoted material, the term *Black* is capitalized to convey a shared sense of history, identity, and community among people who identify as Black. When writing in my own voice, I seek to use language more consistent with twenty-first-century usage, recognizing that linguistic practices continue to evolve.

Scarlett

BEFORE

In the hush of a late winter afternoon in Brunswick, Georgia, a man sets off on a run. This particular day happens to be a Sunday in the second month of the year 2020, but it could be any day, for humans have inhabited this stretch of coast for thousands of years. When the Philadelphia botanist William Bartram visited this part of North America in the late eighteenth century, he found trading paths cut by Indigenous people and the remains of Spanish forts. He slept in English towns and was rowed through rivers by "sooty sons of Afric" who had been brought here on ships with names like *Christ the Redeemer* and *Trinity* and *Blessed*. As the Africans rowed they sang, and to Bartram it seemed they were "forgetting their bondage."

By the time Bartram visited the young colony of Georgia, Quakers in his native Pennsylvania were publishing tracts decrying the enslavement of human beings, and their views were spreading; the state would soon become the first in the nation to abolish the system. Even Bartram, who bought and sold a woman of color shortly before embarking on his journey south, thought the enslaved people he encountered in Georgia and neighboring colonies were the "most abject creatures we can possibly imagine."

His contemporary John Wesley, who lived and preached in Savannah in the 1730s, believed it would be better for this portion of the American coast to be sunk into the sea than for it to "be cultivated at so high a price as the violation of justice, mercy, and truth. It would be better that none should labor there, that the work should be left undone, than that myriads of innocent men should be murdered, and myriads more dragged into the basest slavery."

Of those myriads of innocent men, women, and children dragged into slavery, many also ran. Ran not because it gave them pleasure but because they were desperate. Ran together and alone, with babies on their backs and inside their bodies, through fields and creeks, swamps and woods, along secret paths and hidden routes. Praying for luck or darkness. Grateful for rain, clouds, fingernail moon, no moon. Running toward hope and away from hoofbeats. Away from shouts, guns, dogs. From people—my people. Fleeing my kind.

In the hush of a late winter afternoon in Brunswick, Georgia, a man sets off on a run. I see him now: darting in and out of shadows, down the road, across the highway, into the woods. Pine, cypress, laurel. Through canopies of gray moss, past salt marshes and mud flats, beyond the trees where egrets nest. He turns, pauses, breathes. Crosses the road, vanishes onto a sun-dappled street. Now there is only ocean left, only sea: the one he crossed all those years ago with his one body. Singular, precious, stolen.

WANTED TO PURCHASE—A GANG OF ONE HUNDRED NEGROES, for which the Cash will be paid.

F. M. SCARLETT, Oak Grove, Glynn Co., Georgia, June 15, 1837

PART 1

Myth

1

MIDNIGHT

Quiet at last. Just the flutter of leaves in the breeze outside and the sound of my companions unfolding their sleeping gear. We've arranged our belongings so as not to disturb the museum exhibit that occupies the room by day. A gardening basket in one corner. A pine table set, as if for breakfast, with two plates and a bowl. A massive brick hearth.

Except *hearth* isn't quite the right word, not here at least. Not inside this pine cabin on the Georgia coast, fifteen miles north of Brunswick. As I unzip the sleeping bag I've borrowed from my stepson, it occurs to me that nothing in this space is what it claims to be. Not the faux table setting or the curtained windows or the wicker chair or the narrow cot with the chenille spread and embroidered pillow in the pseudo-bedroom to my left and not the sign outside on the path to the door: "Servants Quarters."

I know the kind of scene we're meant to conjure: a plump Mammy in a kerchief standing at the fireplace, stirring a pot of something while children frolic on the floor behind her—the same pine floor where I've laid out my make-believe bed on top of a yoga mat, which, I now realize, does nothing to cushion my back against the hard wood planks.

It's been decades since I've come this close to roughing it. I spent the past two nights under a chintz duvet on a queen-sized canopy bed in an air-conditioned Savannah hotel room. Before heading south on I-95 today, I treated myself to lunch in the hotel restaurant, a restored eighteenth-century tavern. Glass of sauvignon blanc, locally sourced fried-green tomato sandwich with aioli, espresso.

I crawl inside the flannel interior of my camping gear and try to court sleep, but I'm distracted by my two companions. Joe's stretched out behind me on the floor, posting updates to his Facebook page. Prinny's half-asleep beside me, breathing softly. It's her tenth or eleventh overnight in a cabin, and she's got the drill down. Flashlight neatly positioned on a nearby chair, on top of her neatly folded clothes. Thick foam pad under her back.

I close my eyes and listen to the mournful pings of Joe's phone as he sends the last of his missives into the world. Then silence. The room goes dark. Just the three of us arrayed like mannequins on a moonlit stage set on the Georgia coast. This is why I came, isn't it? Except I can't get comfortable. Roll to one side, yank at my T-shirt, imagine I'm back home in Michigan with my husband.

"I don't know why I'm doing this," I snarled a week ago, as I stood over my open suitcase, fretting.

"You'll figure it out," he said.

But I haven't. Lying here, feigning sleep, my mind hurtles into its familiar spin cycle. What if I'm awake all night? What if I step on a snake on my way to the bathroom? There are rattlers on the plantation grounds, alligators in the marshes where they used to grow rice. Ticks. Spiders. Joe likes to tell about the time he woke in a cabin to find spiders crawling all over him. He's never seen a ghost on a sleepover, but spiders, yes. They terrify him.

"You have to visit these places to see what they endured," he said earlier tonight in a talk to docents inside the visitors' center of the plantation. He wore narrow, wire-rimmed glasses and a collarless white shirt under the thick blue wool uniform of a Union soldier. A dozen people, all white, mostly retirees, sat attentively in rows of plastic chairs. On the screen above his head, he unveiled slide after slide of the kinds of places he meant: weatherbeaten shacks in Tennessee, wooden cabins in South Carolina, a two-story brick tenement behind an urban mansion in North Carolina, attic rooms in New York and Pennsylvania.

"Because they hung in there," Joe said of the people who once lived in these spaces, "we're here today. African Americans. They acquiesced because of us, their descendants. Anything beyond acquiescence could be their death."

This morning's *Georgia Times-Union* had advertised his talk and our overnight stay, noting that, as a descendant of enslavers from the region, I'd be joining Joe McGill, founder of the Slave Dwelling Project, and Prinny Anderson, a white descendant of Thomas Jefferson, on the latest of Joe's sleepovers in a slave dwelling, this one at the Hofwyl-Broadfield State Historical Site in Glynn County. I was startled by the front-page coverage, the realization that, without meaning to, I had exposed my family—the distant cousins who don't return my texts or emails when I visit the area, the nameless person who planted a Confederate flag in front of the granite obelisk that marks my ancestors' cemetery in Brunswick. "Sleepover Puts Spotlight on Glynn's Slave-Holding Past," the *Times-Union* headline announced.

And now here I am, rolling onto my left side, scrunching the single pillow I've remembered to bring with me, wondering how long my bladder will hold out before I have to make my way in the dark with Prinny's flashlight to the bathroom that's been installed on the other side of the wall behind the fireplace, in another tiny space originally built to house as many as twelve people. Who knows what I'll trip over on my way there? I've learned to step gingerly in this part of the world. My grandmother, born in Brunswick in 1898, was taught as a child to kill any snake she found that wasn't poisonous and to call for an uncle with a gun whenever she spotted one that was. In her seventies, on a visit to the family homestead in the woods outside Brunswick, she nearly stepped on a diamondback one day as she was getting out of her car.

She loved this hardscrabble strip of Atlantic coastline, halfway between Jacksonville and Savannah. Although she and my grandfather retired to a small town in tidewater Virginia, she never reconciled herself to the place. "Virginia is as far north as I will ever go," she declared and pressed her tiny foot into the carpet as if to mark a line.

She had a bird's beaked nose and mouth and wore her hair in long, graying ropes looped around her skull. She dressed in brown or at most a drab olive. Much of the time she terrified me: the stern reminders to buckle my seatbelt, the drumbeat of her shoes climbing the stairs to inform me of yet another unwitting household infraction. The stories of ancestral hardship meant to show me how good I had it. The Scarlett O'Hara prettiness of what *life was like* before the war versus the shabbiness of what came after. Her own widowed mother, forced to open a boardinghouse and take in strangers to make ends meet.

Mary King Hilsman Pettigrew, my maternal grandmother—whom we called "Mamie." She's the reason I'm here tonight, twenty minutes up the highway from her birthplace. She's the one who insisted I know the kind of people I came from: strong people—strong women in particular. Like my grandmother herself, who knew more about roughing it than I'd ever learn. She spent twenty years living in the Caribbean with my Navy-officer grandfather, braving scorpions and malaria while raising three children. At the end of it all she only wanted more—more island sunsets and patois songs, more solitary rambles in the countryside searching for pre-Columbian relics. My grandmother, the excavator.

Except when it came to our family. She and her sisters devoted years to assembling the ancestral story, compiling photos, deciphering letters, filling in cemetery maps and genealogical charts. It was no secret we had "owned slaves," as they put it. But it wasn't something they dwelt on. "There are things we don't talk about," Mamie said briskly and often.

Little room in this scenario for what I'm doing tonight. My grandmother would have winced at this morning's front-page coverage. She and her sisters gave their share of interviews to the local press, but always with an emphasis on the salutary: the family patriarch, Francis Muir Scarlett, a penniless British immigrant who made his way to Georgia as a teenager in the late eighteenth century and became one of Glynn County's richest planters; his eleven exemplary children; their illustrious twentieth-century heirs.

And the story everyone liked best: the coincidence that Margaret Mitchell chose our family name for her infamous heroine.

Born in the last years of the nineteenth century and raised on the same postwar brew of recrimination and regret that nourished Mitchell, my grandmother Mamie could not forget. "It still makes me angry at the Yankees stripping the Southern families," she said in her late seventies. She preferred the golden age that preceded her birth, the years when the family fields stretched to the edge of the ocean that spelled misery to millions and wealth to us, when palmettoes shimmered in the twilight, and blushing belles cavorted with suitors at parties like the ones Scarlett O'Hara attended, she who carried our name.

Or maybe I've got it wrong. Maybe my grandmother and I aren't so different after all. I can remember times when I sensed a touch of hesitation or doubt—remorse, even—beneath her arctic veneer. In the spare bedroom she used upstairs as a studio, she painted portraits of women, some of them Black, which she had copied from newspaper clippings: mothers grieving lost children or slain civil rights leaders; young girls staring pensively into space.

In 1982, during her last feverish years of work on the family saga, in one of her many letters to me, Mamie asked if I could get her a copy of *Uncle Tom's Cabin*. "I saw a copy once when a child," she wrote, "but someone said something like this: 'Chile you don't want to read that old Yankee book.' I did want to read it, but didn't." She had gone decades without satisfying her curiosity. But recently she had picked up a biography of the Beechers that referred so often to the novel that my grandmother now wanted to read it. She was eighty-four. "It will make me angry, of course, but I will have to risk that."

I was too busy with school to send the book, and she didn't ask again. Her letters to me grew shorter and shorter until they dwindled to near incoherence ("I have been trying to write the things I seem to remember") and then stopped.

Decades later I learned that my grandmother had been haunted her whole life by a childhood memory. Specifically, she remembered sitting inside the family house in Brunswick at night with the Scarlett women while they waited for the Scarlett men to come home from some clandestine outing—a "night ride," presumably, of the sort Mitchell depicts in *Gone with the Wind* and that terrorized Blacks throughout the South in the first half of the twentieth century. In her final year of life, my grandmother tried to communicate what she remembered to my mother and uncle. They were with her in the hospital room to which she had been confined for months, mind sliding in and out of consciousness. One day my grandmother's eyes abruptly flickered open, and she looked up at her children as if gripped by a vision. She tried to say something—to "make a confession," my Uncle Bob thought—but then shut her eyes and sank back into the pillows. My grandmother died shortly before Christmas 1994. With her I lost my last breathing link to that distant world.

I'm here tonight—spring of 2015—because I want to know what my grandmother could not bring herself to say. Over dinner this evening, Joe and Prinny and I talked about slavery's shadow past. After Joe's presentation at Hofwyl-Broadfield, we'd driven up the road to a waterfront bar on another old rice plantation, Butler Island, once owned by a planter named Pierce Butler—known in part for his troubled marriage to the celebrated British actor Fanny Kemble. We'd ordered shrimp and oysters, lemonade and beer, and, as we ate and drank, we'd talked well into the night about our respective ancestral links to slavery. Joe said he'd started spending the night in slave dwellings in 2010 as a way of calling attention to these neglected structures and honoring his enslaved forebears. He reminded us that twelve U.S. presidents had been enslavers, eight of them while in the White House. One of those men was Prinny's ancestor, a man who decried the tyranny of slavery while pushing for its expansion. At his picturesque hilltop property in Virginia, Thomas Jefferson had enslaved hundreds of people he regarded as inferior to white Americans "in the endowment both of body and mind." Some of those individuals were his own offspring.

I had spent the previous two days at the Georgia Historical Society in Savannah, paging through the papers of a slave dealer who did business with my ancestors during Jefferson's lifetime. Inside box after acid-free box, I had touched the moth-eaten remnants of plantation inventories, shipping manifests, contracts, mortgages, sales agreements, and receipts, including one for a seventeen-year-old "African-born" girl named Margaret, who was sold to settle a debt.

"As a nation we like to preserve buildings, but it's usually the house on the hill," Joe had told the docents at Hofwyl-Broadfield earlier that evening. "We tend not to preserve those places that take us out of our comfort zones." At the start of the Civil War, he'd gone on, some four million enslaved Americans were living in cabins like the ones at Hofwyl-Broadfield. Few of those dwellings survived. "One reason," Joe surmised, "is because of that intent to erase our history."

"It's always been complicated," I had scribbled that morning in my journal.

Lying here at midnight, inside a slave cabin fifteen miles north of where my ancestors built a fiefdom based on enslaved labor, I am newly aware of those complications—all the reasons my grandmother Mamie had to brush aside our history. All the reasons I'd rather be somewhere else tonight. Even now, eyes shut, I'm counting the hours until I can get in my car and drive home to Michigan, the easy North. Patterns drift across my eyelids—stars, waves, circles opening and closing like a kaleidoscope. That's what I'm looking for, I think: patterns. All the ways my grandmother's life, and mine, reinforce the world our ancestors built. The world I saw inside the archive in Savannah this week. The world my family refused to acknowledge.

2

THE FAMILY ALBUM

I have a single photograph of my grandmother taken during her first year of life at the turn of the twentieth century. She and her family are posed together in front of the Scarlett house on the outskirts of Brunswick, Georgia. They're all dressed for the occasion—the adults in starched shirts and wasp-waist skirts, the children in black stockings and high-topped shoes. Everyone is looking stoically in the direction of the photographer as they wait for the long exposure to take. Only one person moves, and that's the nurse, Mattie (the caption gives no surname), who is bent low over a huge wicker carriage that contains a squirming infant in a white cap and gown.

The baby is my grandmother Mary King Hilsman—Mamie—born on November 11, 1898. The picture was likely taken in 1899. Mattie is the only person of color in the photograph—although not in the image itself, for the photograph is a double exposure. Layered behind my grandmother and her family is a second picture, a shadow likeness of a house under construction. You can see the two-story frame structure, wooden porches, chimney, windows, and the brick pylons on which everything rests so that air can circulate underneath. You can see the silhouette of a tall ladder and the faint outlines of two or three men at work, presumably African Americans hired to build a new Scarlett home after the old one burned in 1897. The fire happened so quickly the Scarlett children had to be rolled down the stairs onto a mattress made of sheep wool. (Mamie later stitched me a rag doll stuffed with a portion of that wool, and she attached a note explaining the doll's origins.)

It's a strangely oracular photograph. Taken just a few decades after the Civil War, it suggests not the poverty my grandmother talked about incessantly but a family with the means to afford a new two-story house and at least a few fancy clothes, never mind a photographer to immortalize everything. Maybe there's a trace of hardship in the bearded man—

Mamie's grandfather George Scarlett—who looks as if he has just slapped a jacket over his farm shirt. Or in the woman who stands beside him in a calico dress—Mamie's grandmother Virginia Scarlett—but that dress has a ruffled bodice and extravagant muttonchop sleeves, as do the dresses of the other women in the picture, and I can't help thinking these are people of at least some leisure. Everyone except Mattie, of course, the one person in the photo who is actually working—she and the men in the shadow image behind her, the carpenters and bricklayers at work building the Scarletts' new house. I assume they, too, are people of color and, as such, bit players in the greater drama of my ancestors' lives.

A similar arrangement marked my own childhood. I was born in December 1955, on the same weekend Rosa Parks refused to give up her bus seat in Montgomery, Alabama. I came of age in the 1960s during the civil rights movement. But the sit-ins and marches of that era were only a backdrop to my middle-class life in the white suburbs of southeastern Pennsylvania. I spent a portion of every summer with Mamie and my grandfather in Tidewater, Virginia, without once realizing I was in the segregated South. My grandparents' housekeeper and cook, an African American woman named Carrie Johnson, lived over the garage in their riverfront house, in a narrow bedroom with an attached bath. What little I knew of Carrie's life came from glimpses filched on my way up and down the back stairs. It was dizzying to behold this small and forbidden space, to think of Carrie as someone who watched TV, fussed with her hair, talked on the phone with friends, made plans that didn't include us.

But I liked hanging out with Carrie in the kitchen. She seemed to welcome my presence (what choice did she have?). I liked standing next to her at the sink and watching her toss a basket of blue crabs under the faucet and turn on the hot water. "I love to watch 'em squirm," she'd cry and shoot me a jubilant look. I assumed she had no ambition other than to cook and clean and press our disordered lives into order. Even after she married and moved into her husband's house in another part of town, Carrie continued to show up on weekdays before sunrise to set out our breakfasts and begin the noon meal. She went on using the room above my grandparents' garage as her own, and she kept a separate set of dishes and glassware in the kitchen cupboards for her meals, as she had done before her marriage. In the evenings, after she went home, we'd find our suppers waiting for us on china plates in the refrigerator.

In the privacy of their living room, I sometimes heard my grandparents talk in hushed voices about the "colored people." Not unkindly, but with the clear understanding that we inhabited separate worlds. It was understood that my brother, sister, cousins, and I would go to college (my grandfather had seeded funds for each of us) and that we would one day inherit the porcelain and crystal that surrounded us in their home, as indeed we did. But Carrie? If my grandparents made provisions for her education or health care or retirement, I'm not aware.

There she would be, arms wide, waiting to hug us the moment we got out of our car after the four-hour drive south from Pennsylvania. I'd run from Carrie's arms into the house and up to my bedroom, then back downstairs for lunch in the dining room, where Carrie served us with regal ceremony. She'd stride around the table, lowering plates of chicken and butter beans onto our place mats, then disappear into the kitchen to await the next summons from the little bell my grandmother kept at her side.

"Ma'am?"

"You may clear the dishes now and bring dessert, Carrie."

"Yes, ma'am."

And so I learned my place. It was in the dining room, with the matching china and monogrammed silverware, not at the kitchen table with Carrie, eating leftovers on dime-store dishes. It was with my grandparents: Robert Leslie Pettigrew, for whom I was named, and Mary King Hilsman Pettigrew. Mamie. I don't know where the nickname came from, but that's what my brother and sister and I called our grandmother. Decades would pass before I learned about a second Mamie, a woman from Chicago with a beatific face whose fourteen-year-old son, Emmett, was lynched in Mississippi in August 1955, three months before my birth.

In her last years, when my grandmother again needed tending, another nurse, this one white, began signing Mamie's letters to me "Mammie." The error amused me, as I imagine it would have amused my grandmother if she had been aware. I was in my twenties, and the only Mammie—or Mammy—I knew was the one in *Gone with the Wind*, a book my grandmother bought the year it came out. Her 1936 edition sits on my shelves.

What my grandmother thought of Mitchell's novel I don't know. She must have seen something of her own family in the postwar penury of the Wilkeses and O'Haras. She'd have wanted to identify with virtuous Melanie, I suspect, though my grandmother had more than a touch of Scarlett's notorious gumption. What drew her most to the book, though, was the name of its heroine. As my grandmother never tired of reminding me, we were *Scarletts*—descendants of London-born immigrant Francis Muir Scarlett, who came to America in the late eighteenth century at age fourteen and went on to build a small cotton empire on the coast near Brunswick. My grandmother had papers proving the nobility of our lineage; supposedly we descended from Will Scarlett of Robin Hood fame.

Mitchell's Scarlett was a different breed of character—ruthless, materialistic, brash, an exemplar of the Yankee virtues my grandmother had been bred to despise. The year the novel came out, Frances Scarlett Beach, one of Mamie's aunts, wrote to Mitchell demanding to know why she had given our name to her scandalous heroine.

"Of course I have heard of your family," Mitchell wrote back gently, "for it is so well known in the records and old legends of our Coast. I hope my choice of this name has not been embarrassing to you or to your family."

Frances Scarlett Beach burned the letter. But Mitchell had made a carbon, so her reply survived.

I first saw *Gone with the Wind* in 1967. The film had just been rereleased, and we went to a matinee in a crowded single-screen theater in downtown Philadelphia. I was twelve and fell for the movie wholesale: the tragic love story, the epic war scenes, those endless crinolines. I laughed at Mammy packing Scarlett into her whalebones and at Prissy's antics, oblivious to the movie's racial politics. Years went by before I saw Scarlett for what she is: a woman, like Mitchell herself, heedless "to the most fundamental reality of all," writes historian Drew Gilpin Faust, "that southern civilization rested on the oppression of four million African Americans whose labor made southern wealth, gentility, and even ladyhood possible."

The same year I saw *Gone with the Wind*, violence erupted in Newark and Detroit and a dozen other American cities plagued by institutionalized poverty and racial injustice. The following spring, Martin Luther King Jr. was murdered. I learned about his death from a couple of junior high school friends who'd snuck out of school to smoke cigarettes during a choir concert. We were crouched under a tree near the parking lot when one of them mentioned that King had been shot. I remember thinking I should feel sadder than I did.

King's assassination sparked civil unrest in more than a hundred cities, including Baltimore, where my ten-year-old sister, Mary, born with cerebral palsy, was living in a rehab institute. As soon as we could, my father and I made the ninety-minute trip by car to retrieve her. Inside the city we drove past army tents, scorched storefronts, soldiers with rifles, blockaded streets. A sheet of plywood covered the entrance to the rehab institute itself. Someone wheeled my terrified sister out through a side door to our car, and we buckled her into the front seat and sped back to Pennsylvania and our quiet house in the suburbs. My parents lived beside a fairway that belonged to the country club where my dad played golf on weekends, and my brother and I took swimming lessons. Membership was restricted to white Christians—no Jews or Blacks allowed. There were no people of color in my school, either, except for three African American siblings who showed up in seventh grade and stayed for a year or two, then disappeared. Years later I heard rumors that someone had burned a cross on their lawn.

Is it a coincidence that *Gone with the Wind* was rereleased while King was marching and the fire hoses blasting? I knew which story felt real to me. Upstairs in my bedroom, I brooded over the doomed quartet at the heart of Mitchell's story and wondered if Scarlett would ever get her man. I dreamed of snaring a Rhett of my own to sweep me up a staircase and into wedded bliss. (According to a survey, I was not alone: three-quarters of American high school girls in 1970 identified with Scarlett.)

I kept on dreaming. I took up acting, and in my junior year of high school joined a Christian theater troupe. That summer we toured the country, performing plays in churches. I kept a diary. Georgia, I wrote, was "flat and hot, with mostly shacks." Alabama, which we crossed by night, was "very poor—lots of dogs, foxes, and police." In Mississippi ("poor like Ala."), we drove by "a cotton factory and saw wire trucks full of cotton." It was 1972—four years after King's death, eight years after passage of the 1964 Civil Rights Act. As young white Americans, we drove fearlessly all night across these states.

We spent two days in Memphis as guests of a Baptist megachurch. One member of our company stayed with a family who took her to see the site of King's murder. "A motel in the black section (or 'coons' as we sometimes call them)," I jotted airily. I can see my sixteen-year-old blond self, hunched over my diary in a guest room somewhere in Memphis, trying to be cool. We all talked that way—all across the South, from one barely desegregated state to the next. After Memphis we moved on to Arkansas, "just generally a poor, rundown area with lots of peach and melon shacks." When we crossed the Mississippi, we tossed pennies into the river as if strewing alms.

I knew I had family in the South, but I felt no connection to the region's history. Growing up in Pennsylvania, I thought I was one of the good guys. I had no inkling the North had been built with enslaved labor or that my own city of Lancaster, famously home to the abolitionist Thaddeus Stevens, had profited handsomely in the mid-nineteenth century from cotton grown and harvested by captive African Americans. (Even Stevens praised Lancaster's lucrative cotton mills.) I was in my forties before I thought seriously about any of these facts.

The assumption in my family throughout my childhood was that the Scarletts were "good" enslavers—as good as, if not better than, Mitchell's Gerald O'Hara, who never sold anyone and only once whipped a man "for not grooming down Gerald's pet horse after a long day's hunting."

3

FANNY KEMBLE

Some people did speak out. One of them was the British actor Fanny Kemble, another of my grandmother's obsessions, who witnessed the cruelties of plantation slavery firsthand when she spent six months on her husband's plantations in Glynn County, Georgia, within twenty miles of the Scarletts. She was, my grandmother said coyly when she sent me a book about Kemble, "an interesting woman."

A quintessential Victorian—with looks and crinolines to match the queen's—Kemble came to the United States in 1832 as a young actor and two years later married one of the country's biggest enslavers, Pierce Butler. My grandmother thought that since I too wanted a stage career in my teens, I should know about her. "What an unusual person she must have been," Mamie mused. "A beautiful English actress with a mind of her own." A nineteenth-century phenom who had lived for a short time near the Scarletts and gone on to excoriate their world. Mamie sent me her copy of a 1938 biography of Kemble, *Fanny Kemble: A Passionate Victorian*, a book so turgid I never read it. My grandmother also gave me her leather-bound first edition of Kemble's 1863 *Journal of a Residence on a Georgian Plantation*, a book Mamie termed "interesting reading."

It's not clear whether my grandmother had read these books herself—there's no trace of her hand in either volume. She may have been content, like I was for years, to pick at them piecemeal out of curiosity. I finally dug seriously into Kemble's *Journal* for the first time when I was fifty and on vacation with my family in Glynn County. I tucked a paperback edition of Kemble's book into my carry-on and during the flight home began reading.

The Scarletts must have talked about her. I can envision my grandmother's widowed mother, Minnie, summoning Kemble's name as an example of a woman who had used her wits to earn a living. After her husband's death in 1905, Minnie ran a boardinghouse and baked cakes to support herself and her three daughters. "I see so much that makes my heart ache for young girls who have to work," she told her mother.

Kemble was luckier, at first. Born into a theatrical family in Britain in 1809, she grew up expecting to work. At nineteen she made her London debut as Juliet. At twenty-two she sailed to the United States with her actor father, and the pair toured the Northeast for two years, from 1832 to 1834. A young Walt Whitman saw her and swooned. Girls bought "Fanny Kemble caps"; shops put portraits of the doe-eyed actor in their windows.

Like so many women over time, Kemble had originally nurtured other dreams. She'd wanted to be a writer—a novelist—not an actor. But her father's precarious finances pushed her onstage, and once she realized she could bankroll her family, she stayed. The oldest of four children, she made that first fateful trip to North America with her father because duty called. As their ship approached New York's harbor on September 2, 1832, Fanny, already homesick, scrawled in her journal, "Hail, strange land! My heart greets you coldly and sadly!"

In Philadelphia she met Pierce Butler—a self-indulgent socialite, gambler, and heir to a trio of cotton and rice estates on the Georgia coast and to the nearly one thousand enslaved African Americans who worked those properties. "He is, it seems, a great fortune," Fanny wrote cannily of the short, dark-haired suitor who turned up at her door, nosegay in hand, after her Philadelphia debut. "Consequently, I suppose (in spite of his inches), a great man."

They married in Philadelphia on June 7, 1834. No sooner had the papers been signed, then Butler, then twenty-four, demanded that his wife quit the stage and devote herself exclusively to him. Kemble soon chafed. She'd never thought herself fit for marriage or motherhood, and Butler, with his insistence that she "honor and obey" him, did little to reassure her. Four months into the marriage, Fanny walked out on him one night; hours later she returned home, cold and upset.

She had married Butler knowing he and his brother stood to inherit their grandfather's Georgia plantations, together with their human captives, and that, as a planter's wife, her livelihood would depend on the unpaid labor of those people. Her own country had banned the slave trade in 1807 and slavery itself in 1833. Kemble declared herself, "as an

Englishwoman," intractably opposed to the system. But she reconciled herself to life as an enslaver's spouse.

She was herself just twenty-four when she married and desperate for the kind of financial and other security Pierce Butler offered. Their courtship took place entirely in Philadelphia and parts north. Kemble never set foot in the South—never clapped eyes on her husband's Georgia properties—until four years after her wedding. By then she had two daughters. The compromises she made were part and parcel of her time and place. (Numerous Scarlett women made the same deals, shutting their mouths and heeding the men who paid the bills.) Kemble seems to have convinced herself that her husband and brother-in-law were "good" slaveholders. But it tormented her to realize her income now came ("disgracefully, as it seems to me") from enslaved labor, and she begged Butler to at least let her earn enough money to pay for her wardrobe. He refused.

In 1835 Fanny drafted what she described as "a long and vehement treatise against negro slavery." But she made no effort to publish it lest the citizens of Philadelphia "tear our house down, and make a bonfire of our furniture—a favorite mode of remonstrance in these parts with those who advocate the rights of the unhappy blacks." The treatise has not survived.

Pregnancy and other complications kept Kemble from visiting her husband's plantations until late 1838. That December the couple traveled south to Georgia with their two young daughters, Sarah and Frances. On the eve of her departure, Kemble wondered if she would succumb to yellow fever or be swallowed by an alligator or "shot at from behind a tree for my abolitionism." She hoped her presence on her husband's properties might do some good. "I am about to go among these people the amelioration of whose condition I have considered as one of my special duties," she confided to a friend. But as the trip neared, and the coarse realities of life in the deep South became apparent, that fantasy died. "I have, alas! no longer the faintest shadow of hope," Kemble admitted.

On December 30, 1838, Fanny and her husband and children at last reached Butler Island—a vast, industrialized rice plantation just south of the town of Darien, where hundreds of enslaved African Americans labored in swamps and mills. From the deck of her boat, Kemble saw yellow marshes and beyond them huge cypress trees wreathed in Spanish moss. The funereal garlands reminded her of cobwebs. As they drew close to land, shouts of "Oh, massa!" and "Oh, missis!" broke out along the shore. The actor burst into tears.

Butler Island is today a twenty-minute drive from Brunswick and from the patch of land in the woods where my grandmother spent much of her childhood. The Scarlett homestead in Brunswick is long gone, but the family graveyard remains—a small plot anchored by an obelisk and draped in the same kind of eerie moss that spooked Kemble.

I saw the cemetery for the first time when I was seven or eight, and my mother took us to Brunswick for a family vacation: my only trip to Georgia as a child. I remember the old gray Scarlett house, with its sagging porch and assortment of white-haired residents—my grandmother's surviving aunts and uncle. I also remember the graveyard. The details are hazy, but at some point an adult must have taken me by the hand and led me along the short path from the house to the cemetery and pointed to the tombstones and told me I was related to these people.

One grave stood out from the rest. It sat outside, not inside, the wrought-iron fence surrounding the other Scarlett graves, and its inscription was notably different from theirs:

IN

Memory of

Our

Old nurse

Maum CHARLOTTE

Died 4th day of May 1856

Aged 91

Charlotte was a "slave," I would learn. I am not sure if I was told then or later or whether the person who told me—probably my mother—explained what the word meant or left me to draw my own conclusions. I don't recall thinking there was anything odd about this information, just that it happened long ago.

I did not visit the cemetery again until 2006, when I spent the week in Glynn County on vacation with my family. We stayed with my mother's cousin on Saint Simons Island, and one day he drove us across the causeway to Brunswick to see the graveyard. There was Charlotte's tombstone, more or less as I'd remembered it, almost but not quite touching the fence that encased my ancestors. (I would later learn it is one of countless such tombstones across the South, all of them honoring an enslaved person "beloved" by the family who held them captive.) I wondered what kind of person Charlotte was, what she had looked like, where she had been born. How she had spent her days. Did she have children or a husband or siblings and, if so, what had happened to them and their descendants? I wondered what she would say about being buried next to people who had professed to own her—enslaved in death, as in life, to their wishes.

On the flight home to Michigan I thought again about Charlotte as I opened my copy of Kemble's *Journal*. The actor had written most of the book while visiting her husband's plantations in late 1838 and early 1839—during Charlotte's lifetime—but waited until 1863 to publish it. By then Charlotte was gone, and Kemble had divorced Butler and was living in England.

As we flew north over the snow-covered fields of Ohio—that state on which so many African Americans fleeing slavery had once pinned their dreams—I read about the suffering Kemble found on her husband's properties. Disease, hunger, filth, whippings, rape. Punishing labor in snake-ridden creeks. Men ripped from wives and children and marched west. Women sent back into the fields within weeks—or even hours—of giving birth. Crippling rheumatism, swollen joints, flayed muscles, ruptured internal organs, tumors, hysteria. Kemble was so stricken by what she saw she prayed for the "wild waves of the Atlantic" to carry off "this evil earth and these homes of tyranny, and roll above the soil of slavery, and wash my soul and the souls of those I love clean from the blood of our kind." "Our kind," I realized as I sped through the sky toward home, my husband and stepson dozing beside me, included my forebears.

By the time Kemble visited Glynn County in the late 1830s, my great-great-great grandfather Francis Muir Scarlett had accumulated thousands of acres of land in the same county, along with scores of human beings. He'd gone from penniless immigrant to moneyed planter and further enriched himself by branching into law and government. He had served as a justice of the inferior court in Glynn County and delegate to state conventions and as both a representative and senator in the state legislature.

It's not certain Scarlett knew Pierce Butler except by name—Butler spent most of his time in Philadelphia. But the two had neighbors and business associates in common, and Scarlett represented Butler and his interests in Milledgeville. Butler's three coastal plantations (on Butler Island and nearby Saint Simons and Little Saint Simons Islands) made Fanny Kemble's indolent young husband one of the richest enslavers in Georgia. The Scarlett plantations on the Georgia mainland, in and around Brunswick, were comparatively modest. But both Francis Muir Scarlett and Pierce Butler mined their wealth in the corrosive pits of the human slave trade.

As I worked my way into Kemble's *Journal* on that flight home in 2006, I kept asking myself whether my grandmother had in fact read the book. She had said plenty about Kemble but nothing about the contents of the *Journal*, its blistering attack on "homes of tyranny" like the Scarletts'. There was just Mamie's odd remark that the book was "interesting reading." A different grandmother would have dismissed the traitor actor—thousands of southerners did. For more than a century after the Civil War, Fanny Kemble was vilified, especially in Georgia, especially in Glynn County. Is it possible Mamie admired her? I've long thought a rebel spirit brewed inside those plain brown dresses she wore like a uniform. I could sense it in her efforts to poke fun at southern decorum. (In the front hall of her Virginia house, where most women of her status placed an ornate flower arrangement, Mamie put out a cactus. She liked being the only woman in town to greet visitors this way.)

Not long after my mother's death in 2013, I found a pad of paper on which she had jotted down notes from conversations with her mother—my grandmother Mamie. I could make out the names of relatives and hurried descriptions of ancestral talents ("poetry") and vices ("tippled"). And then, squeezed beside a list of Mamie's many aunts and uncles in Georgia, the words "dark mistresses"—an allusion, surely, to the sexual proclivities of Scarlett men, predations of the sort Kemble recognized.

Mamie's own mother, Minnie, was equally circumspect. Sick in bed with some ailment in the early 1950s, she startled my mother, who was visiting, by whispering that there were "dark secrets" in the Scarlett family. "Lots of them." My mother understood "dark secrets" to mean the mixed-race offspring of Scarlett men. But Minnie would not elaborate—she merely slid back under the covers and giggled.

Of course they knew. Both my grandmother and her mother knew that Scarlett men had sired offspring with African American women, but they kept quiet.

Mamie wasn't the only woman of her generation to find Fanny Kemble interesting. As a reporter for the *Atlanta Journal* in the early 1920s, Peggy (soon to be enshrined as "Margaret") Mitchell wrote a series of Sunday features on "Georgia Romances That Live in History." One of those was the marriage of Fanny Kemble and Pierce Butler. In a florid article Mitchell traced the couple's "impetuous courtship, such as only the gay blades of the Old South were capable." She described Butler's "violent" infatuation with the actor and Kemble's loneliness while visiting her husband's Georgia plantations, "surrounded by gloomy old trees trailing their burdens of gray moss."

The twenty-two-year-old reporter paid little attention to Kemble's graphic record of plantation brutality—except to note that "the question of slavery irked" the actor. After divorcing Butler and returning to Europe in the 1850s, Kemble "began her now famous book, *Life on a Georgia Plantation* [*sic*]," Mitchell reports. "Next to Harriet Beecher Stowe's *Uncle Tom's Cabin*, this book had more influence in arousing antislavery sentiments than any other book published at the time."

The summary ends here. Far more interesting to the newlywed journalist was the story of Fanny Kemble and Pierce Butler as tragic love affair. "For in broken hearts and undying devotion to lost sweethearts through the years, in tempestuous doves and thwarted desires triumphant over obstacles," Mitchell rhapsodizes, "Georgia's history contains stories as compelling as any of those in poetry or drama."

PART 2

Excavation

4

LETTERS

My grandmother Mamie believed in the power of the written word. Most mornings after breakfast, she would descend into the basement office she shared with my grandfather and take her seat at the big desk he had built for her and set to work on the day's correspondence: a pilot at the wheel of the family barge. Upstairs, whenever I visited, I would hear the rhythmic click-click of her typing, the pauses for thought, the longer breaks as she stopped to retrieve something—a card or newspaper article from the pyramid of papers she kept in a basket beside her typewriter—and then the steady resumption of her mind in action. So much to report, so many rumors to magnify or quell, so much fresh intelligence. (Once, as I was idling upstairs near the door to the basement, I heard the typewriter stop and a quiet voice in a Georgia drawl murmur, "damn." It's the only time I ever heard my grandmother swear.)

Her letters landed in our Pennsylvania mailbox as predictably as the morning newspaper. My mother would slice into a fat envelope and spread its contents on the kitchen table like a hand of cards: typewritten missives from my grandmother, photographs to which she had paper-clipped handwritten asides, magazine articles. And then the main draw, family letters deemed suitable for sharing. One family member had dubbed this endlessly forwarded correspondence "peas and carrots," and the moniker stuck. Whenever my mother sent the latest round of letters on to the next family member, she would sketch a tiny mound of vegetables on the envelope. I soon learned that anything I wrote to my grandmother would be shared with a network of relatives, many of them strangers. I had no choice. Mamie made it clear correspondence was a discipline. Until I answered her last dispatch, she'd withhold the next. "Letter writing is something some people do and some don't," she informed me when I was twelve. "Fortunately for us you do." My eleven-year-old brother, on the other hand, "surely doesn't and we hardly know him which is a pity. Letters hold families together somehow. Southern families cherish them—sometimes for years."

In 2010 my Uncle Bob sent me an old Harry and David pear crate stamped with the words "Perishable Fresh Fruit" on its lid. He and his wife were downsizing, and my uncle wanted me to have his share of the Scarlett archive. (In time he would send even more boxes.) "I am so pleased to place all this in younger hands," he scribbled on a slip of paper taped to the outside of the crate. "Altogether this material constitutes quite a remarkable history of the Scarlett family."

Inside the crate I found letters, postcards, sympathy notes, birthday cards, Christmas greetings—most of them written by women and for women, just as it had been in my childhood. Mothers and daughters, sisters and grandmothers, kept families together with their epistolary compulsions. Peas and carrots—read, reread, shared, and at last packed up for the next generation—secured us to one another.

By the time I began seriously trying to sort the contents of the pear crate, my grandmother and her sisters were gone, but their voices were not. Inside envelope after envelope, I heard them exulting over new finds, wrangling with genealogy, tracking the Scarlett legacy. Those indefatigable historians—there they were, filing applications to the Daughters of the American Revolution and sketching coats of arms. All those years Mamie and I overlapped, my grandmother had been toiling over the family archive. Most of what she had cataloged was benign: wedding announcements, her mother's autograph book, long lists tracing our lineage back to the Magna Carta.

But buried among all that sweet-smelling fruit, I found the first glimpse of another story: transcripts of letters written to my great-great-great grandfather Francis Scarlett in 1812 and early 1813. Letters addressing him as "overseer." I picked up one and read, "Sir, I understand the negroes are in want of corn." I had entered Fanny Kemble's world.

I looked up the word "overseer." "Whipping man. Negro-breaker." More benignly: a man, usually white, who supervised the cultivation and harvest of crops on large plantations, the repair of equipment, and the management of large numbers of enslaved workers. A person responsible for the health of those workers (or as one business-minded nineteenth-century planter put it, "the excess of births over deaths").

The first of the letters I read said as much. "You must write me by mail every fortnight the state of the crops and the health of the negroes," Scarlett's correspondent instructed. The sender's name was Richard Stites. He was writing from Savannah in the summer of 1812, by which time the number of enslaved persons in Georgia exceeded one hundred thousand.

How many "negroes" did Francis Muir Scarlett have under his charge? What did it mean to "oversee" a human being in this context? "WANTED," I read in an ad from an 1807 edition of the Savannah *Public Intelligencer*, "a sober, industrious and active MAN of a good character, to attend as an OVERSEER, on a Plantation, who understands the management of 30 or 40 taskable hands."

Those taskable hands had to be disciplined. If an enslaved worker overslept, it was up to the overseer to make sure he didn't do it again. If a fieldhand failed to pick her quota of cotton, it was a man like Francis Muir Scarlett who determined her punishment. If a house slave ran away, it was the overseer's job to catch her. The title "overseer," recalled the Reverend W. B. Allen, formerly enslaved in Columbus, Georgia, was a synonym for "slave driver, cruelty, brutishness." Frederick Douglass would long remember the "disgusting swagger and noisy bravado" of the overseer "fraternity."

Francis Muir Scarlett was in his early twenties by the time he joined that fraternity as an employee of Richard Montgomery Stites on a plantation called Crawford's Dyke, several miles southwest of Brunswick on the Little Satilla River. That much was clear from the letters in the pear crate. But Scarlett likely became an overseer even earlier, possibly in his teens. The family story, lovingly tended by my grandmother and her sisters through another sequence of letters inside the pear crate, was that Francis Muir Scarlett, a London grocer's son, had left England in 1799 as a fourteen-year-old boy after someone—a teacher, perhaps—whipped him (the irony is not lost). Young Francis Muir stowed away on a ship to Charleston, South Carolina, and from there made his way south to Georgia, to a two-hundred-acre cotton plantation owned by a man named David Crum. How Scarlett found Crum is a mystery—maybe the teenager answered an ad like the one in the Savannah *Public Intelligencer*. Maybe there was a family connection; Scarletts had emigrated from Britain to Jamaica in the seventeenth century and north to Georgia in the late eighteenth century. Whatever the link, young Francis went to work for Crum, probably as an overseer for the twenty or so African Americans Crum held captive on his property. It was Scarlett's apprenticeship to the trade.

Descriptions from the period make the job sound almost genteel. One mid-nineteenth-century plantation manual calls for the overseer to be a "fair English scholar" with the "sense and firmness" to enforce "the observance of morality on the farm." But twenty-first-century historian Edward Baptist reports that overseers were most often chosen for their "hardness." In *The Half Has Never Been Told*, his fierce exposé of slavery and the rise of American capitalism, Baptist shows that the overseer was critical to the "pushing system" by which enslaved workers were systematically tortured to boost profits.

There's just one existing portrait of Francis Muir Scarlett, as an older man. Portly, with thick features and a lantern jaw. Gently curling sideburns soften an otherwise granite face. He wears a black jacket and vest, starched white shirt, and black cravat. It's hard to picture the Dickensian runaway of family legend, much less the twenty-something overseer policing the fields at Crawford's Dyke on horseback. Maybe Scarlett delegated the less savory parts of his job to a driver or foreman—typically an enslaved Black man, or "head Negro," tasked with the actual running of a plantation. "Drivers are, under the overseer, to maintain discipline and order on the place," counseled one Lowcountry planter. "They are to be responsible for the quiet of the negro-house, for the proper performance of tasks, for bringing out the people early in the morning, and generally for the immediate inspection of such things as the overseer only generally superintends."

Surely my grandmother Mamie and her sisters would have preferred that our patriarch merely "superintend" the "quiet of the negro-house" and "the proper performance of tasks"—that he have nothing to do with the implicit, let alone explicit, violence that governed daily life at a place like Crawford's Dyke. One year before Francis Scarlett signed on with Stites, over a hundred enslaved people of African descent staged a two-day rebellion outside New Orleans. The uprising failed, and most of the insurgents were murdered, their heads impaled on spikes along a fifty-mile stretch of road leading to New Orleans. The event shocked enslavers across the South, already unnerved by a bloody slave revolt in Haiti a decade earlier. (Never mind another failed uprising along South

Carolina's Stono River in 1739.) Scarlett became an overseer at a moment of heightened vigilance.

Scarlett must have viewed his new job as a necessary first step on his way to prosperity. He was a striver. At twenty-one, just a few years after sailing to America and going to work for David Crum, he'd joined the Glynn County militia and become an administrator for an estate Crum had helped to appraise. At twenty-six Scarlett married Crum's oldest daughter, sixteen-year-old Nancy Ann, called Ann. Their wedding took place on September 26, 1811. Ten months later Francis Muir Scarlett was working for Richard Stites at Crawford's Dyke, and his teenage wife was pregnant with their first child.

To judge from Stites's letters, Scarlett's chief duties as an overseer were to feed and clothe his enslaved workers and to ensure their safety in the event of "any alarm." Coastal Georgia was at the time under threat from both British battleships and warring Creek tribes. If anything should happen, Stites warned Scarlett in the summer of 1812, "you are to order the negroes from the lower plantation to take [to] the woods and to collect somewhere back of the upper *plantn.*" (On the topic of Native Americans, Scarlett's boss was firm: "I am for exterminating them or removing them west of the Mississippi.") The young overseer was also to produce a decent yield of quality cotton. "I shall expect your punctual attention to all my orders," Stites advised.

There were nine surviving Stites letters in all, written over the course of six months, from July 1812 to early February 1813, when Richard Stites suddenly died. The letters in the pear crate were actually handwritten transcripts, written out by my mother's sister, Florence, in the 1970s, after she had chanced to meet a man who happened to own a ledger containing the original correspondence. The man and his ledger had disappeared not long afterward (I've found no trace of either), but Aunt Florence sent photocopies of her transcripts to my grandmother, and, like every other document that fell into Mamie's grasp, these too were rephotographed and distributed through the Scarlett network. Aunt Florence died in 1977.

In time I would find the rest of Stites's archive in the collection of the Georgia Historical Society in Savannah, and in 2015 I spent three days there—days leading up to my overnight stay in the slave cabin at Hofwyl-Broadfield—paging through the papers of Richard Montgomery Stites.

They filled seventeen acid-free file boxes. A Savannah lawyer, enslaver, and all-round wheeler-dealer in his midthirties, Stites did business with planters and overseers up and down the Georgia coast. One of his correspondents was Maj. Pierce Butler of Saint Simons Island, grandfather to Fanny Kemble's husband, Pierce Butler.

Another correspondent, I saw at the top of a tall sheet of tobacco-colored paper, was Francis Muir Scarlett:

> 1812. Sept 27. Cash pd Francis Scarlett pr order (overseer) 7.50

And directly below that entry:

> Paid Sugar for sick Negroes: 1–

The entries in the archive matched details in my aunt's transcripts and confirmed that Francis Scarlett had begun his climb to prosperity by working as an overseer.

"Whipping man. Negro-breaker." As I pored over Stites's papers in the air-conditioned comfort of the Historical Society, I marveled at the world he and my ancestor had worked to build. Stites, who doted on his young daughter and once offered a five-dollar reward for the return of his lost dog—a black terrier named Cockroach—spent his days trafficking in merchandise and human beings. In the summer of 1807, he promised to sell an enslaved Savannah man named Sam to planter William Crawford of Brunswick. Just as Stites was about to close the deal, Sam ran away. Stites caught him a few weeks later and shipped him south to Crawford. "I hope he may arrive in safety, and I believe he will please you," Stites assured his client. "The sum I gave was $550 which is very cheap."

William Crawford died two years later, in 1809, and Stites became the trustee of his estate at Crawford's Dyke. The property included seventy-one enslaved African Americans. It's likely some of those individuals—possibly the carpenter Sam—were still there in 1812 when Francis Scarlett agreed to become Stites's overseer.

Throughout his correspondence Stites was usually in a hurry. Scuttling about like the insect for whom he had named his dog, he bought and sold and leased and bartered and sued and bullied his way into the ranks of Georgia's planter aristocracy. It was all there in his papers in the Historical Society. Stites had a home in downtown Savannah and a plantation on the city's outskirts and who knows how many other properties under his charge. His account books showed receipts for topcoats, pantaloons, shoes, brandy, soaps, parchment writing paper, and monogrammed fire buckets. Among his letters to Scarlett was an almost tender sequence in which Stites directed Scarlett to ship a pet fawn to his daughter in Savannah. "See to have it well penned and or in a good cage or box," Stites wrote. Tell the captain "to take good care of it."

Stites's letters to Scarlett were filled mostly with references to cotton production and plantation supplies: camphor oil, salt, molasses, cotton bagging, coffee, sugar, tobacco, rum, and, most crucially, corn. After sending fifty bushels of corn to Scarlett in August 1812, Stites cautioned his new overseer that "it will be dangerous to feed the negroes too early on new corn until it is dry." Better to store the "fodder" (Stites's word) in dry rooms or pile it "onto stacks to keep out the weather." Find a place that's secure and sufficiently dry. "I fear the old corn house is so full of dust and weavel that it will be improper to put the corn there."

In her *Journal* Fanny Kemble reports that the enslaved Blacks on her husband's properties received two meals a day of corn or hominy to fuel hours of labor in withering heat. Animal protein was given only to the hardest-working laborers "and to them only occasionally, and in very moderate rations." As Kemble walked among the African Americans on her husband's lands, children often raced after her, begging for meat.

In a 2013 talk at the University of Michigan School of Public Health, where I worked at the time, economic historian Richard Steckel detailed his research probing nineteenth-century plantation records for data to illuminate twentieth- and twenty-first-century health disparities. Fewer than half the children born to enslaved women in the American South survived to age five, Steckel said. He cited multiple culprits: low birth weight, diarrheal disease, malaria and other fevers, poor nutrition, and contaminated water and food. Because new mothers typically went back to work within weeks or often days of giving birth, few babies were breastfed. And because protein was reserved for active laborers, as Kemble knew, both the very young and the very old subsisted on corn and whatever could be grown or foraged outside of work hours, which often extended late into the night.

Steckel's scrutiny of plantation account books had led him to see that enslaved African American children were "very malnourished" and as a result exceptionally short—as much as five inches below modern norms, according to some records. It was only after they reached adolescence and became full-time laborers, with a daily allotment of protein, that kids "caught up," he said. The deprivation had gone on for generations, and Steckel was trying to gauge its long-term impact on the health of African Americans today. But the immediate effect was plain. "Slave parents," he said quietly, pausing for emphasis, "could not protect their children against hunger, which is one of the fundamental functions of parenthood."

In late August 1812, Richard Montgomery Stites sent another shipment of corn to Francis Muir Scarlett. "I fear the new corn will make the negroes sickly," he informed Scarlett. "As soon as that I sent you arrives, give half allowance of the old mixed with half the new." In early December of the same year, Stites ordered "one good beef from my cattle" to be delivered to Crawford's Dyke "for the use of my negroes on Little Satilla owing the holidays now approaching." How Scarlett felt about this sudden show of generosity is unknown.

And Charlotte, the enslaved nurse beloved by the Scarletts? What nourishment did she receive? If the tombstone outside the Scarlett cemetery is accurate, she died at ninety-one. Was she, too, forced to survive in old age on cornmeal and garden scraps and foods scavenged from nearby forests and swamps? Squirrel, raccoon, oysters, turtle. In her childhood my grandmother and her sisters used to watch the African American farmers who lived behind her grandmother's house eat roasted sweet potatoes and possum, and "we wanted a taste so bad." But the farmers gently shooed the little girls away so they could eat in peace. In my own childhood, I watched Mamie's housekeeper, Carrie, fry catfish and greens for herself in the kitchen while we sat in the dining room eating the roast chicken or beef she had prepared for us.

Where, in all of this, is the image of a rotund Mammy spooning pancakes into a near-anorexic Scarlett O'Hara?

Francis Scarlett and Richard Stites rode their way into the ranks of privilege on the famished bodies of captive African Americans. When he died of a fever on January 15, 1813, less than a month after sending that

Christmas beef to his captive workers at Crawford's Dyke, thirty-six-year-old Richard Stites left behind—in addition to three children—silver, linens, chimney ornaments, maps, catalogs, and a personal library of more than nine hundred books. He also left, in his downtown Savannah home, twenty-four "house servants," valued collectively at $14,603.

To the enslaved laborers under Francis Scarlett's watch at Crawford's Dyke, Stites had sent an annual supply of "Negro cloth" to be turned into "wenches petticoats" and "fellows jackets and overalls." If they were lucky, the women at Crawford's Dyke received enough fabric to make four dresses and a kerchief, the men enough cloth for four shirts and four pairs of pants.

Stites also sent a yearly stock of footwear, probably brogans: ankle-high shoes built for heavy outdoor toil, with no distinction for gender. In late October 1812, at about the time his first child, a son, was born, Francis Scarlett received orders from Stites to "get ready the negro shoe measuring." A month later Stites sent "52 pair Negro shoes for the negroes under your charge." Two of those pairs, worth a dollar apiece, were for Scarlett himself. Like most overseers on relatively small plantations, Scarlett undoubtedly worked alongside the African Americans he managed, and he therefore needed brogans.

How he must have bristled at the indignity. Mud on his shoes and under his fingernails, back stooped and sweating as he labored. Little wonder he got out as soon as he could—began procuring land and slaves of his own, went into local and then state politics, got himself that debonair frock coat and pristine shirt made of the airy white fiber that by 1820 was the world's most widely traded commodity and the dominant driver of economic growth in the United States.

Was this the turning point? The moment my great-great-great grandfather chose to stick with the slave business rather than turn his back on the system and go elsewhere? Was he beholden to his father-in-law and first employer, David Crum? Indebted to Stites? Did Scarlett enjoy the gamesmanship involved in subjugating people of African descent? (Did he recognize their humanity?)

To wear "Negro shoes" was to be on a par with men like Jonas Wilkerson, the lowborn overseer in *Gone with the Wind*, for whom, as Mitchell writes, "there was no family of any standing into which he could marry." Francis Scarlett sought a different future for himself, and the color of his skin made that possible. A century earlier in the American colonies, indentured whites and enslaved Blacks had had much in common. But by the time Scarlett ran away from London and settled in the new state of Georgia—founded in 1733 as a slave-free colony, an experiment soon abandoned—even the Jonas Wilkersons of the white world were viewed as superior to servile Blacks. British-born Fanny Kemble saw this at once. "The prejudice against these unfortunate people is, of course, incomprehensible to us," she wrote after learning that the African American steward she had met aboard the ship that carried her and her father to the United States would have to sit in the gallery if he wanted to see Kemble perform onstage in New York. It was the law. In the South, Kemble brooded, "to teach a slave to read or write is to incur a penalty either of fine or imprisonment."

Another family legend claims that Francis Scarlett had a younger brother who immigrated to the States not long after Francis. This second Scarlett supposedly went to Georgia and lived for a while with Francis, but he quickly realized he disliked slavery and moved north. The story—for which I've found no proof, not so much as a name—circulated for a time among members of my grandmother's generation. It's as if they needed an apocryphal "Other" Scarlett to offset the crimes of our founding ancestor.

Because he was white and ambitious, Francis Scarlett found a way to shed those "Negro shoes" and, like the Irish-born Gerald O'Hara of Mitchell's fantasy, ascend the ranks of the white working class into the planter gentry. Within four years of becoming Stites's overseer, Scarlett had acquired land of his own not far from Crawford's Dyke, a place he called Oak Grove. On it he would build a house and plant cotton fields and construct a cemetery in which to bury his firstborn child, William, who died from unknown causes on July 10, 1813, at the age of nine months.

Or rather, Francis Scarlett ordered his enslaved workers to build a house and plow cotton fields and carve out a family graveyard in which to bury his infant son.

Among the items my Uncle Bob sent me when he and his wife downsized was a map of Oak Grove, painted by my grandmother's sister Ginger in 1936, the year *Gone with the Wind* came out. The map shows a white-columned house like Tara and a row of delicate white cottages labeled "slave cabins." It's not hard to see why Mamie and her sisters embraced this imagery. To do otherwise would be to betray the people who had raised them—men and women who had come of age before the war on slave-labor camps with pretty names like "Crawford's Dyke" and "Oak Grove"—and who looked back nostalgically on the comforts and customs of that era.

5

PROPERTY

Loyalty to the tribe: my grandmother preached it to the end. Lying there in the hospital in her last months, teetering between worlds, she roused herself to shed some long-buried truths but then stopped. My mother and Uncle Bob watched her head fall back onto the pillow and her body curl against the light, its secrets locked. What did she know?

Or what did she know that she *did not* know? All those details she suppressed—or never learned—but somehow, still, managed to pass on. I wonder that she didn't destroy the evidence but instead dedicated herself to amassing it.

"What haunts are not the dead, but the gaps left within us by the secrets of others," the French psychotherapist Anne Ancelin Schützenberger writes in her 1998 book, *The Ancestor Syndrome*, an exploration of the way family secrets pass unconsciously from one generation to the next. Schützenberger describes children of Holocaust survivors who themselves suffer nightmares about events their parents never divulged. The "unspeakable grieving" associated with these events—the "unfinished mourning"—can get locked inside a person's psyche, Schützenberger suggests, and passed on. This buried trauma, this "secret too shameful to be mentioned . . . can be transmitted from a parent's unconscious to a child's unconscious, from one generation to another."

Perhaps that's what I experienced on the morning after my night in the slave cabin at Hofwyl-Broadfield. I had slept more soundly that night than I had expected—got up once to tiptoe to the bathroom next door but then dozed until a dream woke me just before dawn. It wasn't so much a dream as an image: of a hawk perched in a tree eyeing two cats in a yard below. The cats were oblivious to the bird. Suddenly the hawk swooped down and seized one of them in its talons and hoisted it skyward. Blood streamed from the captured animal. In the incomprehensible way of dreams, the second cat dissolved with a scream into two pairs of shoes—

one adult, one child-sized. Somehow all this became Shakespeare's *Winter's Tale*, and I was aware that I was sleeping in a slave dwelling and that Joe and Prinny and I were inside the play, waiting for Hermione to make her unearthly life-after-death appearance. That's when I woke, conscious that in some recess of my mind I had been dreaming about slavery.

Maybe it's the kind of nightmare my grandmother knew—predatory behavior coupled with inexplicable suffering and the hope of a miraculous deliverance that does not come. All those secrets she refused to divulge but nevertheless retained. This was women's work too, wasn't it? Guarding the family legacy. But at what cost?

Rereading the documents my grandmother passed on, I am struck by how little the Scarlett women revealed about themselves, especially the women in Francis Scarlett's immediate orbit. His wife, Ann, for instance. Married at sixteen, a mother at seventeen, nearly eighteen when her first child died and soon pregnant again. Her second child came within the year: Francis Dunham Scarlett—later known as Frank—born April 18, 1814, and named for his father. An heir. Two years later a daughter: Mary Ann. And so it went, every two years a child, until the last of them, George, my great-great grandfather, born in 1838. And then forty-two-year-old Ann Crum Scarlett ceased reproducing.

Aside from her offspring, Ann Scarlett left no trace of herself. I don't know what kind of mother or wife she was, whether she married Francis Scarlett because she loved him or because her father willed it. I don't know what she did for companionship, living as she did in the marshy outskirts of Brunswick, a town Fanny Kemble dismissed as a "wretched hole" unfit for civilized existence. I have no idea how Ann Scarlett sounded or looked. No picture survives, although she lived well into the age of the photograph, dying in 1879 at age eighty-three. Who knows what twenty-six years of near-constant pregnancy did to her looks? Perhaps she did not want to be immortalized.

She had grown up among cotton fields and pine forests in an even more remote part of colonial Georgia than Brunswick, the oldest daughter and presumed helpmate to her own mother, from whom she would have learned the arts of sewing and gardening and putting up preserves, but little, I suspect, of literature or languages or mathematics, topics reserved for boys—and then mostly rich ones. It's doubtful David Crum hired a tutor for any of his children, let alone a girl. Besides, Ann married at sixteen. What need had she of books outside the Bible? Hear what Saint Paul says: "Let a woman learn in quietness with all subjection, but I permit not a woman to teach, nor to have dominance over man."

Childbearing was her job, as it would be for her daughters. The first of them, Mary Ann, born in the summer of 1816 at Oak Grove, was promised in marriage on the day of her birth. Family custom has it that Francis Scarlett said yes when his wealthy neighbor, John Parland, a thirty-eight-year-old bachelor planter from Scotland, showed up that day asking for the newborn's hand when she came of age. Picture the two men sealing the future of a girl not twenty-four hours old: shaking hands over shots of whiskey as they gaze into the August sky and contemplate the riches this union will bring—adjacent fields, acres of dredged land for cotton, scores of Black bodies to plant and weed and harvest. Parland was one of the richest men in Glynn County, owner of thousands of acres of land, including two islands, and hundreds of enslaved people. Why wouldn't Francis Scarlett acquiesce? Or his twenty-one-year-old wife, for that matter? Scarcely out of adolescence herself, holding no legal rights, exhausted from childbirth, lying prone somewhere in a bed in the dank coastal heat, Ann Crum Scarlett would have had little will or no reason to resist the agreement, calculated as it was to ensure the family's prosperity. In fact, she may have welcomed it.

It's precisely during the decades when Ann Crum Scarlett was producing children that the state of Georgia, abetted by the federal government, was evicting the land's Indigenous people to free up property for men like Francis Scarlett to settle. Scarlett took ownership of Oak Grove not long before his daughter Mary Ann's birth, and he soon added to it. If he was going to grow cotton, which depletes nutrients from the soil, he needed land—lots of it.

The website Our Georgia History spells out the mechanism by which white men of Scarlett's ilk scaled the state's socioeconomic ladder: Georgia's headright system, established in the late 1700s to "strengthen the state." Through it every white male head of a family was entitled to two hundred acres of land, gratis, plus an additional fifty acres for each female and enslaved dependent in his household, up to a thousand additional acres. The landowner had to pay only survey and recording fees, and he could purchase further acreage at nominal cost. The goal was to populate and cultivate Georgia's land and to buffer coastal planters from attacks by native tribes.

Scarlett received his first 200-acre headright grant in 1819 and by 1838 had secured another 297 acres through the system; as late as 1853, according to records in Georgia's online Virtual Vault, he was still getting land from the state. Three times Francis Muir Scarlett was a "fortunate drawer" in Georgia's lottery, another system devised to people the state with white persons of European descent. Scarlett supplemented all this with real estate transactions of his own, recorded in the Glynn County courthouse in Brunswick. Like his late boss, Richard Stites, and his father-in-law, David Crum, Scarlett not only bought land but administered estates for absentee planters who later bequeathed him land, farm equipment, livestock, and "Negroes."

By 1817 Scarlett was a justice of the peace in Glynn County. By early 1819—as members of the U.S. Congress were debating the expansion of slavery into the proposed state of Missouri—Scarlett had enough money to be a co-lender on a $4,000 mortgage, with ten "negro slaves" as collateral. Lest Scarlett's debtor renege on his payments, the mortgage agreement spelled out the names of those ten individuals in florid script: Bill, Peter, William, George, Polly, Fanny, Betty, Eliza, and two indecipherable names.

The following year, when federal census takers came through Glynn County to tabulate the number of people living in the area, they found Francis Muir Scarlett in charge of a household with a white wife, three white children, and fourteen enslaved African Americans, seven of them children. (That same year, eyeing a run for the presidency, John Quincy Adams wrote in his journal, "Slavery is the great and foul stain upon the North American Union.")

In 1821 Francis Muir Scarlett won his first term to the state's General Assembly in Milledgeville. He would continue to represent Glynn County in the assembly, alternating as senator and representative, for the next twenty years.

The records of Scarlett's legislative activity, together with scores of his land and business transactions, can be found in the Georgia Archives, a sleek stone-and-glass library just south of Atlanta in Clayton County—the red-earthed landscape where so much of *Gone with the Wind* takes place. Margaret Mitchell's grandmother Annie Fitzgerald grew up in Clayton

County, in a two-story clapboard house that became the inspiration for Tara. Photos of the Fitzgerald place, with its low front porch and shutterless windows, remind me of the old Scarlett house in Brunswick I saw as a kid. There's no record of what Francis Scarlett's original house at Oak Grove looked like—there are no photos, and the place burned in 1897—but I imagine that, like many coastal Georgia planters' homes, it was a relatively small wooden structure raised a few feet above ground to let air and animals circulate below. So much for David Selznick's pillared megamansion. (Mitchell begged the director to "please leave Tara ugly, sprawling, and columnless.")

In her 1936 rendering of the Scarlett property at Oak Grove, my grandmother's sister Ginger envisioned a grand white residence of the sort Selznick favored. She was clearly in thrall to the antebellum imagery that captivates fans of *Gone with the Wind* even today. When I went to Clayton County to work the Georgia Archives in 2017, I didn't have time to visit the Road to Tara Museum in nearby Jonesboro, but I peered in its windows after hours and saw rows of porcelain figurines on sale in the gift shop: Rhett carrying Scarlett up the stairs, Ashley and Scarlett in the barn, Mammy lacing Scarlett's corset. Icons from a world that never existed, except to those who insist it did; Mitchell's book still sells a quarter million copies a year.

I spent a week at the Georgia Archives scrolling through microfilm and skimming the leatherbound journals of the Georgia state legislature in search of Francis Muir Scarlett. I came away mostly with the public records of what white men in power did in the first decades of the nineteenth century to advance their cause. Here was the Honorable Francis M. Scarlett voting on the disposition of Creek lands by the U.S. government, wrangling over tax codes, funding prisons and roads and a state university at Athens. Here he was championing the construction of a canal between Brunswick and Darien so the town of Brunswick could compete with Savannah for shipping and—not coincidentally—Scarlett could get his crops to market more easily.

I caught odd glimpses of him. In early December 1826, midway through the annual session of the General Assembly in Milledgeville (Georgia's planter legislators always convened in winter), Scarlett met with a fellow senator in Scarlett's "room" to discuss a banking matter. For a minute I could see the glowing fireplace and upholstered chairs, the two men in their sedate attire conversing in low voices. Three days later, on the floor of the Senate, Scarlett moved to adjourn the assembly in time for Christmas. It was often Scarlett, in fact, who motioned to adjourn the assembly—no fan of bureaucratic dawdling, my ancestor. A pragmatist, he voted against a bill to lower state legislators' salaries, and, whenever the question of divorce came before the legislature, as was then required before a couple could legally split, Scarlett voted to grant it.

Infrastructure was his thing. The Honorable Francis M. Scarlett served repeatedly on the Penitentiary Committee and sporadically on the Committee for Agriculture and Internal Improvement. When it came to debates over slavery—whether to allow the importation of enslaved workers into the state, how to prevent enslaved people from committing theft, whether slavery was even constitutional—Scarlett's name was notably absent.

Did he think about these questions? Maybe he preferred serving in the legislature to the unpleasant business of managing a captive labor force. That's what Amy Hedrick, a Glynn County genealogist and creator of glynngen.com, a website devoted to Glynn County history, suggested to me. "The fact that his name is on almost every single court document during his heyday tells me he was more of a businessman than slave owner," Amy said. "He probably couldn't care one way or the other about slavery. But, that's just my 'psychic' reading on him LOL."

During Scarlett's years in the Georgia House and Senate, the number of enslaved people in Georgia rocketed. His own county of Glynn soon had a population that was 87 percent African American, 13 percent white. Fears of rebellion deepened. In 1822 a free Black man named Denmark Vesey was accused of plotting a slave revolt in Charleston, South Carolina, and hanged. An enslaved man named Nat Turner led a blood-soaked two-day insurrection in Virginia and was executed. North of Virginia, abolitionist William Lloyd Garrison launched an antislavery crusade that so galled Georgia's governor he declared, "[Slavery] may be our physical weakness—it is our moral strength."

If the question of slavery worried Francis Scarlett, he left no clue. I've found only a pair of toasts, delivered at a July Fourth celebration in Brunswick in 1829, in which he raised his glass to the defeat of "Our Enemies, let them be who they may" and volunteered, perhaps wistfully, "May friendship and harmony exist throughout the United States."

All through the 1820s and 1830s and as late as 1851, the Honorable Francis Scarlett made the four-hundred-mile round trip from Brunswick to Milledgeville on horseback and by boat. His family swelled; his wealth grew. By 1830—the second year of the expansionist presidency of Andrew Jackson, whom Scarlett admired—Francis Scarlett had more than doubled the number of enslaved men and women on his lands and now counted thirty-four African Americans among his possessions. In another few years, thanks to the strategic marriage of his daughter Mary Ann, those numbers would soar.

Out on the road in his traveling coat and hat or on the boat from Brunswick to Darien, ocean spray in his face, Scarlett enjoyed a freedom he denied others. An ad, from the *Brunswick Advocate*, on June 8, 1837, stated,

> RUNAWAY—FROM Gowin Swamp on Monday night, two negro fellows,—DICK, a stout black fellow, about six feet high 45 years of age. NED, stout yellow complected about five feet ten inches high 27 years of age. As they both have relatives on the Brunswick Canal it is very likely they may be in that vicinity. Ten dollars will be given for the apprehension of each, on application to the subscribers. / F. M. SCARLETT Oak Grove, Glynn Co.

If Dick and Ned were trying to reach relatives, it's likely because they had been sold away from those relatives. Parent, spouse, sibling, child—any of these could be chained and marched to the auctioneer without notice.

> WANTED TO PURCHASE—A GANG of ONE HUNDRED NEGROES, for which the Cash will be paid. / F. M. SCARLETT / Oak Grove, Glynn Co., June 15, 1837

A month after F. M. Scarlett posted this ad, just as cotton prices were starting to rebound after a catastrophic two-year fall, he was again nominated to the Georgia State House of Representatives. It would be his fifth term in the House, his tenth in the General Assembly. The Savannah *Georgian* called Scarlett "one of the strongest men" in Glynn County.

6

DAUGHTERS' WORK

If the family archive is correct, Francis Muir Scarlett did in fact bargain away his first daughter, Mary Ann, on the day she was born: August 27, 1816. That was when John Parland apparently showed up at Oak Grove and asked for the infant's hand in marriage. Sixteen years later, on April 23, 1833—the year the British Empire abolished slavery—Mary Ann Scarlett and John Parland were wed. According to my grandmother's cousin Frank Scarlett, another family historian unperturbed by the facts, the ceremony at Oak Grove was "the finest wedding in this part of the country." The bride was sixteen, the same age as Scarlett O'Hara when she married the first of her three husbands.

John Parland was fifty-three—six years older than his new wife's father. A popular Robert Burns song, "What Can a Young Lassie Do Wi' an Auld Man," tells of an unhappy bride who rues the day she was sold for "silver and land" to an old man, whom she vows to torment "until I heart break him." Perhaps John Parland, proud Scot that he was, knew the same torment, though it's also possible he and Mary Ann "lived happily," as Mamie's cousin Frank Scarlett insisted. A federal judge in the southern district of Georgia in the mid-twentieth century, Judge Frank Scarlett saw nothing odd about Mary Ann's arranged marriage. "It was the custom in England," he wrote cheerily in 1969, "and I think it was a good custom."

For Mary Ann's father, the girl's union with John Parland brought wealth, prestige, huge tracts of land contiguous to his own property, and nearly two hundred enslaved people to work that land. For years John Parland had lived alone, a bachelor planter surrounded by women and children and men whose fortunes depended on his. He was a tall man, over six feet, with a strong build and a taste for the good life. On yearly trips to Glasgow he bought engraved pipes, English china, bottles of Scottish ale—fragments of which would turn up nearly two centuries later in archaeological excavations of slave dwellings on his former properties. At the time of his marriage to Mary Ann, Parland owned four plantations, among them Crawford's Dyke, where Francis Scarlett had toiled as an overseer. That too must have pleased Scarlett.

The newlyweds moved into Parland's grand house on the largest of his estates, Colonel's Island, a 2,500-acre plantation cut off from the mainland by marsh and estuary and covered in live oaks and palmettos, with fields of lucrative sea island cotton planted at its edges. Within a year of her wedding Mary Ann was pregnant. She gave birth to a daughter, Jean, on December 18, 1834. By early 1836 Mary Ann was pregnant again.

At what point did she learn she was to marry her father's neighbor and bear his children—sacrificed, like Iphigenia, at an altar to advance her father's schemes? (Imagine the fear that must have gripped the sixteen-year-old Mary Ann on her wedding night.) It's what planters' daughters did, of course—put on their fanciest gowns and promise to love and obey the men they married, chiefly for economic necessity or familial need, or both. It's what Fanny Kemble did when she married Pierce Butler, another slaveholding owner of an island estate just off the Georgia coast. Kemble's wedding took place within a year of Mary Ann's, and, although the choice to marry Butler seems to have been hers alone, Kemble's marriage, too, was calculated to lift her family's fortunes.

For Mary Ann the lurch from daughter to wife, child to mother and plantation mistress, must have bewildered. Kemble was appalled by the lives of the slaveholding white women she met on her single trip to Georgia. "I pity them for the stupid sameness of their most vapid existence, which would deaden any amount of intelligence, obliterate any amount of instruction, and render torpid and stagnant any amount of natural energy and vivacity," she wrote. "I would rather die—rather a thousand times—than live the lives of these Georgia planters' wives and daughters."

In March 1836 Mary Ann's mother, Ann Scarlett, gave birth to her tenth and penultimate child. Five months later Mary Ann gave birth to her second child, a daughter, Frances Ann. The infant was two weeks old when John Parland went off for a ride on a newly purchased Arabian horse. In the delicate phrasing of Judge Frank Scarlett, Parland was, at the time, "slightly intoxicated." The horse bolted. In a scene Margaret Mitchell could have scripted, fifty-six-year-old John Parland went flying into a fence with such force that he fractured his skull. Rescuers tried to save him, but his neck was broken.

They dressed his shattered corpse in a nightshirt and placed him, shoeless, inside a wooden coffin, which they sealed into a raised brick vault on a wooded bluff overlooking the South Brunswick River. A marble slab gave the date of John Parland's death—September 7, 1836—and the country of his birth: Scotland. The grave stood not far from the big house on Colonel's Island, where three years earlier he had brought his bride.

Aside from a fleeting reference to a needlepoint fire screen she once embroidered, there is no account of Mary Ann in the Scarlett archive. No portrait, no record of how she looked or thought or spoke, whether she had dark hair or light, was tall or short, humble or vain, wrote letters or read books. Did she know how to put up jams or calm a restive child, or did she delegate those tasks to other women? (Did she harbor any doubts about the system by which those women were hers to command?)

I can imagine Mary Ann donning black garments that sweltering September, maybe a veiled bonnet and gloves, and following her husband's coffin to its grave—although it's possible she stayed home, still weak from giving birth. Because he had no other relatives in the United States, Parland's immense estate went to his young widow and her daughters. Land, house, furnishings, clothing, carriages, livestock, horses, outbuildings, cotton, rice, sugar, financial investments, and nearly two hundred enslaved men, women, and children: all became the property of twenty-year-old Mary Ann and her children, twenty-one-month-old Jean and newborn Frances Ann—which is to say they became the property of Mary Ann's father, since as a woman Mary Ann had no legal right to her inheritance.

Six days after his son-in-law's death, Francis Scarlett applied for the authority to administer John Parland's four plantations; notices of the application were distributed throughout the regional press. For the next twenty years, Scarlett and his sons would continue to manage John Parland's holdings. Francis Scarlett also became guardian of the two Parland girls. In addition to "better securing" their "considerable estate"—as a document in Glynn County's probate court reads—Scarlett pledged to pay for the girls' upkeep and education. The two sisters would in time attend a private boarding school on a working farm near Macon, Georgia—a farm tilled by enslaved workers.

The 1836 inventory of Parland's estate filled pages. For each plantation there were lists of possessions, including names and numbers:

Big Sam	$150
Little Sam	$1000
Mariah	$900
Eliza	$500
John	$300
Sally	$400
January	$500
Silvey	$300
Mary	$800
Quaco	$250

And so on. Many of these people had lived for years on Parland's Colonel's Island plantation, well before John Parland bought the land. What would happen now that Scarlett owned them? Men and women, girls and boys, some of whom Parland had rented out to other planters during their time with him, pocketing their earnings, and some of whom had tried to escape. (Happy people, a friend reminds me, do not run away.)

Elias, assessed at $1,100. A slave driver charged with enforcing order and discipline, the most prized of Parland's workers.

Matilda, a mixed-race girl, fifteen years old, with (I would learn) complicated ties to the Scarlett family. Worth $800.

Charlotte, valued at $700. Is this the Charlotte who is buried outside the Scarlett cemetery in Brunswick? I am not the only one in my family to obsess over her. When our cemetery was vandalized in 2010, the grave everyone worried about most was Charlotte's. Let the Scarletts be hurled and smashed, as they were, but not Charlotte. And she was not. By some long-overdue stroke of *something*—I hesitate to call it justice—her stone was untouched.

But she remains a cipher. If my white female Scarlett ancestors are barely audible, the Black women who labored for them are almost wholly mute, which makes them easy to forget. Count the numbers instead. Tally the rows of erased people.

By the time my grandmother was in her last years and confined to a nursing home in the late 1980s, John Parland's former estate on Colonel's Island had become the second-largest deepwater seaport in Georgia. Drive down the highway that cuts across the island today, and you see rail lines, parking lots surrounded by chain-link fences and security gates, and giant cargo ships from Europe and Asia. (One of those ships capsized in Saint Simons Sound in 2019, with catastrophic environmental consequences.) Cars are the main import and "agri-bulk"—much of it soybean meal and wood pulp—the main export. Not so different from the days when John Parland and Francis Scarlett traded cotton for luxury goods from Britain.

In 2000 the Georgia Ports Authority, which owns Colonel's Island, announced plans to expand its operations on the north end of the island. To do that they had to dig up John Parland's grave and rebury him in downtown Brunswick. State law required the GPA to develop an official "descendant identification and notification plan." The GPA hired a pair of genealogists to search the archives and place ads in the Brunswick and Savannah press. The only descendants to respond were African American Parlands, some of whom claimed a direct line to John Parland. One man said his late wife's relatives had long held that Parland had two families—a legal white one with Mary Ann and one, or possibly more, Black families "with his slave(s)." Post–Civil War U.S. census records support the claim.

It's hard to believe Mary Ann knew nothing about her husband's shadow life. Put a single white man in charge of a plantation, declared an Alabama planter in the early 1800s, "and you will see trouble enough." When he toured the South in the early 1850s as a journalist, the future landscape architect Frederick Law Olmsted recalled hearing that in Louisiana there was no plantation "in which the grandchildren of the owner are not whipped in the field by his overseer." Fanny Kemble was quick to spot the high number of mulattoes on her husband's properties. One man had a "striking resemblance" to Pierce Butler's white overseer, Roswell King. To Kemble's bewilderment, no one raised an eyebrow at this "rather unpleasant state of relationships." She listened to wrenching stories from enslaved women who described being raped, being whipped for resisting rape, and being whipped for giving birth to infants who looked like their white fathers. "I have written down the woman's words," Kemble said after hearing one account. "I wish I could write down the voice and look of abject misery with which they were spoken."

For all I know, Mary Ann Parland, too, studied the faces of the people around her on Colonel's Island, parsing foreheads and eyes and mouths for signs of her late husband. How many half brothers and sisters did little Jean and Frances Ann have? What doubts and apprehensions seeped through the veneer of Mary Ann's young life? Did she, like Mary Chesnut and so many other planters' wives, blame the enslaved women themselves for seducing her husband?

Mary Ann Parland spent what remained of her life on Colonel's Island. Just over a year after her husband's death, she married again—another elderly planter, this one a fifty-eight-year-old widower from Florida with plantations near the Georgia border. The two were wed by candlelight on Colonel's Island. The union produced no children and lasted little more than a year. Mary Ann's second husband died of consumption in 1839, in a hotel in New York City, where the two had evidently gone in search of treatment. Frank Scarlett, Mary Ann's older brother, sailed north to retrieve his twenty-three-year-old sister. Twice-widowed, Mary Ann did not marry again. In the summer of 1850, in her home on Colonel's Island, she herself died of congestive fever, seven days shy of her thirty-fourth birthday.

I want Mary Ann to have been like Kemble, who, despite her biases (the actor describes one mixed-race woman as a "dingy mulatto"), spoke truth to power. But the odds are that Mary Ann, like most of her peers, endorsed the system that gave planters' wives and daughters what Edward Baptist calls "right-handed power."

Mary Ann Parland's oldest daughter, Jean, eventually married an enslaver herself and acquired even more human property. Mary Ann's youngest daughter, Frances Ann, never married. In 1874 she was declared insane and committed to the State Lunatic Asylum in Milledgeville—the same genteel town where her grandfather Francis Scarlett had made his name as a legislator. She was somehow damaged, and I'm tempted to believe it had something to do with the madness of living in a time and place that traded in misery and lies.

In 2015 the Georgia Ports Authority drew up plans for another new parking lot, this one on the south end of Colonel's Island, roughly two miles from what was once John Parland's house. Archaeologists were dispatched to the site to excavate the remains of a slave settlement dating back to the 1830s. They unearthed the foundations of nine cabins and some forty-two thousand artifacts—remnants of plates, bowls, pots, utensils, padlocks, nails, chamber pots, pocket knives, even guns.

I happened to be visiting Brunswick when they were digging, and I went out to the site one day with a member of the team, Carolyn Rock. It was a humid May morning. Carolyn wore a canvas hat, a long-sleeved shirt, and long pants tucked inside her boots. "Ticks," she grimaced. I pulled on my own gear, and we headed into the woods. The site of the old settlement felt eerily empty—oaks and pines, mostly—as it may have sometimes felt in Parland's day. A damp breeze, bird calls. At one point Carolyn bent low to show me the outlines of a tabby foundation (made of oyster shells, sand, lime, ash, and water), and a bright blue skink darted from the ruins and disappeared into the grass.

She told me that she and her colleagues had found an unusual number of material goods around the cabins, among them buttons and pipe bowls stamped with the Scottish thistle.

"Parland and his nighttime predations," I volunteered.

Carolyn nodded. "Could be."

Among the items she and her team had discovered were dozens of beads, mostly blue, a color linked, in the African diaspora, with spiritual protection. The archaeologists also found Native American arrowheads and tools, which Parland's enslaved workers had apparently collected. They wanted, in their bondage, Carolyn speculated, to forge ties with those other abused people: the Indigenous men, women, and children who were even then, in what's known as the Trail of Tears, being pushed out of Georgia to make room for people like John Parland and Francis Scarlett.

Not long after we visited the site, Carolyn and her colleagues wound up their work. They sent the artifacts they'd exhumed to the University of Georgia in Athens for storage. They wrote a four-hundred-page report, which Carolyn eventually shared with me, along with a PowerPoint she designed for conference presentations. She and her colleagues moved on to other excavations at the sites of future shopping malls, neighborhoods, highways, and parking lots. The Georgia Ports Authority poured asphalt over the exposed remains of the old Parland slave settlement, and a new parking lot soon appeared and filled with cars. From the highway you'd never know anything else happened here.

7
SECRETS

On my desk in Michigan is a key: four inches long, rusted iron, twisted at one end. It belonged to my enslaver ancestors and later to my Uncle Bob, who mailed it to me in the early 2000s in a cardboard container whose interior he had rigged to hold the key more or less snugly. A reliquary, of sorts. I keep it beside my desk.

To my engineer uncle, the key's primary interest was structural, not metaphorical. "An intriguing item is the configuration of the combination slots," he wrote in a note attached to the front of the box. He was referring to the key's bitings, or teeth, which form a *T*—a possible reference to a branch of the Scarlett family named Tison. "Could be," he mused, "because those old birds had lots of time on their hands to think about things like that."

Ah, the old birds. Padding about the house, keys at the waist, locking up what belonged to them: smokehouse, kitchen, cupboard, trunks. It's what you do when you live with people you don't trust. Even the men and women my ancestors enslaved had items they secured. Carolyn Rock and her team found the remains of at least nine padlocks in the slave settlement they excavated on Colonel's Island—one at each of the nine cabins they unearthed. Keys too. The archaeologists determined that Parland's enslaved workers had used these to safeguard their belongings when they went out to work. When Frederick Law Olmsted toured the South in the 1850s on assignment from the *New York Times* to document the "Cotton Kingdom," he saw evidence of the same—locks hanging on the outer doors of slave cabins during the day, while their inhabitants were in the fields.

Privacy: that cherished commodity most of us take for granted. Imagine living ten or more to a room measuring no more than twelve-by-fifteen feet, the size of the dwellings Fanny Kemble encountered on her husband's Butler Island rice plantation. Two families, one on each side of the cabin, separated by a wooden partition and a common chimney. Kemble's Victorian sensibilities recoiled at the filth of these "hovels," but her sympathies were real. She saw how in winter the gaping brick chimney at the center of each cabin discharged a blast of bone-chilling air "little counteracted by the miserable spark of fire which hardly sends an attenuated thread of lingering smoke up its huge throat." Families slept together on mattresses stuffed with Spanish moss, with "filthy, pestilential-looking blankets for covering." House slaves had even less privacy. No bedroom—just a spot by the hearth for young boys and a "rough board bedstead, strewed with a little tree moss," for grown women, Kemble reports. "In the North we could not hope to keep the worst and poorest servant for a single day in the wretched discomfort in which our Negro servants are forced habitually to live."

Frederick Douglass never forgot the misery of cabin nights. Old and young, married and unmarried, male and female all slept in the same room, covered with a blanket that did little to ward off cold or wet. They went to sleep drained after a day's labor and woke "at the first gray streak of dawn" to the sound of the driver's horn, Douglass recalled in his 1845 *Narrative of the Life of Frederick Douglass, an American Slave*—a global best-seller that forced readers to confront both the realities of American slavery and the intellect of its author. Some bells rang as early as three o'clock. People who overslept were punished. Douglass recalled the agonized cries of a girl whipped for missing her morning's work. "Oh, don't, sir! Oh, please stop, master! Please, sir! Please, sir! Oh, that's enough, master! Oh, Lord! Oh, master, master! Oh, God master, do stop! Oh, God, master! Oh, God master!"

In the mid-1830s, just as Francis Scarlett was cashing in on his daughter's short and profitable marriage to John Parland, the French historian Alexis de Tocqueville released the first of his eyewitness accounts of American democracy. "The citizen of the Southern states," he wrote of the white planters he'd encountered in places like Georgia, "becomes a sort of domestic dictator from infancy. The first notion he acquires in life is that he was born to command, and the first habit he contracts is that of ruling without resistance."

Tocqueville could have been describing John Parland or Francis Scarlett or Scarlett's sons—in particular his oldest son, Francis Dunham—or Frank—who by the mid-1830s was managing several of his father's properties. Sons like Frank Scarlett grew up spoiled, "indolent," in Tocqueville's phrasing. It was these men and not their enslaved Black laborers, Tocqueville notes, who led slothful lives of dissolution. Raised in a world run by and for whites, Frank Scarlett and his brothers and sisters were taught to regard African Americans as something between human and animal. What reason would they have to think the people they "owned" deserved civilized shelter or clothing or food, let alone something so basic as privacy? Those padlocks on the cabin doors did not stop John Parland from violating his human property.

The first news that the Scarlett cemetery had been vandalized in 2010 came from a stranger. Jennie Kennedy reached out on Ancestry.com in late fall to let me know our ancestral graveyard in Brunswick had been attacked. She was desperate to find a family member, and my name had turned up. It was Jennie who spotted two boys running from the cemetery on the Saturday morning after Thanksgiving. A pair of middle school kids—one white, one Hispanic. Bored on a holiday weekend, it seemed, and not, as I first assumed, an African American bent on revenge. (Some time earlier someone had stolen the cemetery's wrought-iron fence and melted it down for cash. The place was an easy target.) Jennie had called the cops. They had found the children at home in a nearby RV park, watching TV.

"It's just . . . a violation," Jennie said by phone when I responded to her message. In their rampage through the cemetery, the boys had wrested whole tombstones from the earth and flung them against one another with such fury the damage was thought to be in excess of $30,000. Some stones were beyond repair.

"I respect history," Jennie went on. She lived near the cemetery and often took walks there because she found the place comforting. Her parents had both recently died, and she felt them near her as she walked among the Scarlett graves.

Jennie had gone to the Brunswick library and dug up clippings about the Scarletts and traced the provenance of the graveyard's wrought-iron fence (British, ca. 1812). She'd discovered a second Scarlett cemetery a half mile up the road, a hidden plot where the people enslaved by the Scarletts had buried their own loved ones. Few of its graves were visible. Jennie had no idea how many people were interred there. The site itself, as if quarantined, lay deep in the woods on a dirt lane behind a padlocked chain-link fence, on a horse farm guarded by dogs. "You'd have to ask the lady who owns the place to see it," Jennie advised.

Surely the Scarletts in their commodious house down the road knew about this cemetery, maybe even attended burials. (After kneeling among the mourners at a twilight funeral for an enslaved man on Butler Island, Fanny Kemble said she felt "an indescribable sensation of wonder at finding myself on this slave soil.")

Jennie asked if I had seen the Black Scarlett message board on Ancestry.com. I hadn't. She promised to send me a link. Hours later I went online, and there, near the top of a list of inquiries from and about African Americans with a Scarlett surname, was a message from a man named Ed Wood in Atlanta. He was searching for information about his great-great grandfather Madison Scarlett, who he thought was the son of either Francis Muir Scarlett or Scarlett's oldest son, Francis Dunham Scarlett—Frank.

I sent Ed a message. He emailed me back at once, a rush of words that blistered across my screen:

> My great great grandfather's name was Madison Scarlett we believe he was the son of Francis Muir Scarlett or son of Francis Dunham Scarlett. Madison was born in 1845 his mother's name was Susan Banks. He was born in Brunswick, Ga and he worked as a servant on a ship for most of his life. He married Julia Tison (Tyson). Feel free to contact me any time I also have letters as well as photos to share.

Here was a glimpse of the other side—the part of our story my relatives had worked so hard to conceal.

"It sounds kind of weak," I heard myself stammer to Ed Wood over the phone a day later, "but I apologize for what my family did to yours."

"Well, that was a long time ago." Ed's voice was unexpectedly kind.

"Yeah, but still . . . It was an awful time."

Ed paused. "Yeah, it was."

We were both silent. And then Ed turned to his notes. He had been researching his family's genealogy for some time, partly so his two young daughters would know their history. He had compiled a small archive of documents and photos on his phone. From census records he knew his great-great grandfather Madison was the son of a white man in Brunswick named Francis Scarlett—possibly Francis Muir Scarlett.

Or possibly his son, Frank, I said. I pulled up my notes, and we did the math. Francis Muir Scarlett was sixty in 1845, the year Madison was born. Francis Dunham Scarlett—Frank—his oldest son and namesake, a bachelor planter in charge of at least two of his father's big cotton operations, was thirty-one.

"It's gotta be him," I said.

Ed inhaled. "Yep."

He emailed me a photo of Madison. A studio portrait, sepia-toned, showed a handsome man in his thirties or early forties. More white than Black. In fact, if I hadn't known the back story I'd have taken him for white. Light, close-cut hair. Long face and aquiline nose. Thick sideburns and moustache. Dressed in a dark jacket and vest, a white dress shirt buttoned at the collar. I felt an ancestral door unlatch. The same features turn up in the only photograph I have of Frank Scarlett: long oval face and beaked nose. Thin lips. Thick sideburns. Pale eyes beneath two quizzically arched brows. Dark jacket and vest, white shirt.

So this is how that not-so-long-ago world worked—the one Kemble describes in her *Journal*, with its "rather unpleasant state of relationships." The world of Thomas Jefferson and Sally Hemmings, of John Parland and his two families, of ubiquitous "yellow babies," as even Margaret Mitchell acknowledges (though she blames Yankee soldiers, not southern gentlemen, for the phenomenon). A world so commonplace it scarcely drew a glance from the likes of Mary Chesnut, the patrician daughter and wife of enslavers in South Carolina, who observed coolly in her diary: "The mulattoes one sees in every family exactly resemble the white children—and every lady tells you who is the father of all the mulatto children in everybody's household, but those in her own she seems to think drop from the clouds, or pretends so to think."

I told Ed I would scan Frank Scarlett's picture for him, and he promised to send me a copy of Madison's death certificate listing "Frank Scarlett" as Madison's father. We talked a few minutes more, mostly about Madison and his children. One of Madison's sons had earned a law degree from the University of Michigan, where I worked. A daughter had the same name as my mother, Ann Scarlett. The family resemblances went beyond a pair of photographs.

After we hung up, I took another look at Frank's picture. Unlike the elegant Madison, with his earnest gaze and neatly pressed attire, Frank Scarlett looked as if he had just climbed down from his horse after a brisk canter through the fields. His jacket and vest were rumpled, cravat lopsided, hair unruly. There was something rakish about the man. The eyes, above all, signaled *rogue*—those arched brows, the taunting stare, as if daring me to meddle in his business.

Writer Wendell Berry, a descendant of enslavers on both sides of his family, says when he first learned about his family's past, he felt "somehow special, being thus associated with a historical scandal." In time Berry saw that this "hereditary knowledge of hereditary evil"—the racism endemic to American society—had wounded him, just as it has all white Americans. "The wound is there," Berry writes, "and it is a profound disorder, as great a damage in [the white person's] mind as it is in his society."

Berry asks if the reason some white Americans are so eager to disclose their ancestral wrongs is because we're unconsciously hoping we'll tell the story to someone who will forgive us.

Is that what I wanted from Ed Wood?

And yet to say nothing, to resort to my ancestors' silence and euphemisms, would be to widen the wound Berry describes. A wound fed by the self-protecting myths of benevolent paternalism and the deliberate papering over of violence. One of the lies men like John Parland and Frank Scarlett contrived to justify their behavior was that African American women were uniquely sexual and therefore game—as opposed to the ornamental, ladylike, asexual white wives who graced these men's parlors and bore their "legitimate" children. "Beyond the considerable unhappiness it has caused to individuals," Berry writes of this sexual chicanery, "it has poisoned the very heart of our community."

Equally toxic is the myth, so memorably exploited by the writer Thomas Dixon and his protégé Margaret Mitchell, that men of color are innate predators. In his best-selling 1905 novel, *The Clansman*, which inspired *Birth of a Nation*, Dixon details how "the black claws of the beast sank into the soft white throat" of his young victim.

Exactly how, when, and where did these socially sanctioned rapes of Black women by white men take place? In the 1930s a formerly enslaved woman, Mollie Kinsey, remembered how her sister, then "jes a small girl," was forced to "go out and lay on a table and two or three white men would have in'ercourse with her befo' they'd let her git up." (White men had a different word for it, of course. They "used" or "had" or, most sinister, "visited" the women they raped.) The federal census shows that in 1840 twenty-six-year-old bachelor planter Frank Scarlett "owned" 11 enslaved women under his own name and held another 102 women under his command on the properties he managed for his widowed sister, Mary Ann. Of those 113 captive women, 39 were between the ages of ten and thirty-six. Madison Scarlett's mother, Susan—later Susan Banks—was presumably among them.

Frank Scarlett married in 1852, the year his apparent son Madison turned seven. Perhaps Frank's bride, twenty-two-year-old Fanny McDonald, a belle of *Gone with the Wind* charms, agreed, as did countless women across the South, to behave kindly toward her husband's enslaved offspring. But Fanny McDonald Scarlett's letters give no hint she knew about them. She writes instead with piety of the man she called "Mr. S." "All the love we can give him is scarcely what he deserves," she confided dreamily to a niece after ten years of marriage and five babies, all girls. "What have I not to bless the Lord for giving me such a husband."

Ed Wood had asked if I would take a picture of his great-great grandfather Madison's grave the next time I visited Brunswick, and I did. Madison Scarlett and his second wife, Julia, were buried side by side in a cemetery at the city's north end, near the site where Liberty ships were built during World War II. A fitting spot for a man who, as Ed informed me, joined the Union navy during the Civil War and later worked on ships.

Their graves were simple. Plain blocks of stone, each incised with a name, nothing more. A reminder of what a full name meant to people long denied one. Madison Scarlett died in 1923, in his early seventies. He and Julia were among the last Americans to have known slavery's fist. They lived through war and Emancipation, the promise of Reconstruction and the brute reversal of that promise. The shock of Jim Crow. Chain gangs, lynchings—at least three in Glynn County between 1891 and 1895 and who knows how many more that went unreported? (Trawling Amy Hedrick's Glynn County website one day, I found an account in the *Atlanta Constitution* of a Black man strapped to the railroad track in Brunswick in 1884 and beheaded by a train. "Immediately the vicinity was alive with negroes who had doubtless bound the man to the track, and were hypocritically lamenting the occurrence of the tragedy," the paper claimed. A lynching by another name?)

All this time Madison and Julia Scarlett were putting down roots in Brunswick, raising kids, acquiring property. Madison became a porter at the local railroad station and treasurer of his Methodist church. He and Julia lived in a house on Amherst Street. Their son George Chandler Scarlett grew up to be a lawyer in New York City. Their daughter Ann Scarlett Cochran earned graduate degrees from four universities, one of them my father's alma mater, the University of Pennsylvania.

Ann Scarlett Cochran was a strong woman, Ed told me when we met in person the following year in Atlanta. He was younger than I'd expected—thirties or early forties—with pale brown skin, a shy smile, and a phone full of digitized Scarlett documents. We sat across from each other at a booth in a Waffle House somewhere in the city's nest of highways, and Ed scrolled through his archive. Snapshots of his daughters playing in the yard. The studio portrait of Madison he had sent me after our first phone call. A glam shot of Madison's second wife, Julia, in a magenta coat and lambswool hat, looking like a figure from the Harlem Renaissance. A formal portrait of two of their children: son John, pale skin and chestnut hair, dressed in a white sailor's suit and black leggings, and daughter Ann, equally pale, wearing a pink dress and matching pink bow in her red hair.

Ed remembered Ann Scarlett Cochran from his childhood—a handsome, big-boned woman with skin so light "she could have passed for white but didn't." She studied in Mexico and traveled the world and taught at several universities in Georgia. An independent woman of the sort my grandmother admired and urged me to become. "Someone who spoke her mind," Ed said.

He had a story about Ann Scarlett Cochran, one that still circulated in his family. It involved my grandmother's first cousin Frank Scarlett, the man who had thought so highly of Mary Ann Scarlett's arranged marriage to John Parland. ("It was the custom in England and I think it was a good custom.") Born in 1891, reared in Brunswick, one of a long line of Frank Scarletts named after the family patriarch, this twentieth-century Frank Scarlett had distinguished himself by becoming a federal judge for the southern district of Georgia—the first ever from Brunswick.

At his swearing-in ceremony in 1946, Judge Scarlett had placed his right hand on the Bible carried across the Atlantic by Francis Muir Scarlett in 1799 and vowed to impartially discharge the duties of his office. For the next two decades, Judge Frank Scarlett ruled consistently against the interests of African Americans.

One day in the late 1950s or early 1960s, after he had issued yet another discriminatory ruling against Blacks—Ed thought this one may have had to do with a civil rights case against the Savannah Housing Authority—Ann Scarlett Cochran had had enough. She found her way to the judge's office and charged through the door, waving a two-foot-high framed portrait of her father, Madison.

"*This* is your family," Ann Scarlett blared.

Judge Scarlett was unmoved.

"I gather they exchanged choice words," Ed said.

As doubtless they did, this man and woman on two sides of a nearly four-hundred-year divide—our national wound. I had seen pictures of Ann Scarlett Cochran in a book about notable African Americans in Glynn County. An imposing woman, not unlike Fanny Kemble in her older age, with a stern gaze and tight smile, impeccably clothed in tailored suits and pearl necklaces, hair swept off her face in soft waves. I wonder what Judge Frank Scarlett thought of her. This man who, in 1963, eight years after *Brown v. Board of Education*, ruled that Savannah's public schools had a legally "reasonable" right to remain segregated owing to the "distinguishable educability capabilities" of white and Black children. This cousin of my grandmother's, who spent his free time tracing the noble origins of the Scarlett family and whose rulings on Savannah's schools became the basis of a national movement to overturn *Brown v. Board of Education*.

Ann Scarlett Cochran would have known his type. She must have realized, too, when she walked into Judge Scarlett's office, that she was carrying on the work of Frederick Douglass and Harriet Tubman and Sojourner Truth and W. E. B. Du Bois and so many others who had risked everything to unlock slavery's lasting coffles. With no help from Judge Scarlett, Savannah's schools were finally integrated in 1967. Scarlett died four years later. His obituary, a copy of which Ed Wood showed me on his phone, hailed the judge's illustrious career, in particular his 1955 decision "upholding the 'separate but equal' doctrine concerning public housing." That ruling had brought him national attention. "His decisions in the Civil Rights field were marked by courage and diligence during those trying times," the obituary read.

Two years after Judge Scarlett's death, Senator Herman Talmadge of Georgia introduced a bill to name the federal building in Brunswick after his late colleague. President Gerald Ford signed the bill into law in 1975. As of early 2025, the Frank M. Scarlett Federal Building—a dull gray edifice honoring a malignant era—occupies a prominent spot in the center of downtown Brunswick.

8

LOST

During the years that Judge Frank Scarlett was issuing his brave rulings in trying times, I made my first trip to Georgia. It was the early 1960s. My mother drove us south from Pennsylvania, through Virginia and the Carolinas to Brunswick and over to Saint Simons Island, where we checked into a white cinderblock motel with a kidney-shaped pool outside our room. I had no inkling I was in a segregated world. We ate and gassed up and swam where it suited us. Decades later a friend gave me a PDF of a 1949 edition of the *Negro Motorist Green Book*, listing the hotels, campgrounds, barber shops, beauty parlors, gas stations, restaurants, drugstores, taverns, tailors, night clubs, and garages then willing to serve African Americans so they could travel in the United States, Canada, Mexico, and Bermuda without "difficulties" or "embarrassments." "There will be a day sometime in the near future when this guide will not have to be published," its author, Victor Green, wrote hopefully in the book's short introduction. "That is when we as a race will have equal opportunities and privileges in the United States." The first edition of the *Green Book* appeared in 1936. The last came out in 1966, the year I turned eleven.

By then I was a full, if unwitting, participant in the system. There was my grandparents' house in Virginia, where Carrie ate from mismatched dishes on one side of the kitchen door and we sat on the other side with our porcelain plates and sterling flatware. I never saw Carrie come into the living room except to clean or serve, never saw her sit on my grandparents' upholstered furniture, only the wooden chairs at the kitchen table, where she shelled crabs and peas. The town itself—Tappahannock—was segregated, but I didn't know it. Why would I? I could go anywhere. (A childhood acquaintance who grew up in Tappahannock told me he had always been confused by the sign on the front door of a popular downtown restaurant: "White only." He thought it meant the door could only be painted white.) Even in Pennsylvania, the much-vaunted North, I could shop with ease as a middle schooler—shoplift, even—while African Americans knew if they so much as tried on a hat in the local department store they had to buy it.

"IN *Memory of Our Old nurse* Maum CHARLOTTE" was the inscription on the tombstone I saw for the first time during that trip to Georgia in the early 1960s. Another person we loved but kept at an unbreachable distance. The nineteenth-century Scarletts must have felt about Charlotte as my family and I felt about Carrie—loved but "Other." What kind of ceremony accompanied Charlotte's burial in the spring of 1856, four years after passage of the Fugitive Slave Act and nine years before Emancipation? Did the Scarletts, good Methodists that they were, conduct a service? And if they did, how did that service compare to the rites held up the road in the cemetery where the rest of the people enslaved by the Scarletts buried their dead? Eventually I was able to visit that second graveyard, thanks to Amy Hedrick, the Glynn County genealogist and creator of glynngen.com. Amy knew how to reach the woman who could unlock the gate and kennel the dogs that would otherwise make it impossible to get near the old slave burial ground.

"Over there," Amy said, as we pulled up to the site in her red pickup. She pointed to a stretch of pockmarked earth beneath a grove of tall oaks. I could make out a smattering of hollows in the ground, but if Amy hadn't told me they were graves, I wouldn't have guessed. There was no obelisk, as in my family's cemetery, no names enshrined in stone. Wendell Berry speaks of the gaps within the language white Americans used to communicate with Black Americans when he was growing up in Kentucky in the 1930s and 1940s. "When in their presence one did not flaunt one's 'superiority' or use the word *nigger*, one called elderly Negroes Aunt and Uncle, and so on," Berry writes of this coded speech, born of prejudice and segregation. But within that speech, he says, "there was a silence, an emptiness, of exactly the shape of the humanity of the black man."

It struck me that the burial ground in front of me was similarly contoured. Amy and I stepped gingerly across the soil in the direction of the graveyard, alert for soft spots that could twist an ankle. To get here hadn't been easy, and I wasn't sure what I'd hoped to find. Evidence, I guess. Some hint of the lives we had tried to eradicate. But there was only this gently undulating terrain that itself seemed a reflection of the void Berry describes.

The custom among African Americans in Glynn County, as Fanny Kemble learned, was to bury the dead at night, by torchlight, lowering the deceased into the earth with prayers and hymns. Black cemeteries were often positioned near water. The spot where Amy and I stood wasn't far from an estuary of the South Brunswick River, which feeds into the Atlantic by way of Saint Simons Sound. Enslaved people knew they had been brought to America by water, a Gullah-Geechee man, Gregory Grant, told me when I visited his Geechee Kunda Cultural Arts Center and Museum in Riceboro, Georgia, midway between Savannah and Brunswick.

Grant's museum and cultural arts center was dedicated to honoring the Gullah-Geechee people and their language, material culture, food, music, dance, and religion. Descendants of enslaved Africans—principally from West Africa (the term "Gullah" is thought to stem from either Angola or Gola)—the Gullah-Geechee people shaped the Lowcountry landscapes of Georgia and South Carolina. Because they lived and labored on the Lowcountry's barrier islands (in relative isolation from their European masters, who preferred the more livable conditions of the mainland), the Gullah-Geechee developed their own language and lifestyle, a unique blend of African traditional religion and Christianity.

Enslaved Gullah-Geechee, Gregory told me, believed water would carry them home. Or, as he phrased it, "We came by water, we'll go back by water."

An estimated 12.5 million people kidnapped from Africa crossed the Atlantic Ocean between 1501 and 1866. Just over 10 million of them survived the voyage. The dead and dying were tossed overboard without ceremony. "The Atlantic Ocean," Gregory said, "is paved with the bones of ancestors."

Add to those the bones of those who disappeared on North American soil. Not only the nameless people buried in the woods a mile up the road from the Scarletts at Oak Grove but the African Americans throughout the United States who received no funeral at all, or at best a cursory one. "When a slave died," a Texas woman who survived slavery recalled in the 1930s, "masser made the coffin, and sent a couple of niggers to bury the body, and said, 'Don't be long, and no singin' or prayin' allowed, put 'em in the ground, cover 'em up, hurry on back to that field.'"

Historian Edda Fields-Black has described her quest to restore her great-grandfather's otherwise unmarked grave in an unmarked ancestral cemetery in the South Carolina Lowcountry. Fields-Black, who has lived and studied in West Africa, speaks of the "millions of disturbed spirits in our cosmology who have the power to disturb the living." This idea, she says, "comes from a very African place, a place I feel very close to in the Lowcountry." Of her efforts—and those of other descendants of enslaved people—to reclaim the lost, Fields-Black vows, "We will trouble the living until we honor our dead."

As I stood inside the woods on land where my family's enslaved once grieved their dead, in the heart of our American gulag, I began to see what she meant.

Naturally, my grandmother and her sisters, born thirty years after the Civil War, wanted to talk about other things: about loyal and grateful servants, about beaus and balls and coquettes like Fanny McDonald Scarlett, our own Scarlett O'Hara, wife of Frank Scarlett and daughter-in-law to Francis Muir Scarlett. Fanny's letters to friends and family are among the most copied documents in the Scarlett archive. Read Fanny's correspondence from 1850, written at age nineteen, and you're in the opening pages of *Gone with the Wind.*

In her one surviving portrait, Fanny Scarlett even looks like Vivien Leigh. Locks of curling brown hair, dimpled cheeks, almond eyes. A self-conscious tease of the kind Mitchell relished. The prewar, not-yet-married Fanny McDonald reads novels like *The Maiden Aunt* and *The Two Flirts*. She takes "delightful" buggy rides with her "interesting driver" en route to what she calls "frolicing." She writes breathless letters to her girlfriend Carrie, in which she describes herself as "such a 'harum-scarum' thing" and apologizes for the "scribble" of her handwriting. She serves up the gossip:

> I spied a handsome ring on Sue's finger that took my fancy wonderfully. By the way, has Sallie got hers from Steve yet?
>
> It is the current report about here that Mrs. Gignilliat and Mr. Rees are engaged—but I don't believe it.

> Beaux are very scarce in these quarters. Only two of the city gents called on us and they were Mr. Adams and Captain Clark. I did not lose my heart with either. The former thinks too much of himself and the latter not quite enough.

Fanny sends Valentines to suitors and books to friends; she takes singing lessons and goes horseback riding and attends parties. She is shocked when male acquaintances get drunk and thrilled when friends get married. Sundays bore her ("no matter how hard we try I know it is very difficult to spend the Sabbath properly when we are at home all day"), and yet she yearns to be a "better Christian." "Give yourself *all* for Christ," she admonishes her friend Carrie. "You can never know till then *true* happiness."

Fanny's piety appears to have come from her late mother, Margaret—a devout woman who, in the pattern of Mitchell's saintly Ellen O'Hara, steered her tempestuous Scottish husband, Alexander McDonald, away from his "unstable" habits and into the certainties of Christian salvation. The enslaver Alexander McDonald went on to become a church deacon.

His daughter saw no discrepancy between her father's faith and the means by which he made his money. Few in her position did. "Americans reconciled the gap between the ideal and the real" by, among other tactics, "manipulating Scripture to find biblical sanction for slavery," writes historian Jon Meacham. Or, as Frederick Douglass noted in his *Narrative of the Life of Frederick Douglass, an American Slave*, "The slave auctioneer's bell and the churchgoing bell chime in with each other."

Reared in luxury and accustomed to adulation, the corseted and beribboned Miss Jane Frances McDonald—Fanny—trained her gaze away from earthly surroundings (her father's property, for example, held a half-dozen cabins housing nearly forty enslaved African Americans) and toward "that bright home beyond the grave for those who love the Lord—where the wicked cease from troubling and the weary are at rest," she said.

Like other women in the extended Scarlett family, Fanny was raised to marry and breed, a prospect she found romantic. A month before her twentieth birthday she confessed to Carrie that if she were to meet a man who loved her and whom she could love in return, she would welcome it—so long as her admirer kept his mouth shut. "He must not *speak* of it—not even *whisper*, for it would break the charm." The same letter mentions "Mr. Frank Scarlett," who has been ill of late and for whom the community is praying. "I sincerely hope that his valuable life may be spared."

Two years later they married. Fanny was twenty-one, Frank thirty-eight. A bachelor with property valued at over $30,000. A man of enterprise, in his father's mold: estate administrator, postmaster, owner of a turpentine distillery, secretary of a countywide citizens group, past sergeant in the Glynn Hussars, and future board member of the Brunswick and Florida Railroad. Frank Scarlett managed his late sister Mary Ann's estate on Colonel's Island and his own holdings next door at a plantation called Fancy Bluff, where he and Fanny took up residence. He looked after his father's affairs when the older man was in Milledgeville, as Francis Muir Scarlett was again in 1852, the year Frank and Fanny wed. Francis Muir was then sixty-six, and this was his twelfth and final term in the Georgia legislature. Fanny's new husband was also helping to raise his two orphaned teenage nieces, Jean and Frances Ann Parland, and he and Fanny would soon take on a third niece, Meta Long, when Frank's youngest sister, Theodosia Scarlett Long, succumbed to disease in her midtwenties.

Frank Scarlett appears to have savored life as a planter. (Amy Hedrick told me she thought Frank had a zeal for slavery his father lacked.) Press accounts show "F. D. [Frank] Scarlett" sailing back and forth from Brunswick to Savannah and Charleston, South Carolina, staying overnight in hotels, negotiating with cotton factors, mailing samples of Scarlett cotton to reporters in hopes they would promote it, which they did.

The U.S. government slave schedules for 1850 reveal that, in that same year, Frank (listed as Francis Dunham) Scarlett managed a labor force of thirty-six enslaved workers under his own name and nearly four hundred more enslaved people under his father's. The long lists of slaves "owned" by Frank Scarlett take up multiple pages and give only gender, age, and color (*B* for Black, *M* for mulatto)—no names.

Records of his administration of John Parland's estate also track Frank Scarlett in action—purchasing shoes, cloth, and corn by the bushel for his family's fieldhands and overcoats for his carpenter and overseer. Frank doles out cash to his driver and takes in cash from the sale of produce and poultry raised by Scarlett slaves. He buys and sells and rents out his workers and keeps their earnings. When his "negroes" fall sick, Frank buys them bacon. When they flee, he hunts them down:

> ONE HUNDRED AND FIFTY DOLLARS REWARD.—Runaway from the plantation of the subscriber, the following slaves, viz: DICK, a tall black fellow, quick-spoken, intelligent, and about 50 years old; ELIZA, a large woman, yellow complexion, very sensible and about 25 years old. These two have been out about two years. NED, a black fellow, about 30 years old, five feet eight inches high; and HENRY, a mulatto fellow about 20 years old, and five feet ten inches high. Ned and Henry have been out but a few days. They were bought in Charleston, and is presumed they will make for that place.
>
> One hundred dollars will be paid for apprehending and securing Dick and Eliza, and Fifty Dollars for Ned and Henry, and in that proportion for either of them; together with all reasonable expenses for securing them in some jail, or for their delivery to Elias Reed, in Savannah or to me at my residence. / FRANCIS D. SCARLETT, Glynn County, Ga.

"They were bought in Charleston, and is presumed they will make for that place"—where they doubtless had loved ones. The notice ran for days in the Savannah and Charleston papers in the summer of 1844, then stopped in mid-August. In its place:

> Committed, To the Jail of Colleton [South Carolina] District, runaways, NED, a black fellow about thirty years old, and HENRY, a mulatto fellow about twenty years old, they say they belong to Francis Scarlet [*sic*], of the State of Georgia.

Follow-up accounts note that Frank Scarlett paid the South Carolina jailer $4.28 to lock up Ned and Henry and an additional $59.20 to hold the two men for twenty days. He doled out a $50.00 reward and $50.00 more in fees to a South Carolina law firm for "advice and services in recovering two runaway slaves," as well as $299.36 for "expenses on two runaway Negroes."

Also caught that fall—probably in the Territory of Florida—were the freedom seekers Dick and Eliza, who had been missing for two years.

They were presumably found by a slave patrol, one of countless vigilante groups prowling the South in the nineteenth century. Made up of white men like Frank, armed and on horseback, accompanied by dogs, these unchecked posses—forerunners of rural southern police departments in the nineteenth and twentieth centuries—were primed to inflict the kind of punishment that would scar a person for life, or worse. (In 1848 a patrol calling themselves the "Glynn County Rangers" formed in Glynn County with the express aim of acting "as a safeguard, to protect the Community and County from insurrections and invasions.")

After their capture that autumn, Frank had Dick and Eliza shipped from Jacksonville to Savannah and jailed. Shortly before Christmas 1844, Frank or another Scarlett family member sold Dick and Eliza to an unknown buyer for $500. Savannah's auction house stood conveniently near the banks and law firms and cotton factors where Frank did business. Records show that he and his brother David traveled to the city that year and paid for a wagon to transport Dick and Eliza "to and from jail." As the Scarlett brothers strode through town in their dark coats and leather gloves, it's possible they spotted the captive man and woman being hauled somewhere in that wagon—maybe to a slave pen outside the auction house, where Dick and Eliza would have been left to shiver and wait their turn on the block. Or maybe Frank and David Scarlett conducted the sale in private, with a known buyer, one willing to take on two people who had a history of fleeing.

Nor is this the only account of Frank Scarlett engaging in the slave trade. He can be found that same year, 1844, shipping a nineteen-year-old enslaved woman named Lucinda from Savannah to Brunswick and two years earlier selling an eighteen-year-old boy named Jacob to a pair of Florida men for $500. That exchange, like the sale of Dick and Eliza, took place just days before Christmas.

In his dealings with Eliza and Dick, Ned and Henry, Frank would have been no different from his wife's father or brothers or brothers-in-law or any of the men Fanny Scarlett had socialized with in her heyday as a single girl in search of a suitable mate. An able master kept strict control over his labor force. So did his wife. Inside their ample home at Fancy Bluff, overlooking the sunlit marshes of the Georgia coast, Fanny would have relied on a crew of enslaved women to prepare her meals and dust her pictures and arrange the flowers from her garden, where snowdrops bloomed every spring. Practiced in the arts of herbal medicine and midwifery, some of these women surely coaxed Fanny through her five pregnancies and deliveries and nursed her four surviving daughters through measles and toothaches and stomach ailments. (A fifth daughter, born in 1858, died at fourteen months, and surely African American hands also washed this child's body and wrapped her in cotton and laid her in a small coffin for burial.)

The names of some of the women who tended Fanny and Frank Scarlett at Fancy Bluff were Sarah Jane, Mary, Hetty, Dido, Grace, Dolly, and Sary—whom Fanny called, at various times, Big, Old, Yellow, and Maum Sary.

There was also a Maum Matilda, who seems to have come to the Scarlett household by way of John and Mary Ann Parland's two orphaned daughters, Jean and Frances Ann. Matilda's name appears in the 1836 inventory of John Parland's estate, where she is valued at $800. By the time Fanny and Frank married and took the Parland sisters with them to Fancy Bluff, Matilda would have been in her early thirties. Fanny came to depend so wholly on her she trusted her "with anything."

I imagine Matilda and the others wore dresses made of the coarse cotton fabric known as osnaburg, which the Scarletts ordered in bulk, and sturdy shoes, for the Scarletts bought those as well, together with "Negro woollens." Such items turn up in the records of John Parland's estate. But it's impossible to know if the women who worked for Fanny and Frank Scarlett received these materials in sufficient quantity or quality to withstand the damp cold of a Glynn County winter. On her husband's plantation fifteen miles north of Fancy Bluff, Fanny Kemble saw a group of enslaved women in rags struggling to warm themselves around a handful of "powerless embers" one December day. Kemble wept at the sight.

Maybe Fanny Scarlett wept as well, though her letters give no sign of it. She frets about her husband's health, her father's broken leg, her father-in-law's earache, and her daughter's whooping cough, and she grieves when her sister-in-law loses a child—but of the women who serve her, Fanny mentions only their whereabouts and their loyalty.

Charlotte, the nurse buried outside the Scarlett cemetery, would have been known to Fanny, perhaps even worked in her house. Like Matilda,

Charlotte may have come to the Scarletts through Frank's Parland nieces. She was possibly in her eighties when Fanny and Frank married in 1852. Old enough to have earned a rest after decades of suckling Scarlett babies and watching them turn into her masters and mistresses. But there's little reason to think Charlotte got the reprieve she deserved—enslaved elders were typically put to work caring for small children, nursing the sick, washing clothes, and cooking for other enslaved people.

Charlotte died on May 4, 1856, the same month John Brown went on an antislavery killing spree in Kansas, and enslavers across the South responded by clamping down even more harshly on their human property. According to her tombstone, Charlotte was ninety-one. A beloved "nurse" and "Maum"—the Lowcountry term for "Mammy," that grinning emblem of so much postwar wishful thinking. Never mind the intelligence it took to be a nurse: the skills to bring a breech newborn safely into the world or to soothe a teething baby or to brew a special tea for rheumatism.

"Our Old Nurse." Words carved into a block of stone as indifferent as the ocean floor "paved with the bones of ancestors." Did Charlotte and the others ever gaze out at the water beyond the Scarlett plantations and dream of freedom, as the teenaged Frederick Douglass did? "You are loosed from your moorings, and are free," he would think to himself as he watched the boats stippling the surface of the Chesapeake Bay. "I am fast in my chains, and am a slave!"

It is almost certainly by water that Dick and Eliza, Henry and Ned, and who knows how many others fled from Frank Scarlett and his extended family. People and goods along the Georgia coastline all moved by water—still do. Seven years before his death, Frank's brother-in-law John Parland posted a $100 reward for three enslaved men—Harry, July, and August—who had seized a plantation boat and sailed off, either to South Carolina or Florida, Parland thought.

What became of Harry, July, and August is unknown, but, if they were caught, Parland would have brought them back to his property on boats piloted by enslaved men. The Scarletts also rented out enslaved African Americans to build the canals that linked neighboring waterways along the coast. Laboring in snake-infested swamps, a single worker could cut as much as one yard of canal in two days' time. For this he received fifty cents a day—money the Scarletts kept.

Water as punishment. On November 28, 1858, nearly two years after Charlotte was buried in a tract of earth not far from a canal dug by Scarlett slaves, Francis Muir Scarlett ordered eight of his enslaved workers to row him through the marshes to nearby Jekyll Island. Well before dawn that morning, a yacht retrofitted with a warren of decks, each no taller than nineteen inches, had dropped anchor on the landward side of Jekyll and unloaded its cargo—over four hundred human beings abducted from West Africa, most of them men, all of them for sale. Francis Scarlett, then seventy-three, was in a mood to buy. He had brought a grandchild with him—the five-year-old son of his son David. The child's mother had pleaded with her father-in-law not to take the boy, but Francis Muir had prevailed. He believed it would be a "good experience" for the child to accompany him.

The two reached Jekyll Island that morning to find hundreds of malnourished Africans, many of them naked, a few with blankets or strips of clothing, scavenging in a field for mice to eat. The stench from the yacht—an illegal slaver called the *Wanderer*, one of the last to sail the Middle Passage to the United States—was suffocating.

According to the document I discovered in my Scarlett archive—a typewritten oral history—Francis Muir Scarlett paid $1,500 to buy a captive man from the *Wanderer*. A "large magnificent Negro slave," Scarlett's grandson would remember years later. "The Captain informed my grandfather not to purchase this slave because he was a King or a Prince and he persecuted the other slaves on the way from Africa." But Scarlett bought the man anyway and took him back to Oak Grove, where the African apparently refused to work and was thus "severely" punished. Francis Scarlett then tried to turn this captive man into an overseer, but the man resisted. And so, according to Scarlett's young grandson—the five-year-old who went along to Jekyll that morning and who decades later would tell this story to his own descendants—the Scarletts rented this African king or prince out to other enslavers in Glynn County "as a producer of children for $100 a day."

The little boy who accompanied Francis Muir Scarlett on that hellish expedition in 1858 would in time become the father of Judge Frank M. Scarlett, for whom Brunswick's federal building is named. Sometime in the mid-twentieth century—perhaps during the years he was working to uphold segregation throughout the southern district of Georgia—Judge Scarlett typed up his father's story about the *Wanderer*. I found it nestled among my grandmother's papers, next to diagrams of the Scarlett cemetery and copies of Fanny Scarlett's letters. To read it is to be reminded of what I've often heard Joe McGill of the Slave Dwelling Project say: "They were slaveholders. How good could they be?"

The *Wanderer* arrived in Georgia from West Africa precisely fifty years after the U.S. government banned the transatlantic slave trade. For weeks after its landing, rumors of the illegal ship circulated in the American press. But the vessel itself, rinsed clean with vinegar and lye and restored to its original status as a yacht, disappeared. The men behind the *Wanderer* scheme—chief among them a debt-plagued Savannah businessman named Charles Lamar—went unpunished.

Three months after Francis Scarlett purchased his African king or prince, Fanny Kemble's estranged husband, Pierce Butler, sold off 436 of his enslaved workers to pay down gambling and other debts. The sale, fully legal and amply advertised, took place in Savannah on a racetrack owned by Charles Lamar, the mastermind behind the *Wanderer*. The largest-ever slave auction in U.S. history, it became known as the "Weeping Time." Families whose ties to the Butlers and to one another went back generations were hauled to Savannah, housed in horse sheds, and sold. "The blades of grass on all the Butler estates are outnumbered by the tears that are poured out in agony," wrote a reporter for the *New York Tribune* who posed as a buyer so he could report on the two-day sale. "But, then, what business have 'niggers' with tears?"

Later that year John Brown would launch another murderous raid, this time in Harper's Ferry, Virginia. U.S. Marines under the command of Col. Robert E. Lee quelled the insurrection and captured Brown. He was hanged in December 1859. In Illinois a lawyer named Abraham Lincoln, who thought slavery a "cancer," was campaigning to become the new Republican Party's nominee for U.S. president.

Before long Fanny Scarlett would write wistfully about the days when "our dear old homes," untouched by war's deprivations, stood tall "in their loneliness and loveliness, just as they used to be."

Her husband, Frank, would admit grudgingly, "All things must come to an end."

As for the nameless king or prince, stolen from Africa, chained below deck in a space no bigger than a coffin for the forty-two-day ocean crossing, brought to Scarlett lands, whipped for disobedience, and then forced to rape other enslaved human beings—I've found no record of him anywhere, not even his name.

FIG. 1. Francis Muir Scarlett (1785–1869). Born in London, Francis Muir Scarlett immigrated to Georgia as a teenager and became an overseer and then an enslaver, one of America's richest. Scarlett-Tison family collection, Georgia Historical Society.

FIG. 2. *above*: Francis Dunham (Frank) Scarlett (1814–97). When war broke out in 1861, Frank Scarlett organized an armed white militia "to protect our homes." Scarlett-Tison family collection, Georgia Historical Society.

FIG. 3. Jane Frances McDonald (Fanny) Scarlett (1830–63). The wife of Frank Scarlett, Fanny wondered if the enslaved woman who escaped from the Scarletts during the war could be "so depraved as to be happy." Scarlett-Tison family collection, Georgia Historical Society.

FIG. 4. John Mason Berrien Tison (1817–82). A Scarlett relation by marriage and one of America's wealthiest enslavers, John Mason Tison was praised for his exceptional generosity. Scarlett-Tison family collection, Georgia Historical Society.

FIG. 5. (*above*) Alec Massie at Bethel Plantation, circa 1888. Massie, formerly enslaved by the Tison family, was married to a survivor of the illegal slave ship *The Wanderer*. His birth and death dates are unknown. Scarlett-Tison family collection, Georgia Historical Society.

FIG. 6. Tombstone of "Maum CHARLOTTE," a woman enslaved by the Scarletts, early to mid-nineteenth century. The tombstone was placed just outside the fence where white members of the Scarlett family were buried. Scarlett-Tison family collection, Georgia Historical Society.

FIG. 7. Madison Scarlett, probable son of Frank Scarlett. Photo courtesy of Edward Wood; used with permission.

FIG. 8. Julia Tison (Tyson), wife of Madison Scarlett.
Photo courtesy of Edward Wood; used with permission.

FIG. 9. Alec Massie, in front of a former slave cabin on Scarlett property, circa 1888. Free Blacks continued to live in former slave cabins well into the twentieth century. Scarlett-Tison family collection, Georgia Historical Society.

FIG. 10. Millie Polecat (dates unknown). She was enslaved by the Scarletts and worked for them after gaining her freedom. The author's grandmother knew Millie as a "goof doctor," or conjurer. Scarlett-Tison family collection, Georgia Historical Society.

FIG. 11. (*left*) Virginia Sherrod Tison Scarlett (1884–1921). She was the daughter of John Mason Berrien Tison, wife of George Scarlett, and great-great-grandmother of the author. Scarlett-Tison family collection, Georgia Historical Society.

FIG. 12. Annie Belle (Minnie) Scarlett Hilsman (1848–1921), with two of her children: Virginia (Ginger) Hilsman Blanton (*left*) and Mary King (Mamie) Hilsman Pettigrew (*right*), the author's grandmother. Scarlett-Tison family collection, Georgia Historical Society.

FIG. 13. Mary King (Mamie) Hilsman Pettigrew (1898–1994), the author's maternal grandmother. Scarlett-Tison family collection, Georgia Historical Society.

FIG. 14. (*above*) Robert Leslie Pettigrew (1893–1987), the author's maternal grandfather. Scarlett-Tison family collection, Georgia Historical Society.

FIG. 15. Mary King Hilsman (Pettigrew) and Robert Leslie Pettigrew on their honeymoon, 1920. Scarlett-Tison family collection, Georgia Historical Society.

BRUNSWICK TIMES-CALL

BRUNSWICK, GA. SATURDAY MORNING, JUNE 15, 1901. PRICE FIVE CENT

CITY COUNCIL MEETING.

What the City Solons Did at Their Last Regular Meeting.

REGULAR MEETING.

Brunswick, Ga., June 13, 1901.

Present: Hon. N. Emanuel, Aldermen Cox, du Bignon, McGarrey, Briesenick, Smith and Newman. Absent: Bloodworth and Calhoun.

Minutes of meeting June 6th read and confirmed.

On motion the regular order was suspended, and the following routine business disposed of:

Petition from D. W. Krauss and C. Symmes, attorneys for Mrs. E. T. Danforth, offering to arbitrate the question of the value of the property awarded her at the last term of court, etc., referred to Special Committee.

Petition from residents in the vicinity of Union and Prince streets, requesting the substitution of an electric light for the gas lamp in that locality, referred to Light and Water Committee.

Report from Special committee on petition of W. B. Curry was received, stating the city had no Town Commons for lease in vicinity asked for by petitioner, therefore, could not grant petition. Ordered filed.

Report from Taxes and Revenue committee on petition of Brantly & Aiken, recommending that the over payment of $6 43 be refunded, and the Treasurer be directed to make payment on proper vouchers.

Report Special Committee on Sewerage Inspection:

Brunswick, Ga., June 13, 1901.

To the Honorable Mayor and Council—Gentlemen: Your Committee on Sanitation together with a Special committee, composed of two from the Board of Health and Civil Engineer, to which was referred the resolution of Council, its subject being, "To make

GRIFFIN PAYS THE PENALTY

Executed Yesterday Morning for Killing Conductor Latimer.

FRICY GRIFFIN.

Fricy Griffin, the murderer of Conductor Marion Latimer, was hanged in the Glynn County jail yesterday at 12:23 o'clock in the presence of the sheriff, his assistance, several guards, a few newspaper men and several other citizens, who were admitted to see the execution.

Long before the hour appointed for the hanging, hundreds of colored citizens and [illegible] of whites congregated around the jail, looking at the

on Conductor Latimer's train at Everett to come to Brunswick, how the conductor and trainmen tried to drive him from the train, how he was afraid to jump because the train was moving so fast, how the conductor beat him with a broom and threatened to knock him off, and finally to scare the conductor, not intending to kill him, he fired the pistol. He claimed not to have known the conductor was hit until he came to Brunswick after the shooting. He

have done. I have prayed and asked him to forgive me for every idle thing and every wickedness I have done. I never used to believe in angels. I thought people told you of them to frighten you and make you do good, but the other night while I was lying on my bunk, with my eyes wide open, the cell was all lighted up, and an angel of the Lord came and said "Fricy, God has forgiven you your sins." I feel like I am going to die, but I have all the friends I want with Jesus on my side. When I fall through that trap out here God knows the reason I am here is not because I did it intentionally. I know that when I fall through, he is going to catch me up and carry me to my home beyond the skies. "Though I walk through the valley of the shadow of death I will fear no evil." How can I fear? Jesus Christ is with me. They say Fricy Griffin has nerve. It aint nerve. It's Jesus Christ with me. My soul is happy in His word. I am no murderer; I am no slayer. I am ready to die. While I am ready, I want to go to heaven. I would not have a pardon, I don't want a pardon. I want to go to heaven. If I go back into the this world, I am liable to be cut off in the twinkling of an eye and destroyed. I will be happy up in Beulah land."

Told His Friends Good By.

As soon as Griffin finished his statement he went to the window and told all his friends who had gathered around the jail, good by; then shaking hands with those in the jail, he said he was ready. While Sheriff Berrie read the death warrant the negro took a cigarette from his pocket and enjoyed his last smoke.

Steps on the Trap.

Griffin was then led to the gallows, and mounted the trap without a quiver. As the rope was being tied around his neck, the negro sang, and as the black cap was placed over his head, he said:

DAVIS SUSPENDED FOR THIRTY DAYS

CITY COUNCIL MET YESTERDAY MORNING AND TOOK THIS ACTION IN ORDER TO INVESTIGATE CHARGES.

The city council held a meeting in the mayor's office at 10 o'clock yesterday morning to investigate the charges brought against Superintendent of Public Works David Davis, charged with stealing feed from the city.

The evidence taken on Thursday night was carefully examined by the board, and after considerable discussion it was decided that the superintendent be suspended for thirty days, pending a thorough investigation.

This step was taken by the body in view of the fact that no evidence, outside of that of Mr. Hoyt, who preferred the charges, has been introduced to prove that Mr. Davis had a wagon load of feed carried from the city's feed house to his residence.

There is no one who saw Hoyt carry the feed in question, and it is not known by the body whether Hoyt's evidence is true or not, as Mr. Davis flatly denies the charge and says he will prove his innocence.

During the thirty days, the council will thoroughly investigate the matter. Chief of Police Burney has been instructed to also act as superintendent of streets during the time of Davis' suspension.

Mr. Davis has been a resident of Brunswick for a number of years, has always enjoyed a good reputation, and his friends are sure that he will be acquitted of the charge preferred against him.

FIG. 16. Fricie Griffin on the front page of the *Brunswick Times-Call* (June 15, 1901), one day after Griffin's execution. Library of Congress, Washington DC.

FIG. 17. (*top*) Author with members of the Hippard family at their reunion in Brunswick, Georgia, in 2011. *From left to right*: Marjorie Hippard Clinch, Nancy Hippard Cahoon, the author, Gilbert Maxwell (husband of Gertrude Hippard Maxwell), and Gertrude Hippard Maxwell. Author's collection; used with permission from the Hippard family.

FIG. 18. Slave Dwelling Project sleepover at Locust Grove, Louisville, Kentucky, in August 2019. Author's collection.

PART 3

Betrayals

9
TROUBLE

On December 7, 1859, "well knowing the uncertainty of life," Francis Muir Scarlett drafted his last will and testament. He ordered that his body be "decently interred," his soul remanded "to the God who gave it," his funeral expenses and debts paid, and his estate equally divided among his direct descendants. As a special bequest, he willed five hundred acres of land—including the Scarlett homestead and cemetery at Oak Grove—to his youngest son, George, my eventual great-great grandfather, together with a "negro boy named Robert."

The rest of his "negro property" Francis Muir wished to be "subject to a general division" among his survivors.

By the time federal census takers came through Glynn County the following year, Francis Muir had to his name 59 enslaved people and twelve slave houses. His son Frank had 50 enslaved people; his son John, 18; and his son David, 17. Francis Muir's ten-year-old granddaughter, Meta Long, who lived with Frank and Fanny Scarlett, had 3 enslaved people to her name. Francis Muir's twenty-one-year-old granddaughter, Frances Ann Parland, who also lived with Frank and Fanny, had 60 enslaved people, and her twenty-five-year-old sister, Jean, now married to a lawyer named Henry King, had 189 enslaved people and thirty-two slave houses. All told, Francis Muir Scarlett and his immediate heirs legally possessed more than 400 human beings in 1860 and as many as eighty slave dwellings—not one of which survives.

Most nineteenth-century Americans had no slaves at all. On the eve of the Civil War, even in the South, just one in seventy U.S. residents possessed human property, and most of these people had, on average, ten slaves. Families like mine represented less than 1 percent of the total number of enslavers in the United States. But the income we generated drove the nation's economy. In Georgia alone the estimated aggregate worth of enslaved people in 1860 was approximately $416 million—nearly forty times the value of the state's manufacturing output.

Much of my ancestors' wealth came from the financially strategic three-year marriage of Mary Ann Scarlett to John Parland. Their daughters, Jean and Frances Ann, were two of the richest people in Glynn County. (Only James Hamilton Couper, a Yale-educated planter on Saint Simons Island, known for his pioneering agricultural innovations, was wealthier. Pierce Butler once rivaled Couper.) Frances Ann Parland, for whom the Scarletts served as lifelong guardians, was worth $125,000 in 1860.

Francis Muir Scarlett lived another decade after drafting his will, by which time his instructions for the distribution of his enslaved property were moot. I have not found a revised will. By the 1970s the surviving Scarletts in Brunswick were dependent on monthly checks from my grandmother for their health care. When the last of Mamie's aunts, Pauline Scarlett, passed away in 1982, at ninety-seven, and the final sliver of Scarlett land at Oak Grove was sold, my grandmother received $1,400—her share of the Scarlett estate. Mamie used a portion of her inheritance to buy me a silver jelly spoon. In time I inherited more reminders of that past: a trio of Chinese-imported soup bowls, a teapot, a pitcher damaged by fire, a pair of chocolate pots, and a half-dozen monogrammed silver forks, each split in two by some calamity lost to time.

And documents, of course, which my grandmother first tried to pawn off on her only son. Days after her sixty-sixth birthday, Mamie sent my Uncle Bob a fresh batch of papers. "I do not wish to load you down with these things but am so glad to pass them on, knowing I will never do anything with them or put them in order," she wrote with an all but audible sigh. "As a matter of fact, when you come home next time, look through my dreadful box of clippings and copies of letters and take what interests you. The rest I will then burn."

How many possessions did the four-hundred-plus people "owned" by the Scarletts in the nineteenth century have to pass on to *their* heirs? And what kind of possessions would they have been—a garden plot? A cache of sweet potatoes? A handful of buttons? Maybe a hat or a pair of shoes, a few coins culled from the sale of excess produce and hidden in the walls of a cabin, along with mirrors and beads and Indigenous artifacts, such as those that turned up in the archaeological dig on John Parland's former property in 2015.

The woman Matilda, for instance—"Maum Matilda," whom Fanny and Frank Scarlett trusted unconditionally. Where did she live and with whom? Did she, like some enslaved people, horde bacon in her living quarters so her kids would not go hungry? Did she snatch a few minutes at the end of a fifteen-hour workday to weed the patch of land behind her cabin where she had planted okra and greens? Or was Matilda made to sleep in Frank and Fanny's house, to be on call through the night should one of Fanny's daughters—young Jeannie, for example, "our little sunbeam"—need Matilda's ministrations?

Toward the end of her life, my grandmother did burn documents. One day she took all the letters she and my grandfather had exchanged during their courtship and stuffed them into a paper bag and asked my mother to take it into the backyard and set it on fire. Mamie stood off to the side, stooped over her cane. When the letters were ash, she nodded and walked back to the house.

She knew enough to destroy what she did not want seen. But this story was bigger than she was, and for once she let her devotion to history outweigh her devotion to family. She passed on the goods: the incriminating *Wanderer* account; those Stites letters to Francis Scarlett (copies of which she also gave to a local library); Fanny Scarlett's correspondence, in which Fanny names the women and men whose uncompensated labor made the Scarletts rich: Matilda and Dido and Sary. Sary's son Alex. Meta's "man" Levi. George's "boy" Robert. Harry, John, Dick, Tony Cornelius, Charlie, Dave, Sarah Jane, Julia, King. And more. My grandmother passed all this evidence on to her son and through him to me. As if to say, "I can't do anything with this but maybe you can."

When war breaks out in *Gone with the Wind*, there is no question where Black loyalties lie. Mammy and Dilcey and Pork stick with their Scarlett. Trust between Blacks and whites is complete, or so Mitchell would have us believe. (It's not until after the war, when "uppity" Blacks and "high-yellow trash" begin occupying the same sidewalks as white aristocrats, that trust erodes.) Georgia's ubiquitous slave patrols, funded by white planters to keep Blacks in line, are mentioned just once, by an enslaved teenager who jokes that he would rather be caught by the "paterrollers" than by his mistress when she is "in a state."

There's no hint of the viciousness with which white vigilantes policed African Americans in the decades before the war, let alone after fighting began in April 1861. The ropes and chains and branding irons, the spiked metal collars and lunging dogs. With the prospect of a slave insurrection now close to home, paramilitary groups sprang up across Georgia. Mitchell's guileless Tarleton twins help form a militia in Clayton County on the day Georgia secedes; its members do little more than drill, in hopes of one day tangling with a Yankee. The group goes by various names, among them the Clayton Wild Cats.

Two hundred miles south, in real-life Glynn County, in the late summer of 1861, Frank Scarlett formed a militia with more immediate aims. Composed of nearly thirty "old citizens and young men"—one of them Frank's twenty-three-year-old brother, George, who would soon join the Confederate army—the group called itself the Satilla Wild Cats. In a letter to Georgia's then–governor Joseph Brown, Frank explained,

> We have uniformed ourselves and armed with *double barrel guns* and [are] ready to protect our Homes and do service in the County. You will please if possible recognize us in some way and commission our officers. We will be no expense to the government and your sanction of such a company will do us much good and in no way injure the good cause for which we are all much interested. It is a *horse* or *foot* company, just as circumstances will dictate, and the most good can be accomplished.

As captain of the Satilla Wild Cats, Frank Scarlett would have known precisely what circumstances might dictate the need for two dozen white men to grab their rifles and take to the roads on horseback. Surely he had heard about John Brown's raid two years earlier; surely he knew of white planters who had been poisoned or knifed by their captive workers. (Long before Brown's rampage, Fanny Kemble found that "every Southern woman to whom I have spoken on the subject has admitted to me that they live in terror of their slaves." In a segment she later expunged from her published diary, Mary Chesnut fretted about a cousin who had been smothered as she slept "by her own people. Her negroes.") In December 1860, a month after Lincoln's election, an emissary from Mississippi warned members of the Georgia General Assembly that if

Georgia did not secede from the Union, the state would suffer an orgy of rape and murder by "half-civilized Africans." Fieldhands would marry the daughters of white planters, and the white race itself would melt away in a "saturnalia of blood," a "war of extermination."

Georgia seceded on January 16, 1861. The Macon *Daily Telegraph* hailed the move as the first breath of a "white man's Republic." Georgian Alexander Stephens, soon to be vice president of the Confederate States of America, pronounced slavery the "corner-stone" of the new nation, founded "upon the great truth, that the negro is not equal to the white man." Across this "new" Confederate nation, lynchings of African Americans accelerated.

That May three enslaved Blacks fled their owner in Virginia and took refuge in a nearby federal garrison. Union general Benjamin Butler declared them "contraband of war" and refused to return them. By midsummer, nine hundred additional "contrabands," many of them women and children, had joined those first three. In the next four years, their numbers would swell across the South into the hundreds of thousands.

On April 18, 1861, four days after the fall of Fort Sumter and one day before Lincoln ordered a federal blockade of southern ports, Frank Scarlett turned forty-seven. He was too old to be drafted into the Confederate army and too rich to enlist. He was responsible for a wife, four children, a young niece, two elderly parents, thousands of acres of land, scores of farm animals, multiple homes, and hundreds of enslaved African Americans. Inside the spacious house he shared with Fanny at Fancy Bluff there were treasures large and small to guard: tables and bedsteads, rugs, a piano, sheet music, books, almanacs, silk dresses, ribboned hats, cologne, coffee, tobacco, brandy, whiskey, rum—possibly even a dog, for among the family records there is a receipt for a Newfoundland.

Frank also had the property of his heir nieces, Frances Ann and Jean Parland King, to look after. When war broke out, the two women were in the new state of Texas, where Jean's husband, Henry King, had been advised to go for his health and his law career. Before leaving, the three had authorized Frank to handle their affairs in Georgia. This included the proposed sale, in early 1861, of "a certain lot of negro slaves or any part or number thereof being about 200 more or less," according to a deed registered in Glynn County. The same document notes that "said negro slaves" had previously belonged to the estate of John Parland and still lived in Glynn County—doubtless on the same land and among the same people where they had lived for at least twenty-five years. And now, because Jean Parland King and her husband and sister were stranded in Texas, these 200 ("more or less") individuals were to be sold, though there is no indication the sale ever took place. Maybe the commotion over secession or the threat of war distracted Frank. Or maybe he was preoccupied with another transfer of human lives, for, as the legal representative of Jean and Henry King, Frank received, in early 1861, 242 enslaved people in two "lots" as partial repayment of a debt owed the couple by a man named Franklin Holcomb.

So the wheeling and dealing, the shattering of African American families and lives, went on right up to the end. Or more accurately, the beginning of the end, since the "unmaking" of the Scarlett plantation household at Fancy Bluff—the term comes from historian Thavolia Glymph—took another year.

Fanny Scarlett chronicles the disaster in a series of letters written to the Parland sisters from 1861 to 1863. "Jeannie" and "Puss," she calls them. "Puss" is twenty-five-year-old Frances Ann, damaged in some way that would ultimately lead her to be adjudged a "lunatic." She is an enigma in this story—doted on but not knowable in the ways her older sister is. "Oh Jeannie, we are so glad it is all over," Fanny writes in November 1861, seven months into the war. Coastal Georgia was at risk of attack by the Union navy. In Texas Jeannie had just given birth. "Kiss the little darling many times for the dear friends it has away off here in Georgia." The note of melancholy in Fanny's words suggests her fear that she won't see Jeannie or Puss again (and in fact, she did not).

Fanny's letters survive as typewritten manuscripts transcribed in the 1940s by one of Fanny's granddaughters, Fannie Webb Holt. As in a playscript, Holt provides brief descriptions of the settings and characters: Frank and Fanny Scarlett "lived at Fancy Bluff, Glynn County, Georgia, almost in sight of the Atlantic Ocean." Fanny is "tall with dark brown hair and gray eyes"; Frank is "tall, fair and blue-eyed"; Frank's brother George has red hair and a red mustache and stands over six feet tall.

What letters Fanny received from the Parland sisters are lost. Mail was unreliable ("I hope you receive our letters more regularly than we do yours"). It is hard to fathom the chaos that enveloped them all. Even Jeannie and Puss, off in Texas, faced what Fanny coyly called "Indian troubles." In Georgia war was palpable. With southern ports blocked, planters like Frank Scarlett struggled to get their cotton to market. Food imports dwindled. Coffee gave way to parched okra seed and rye, tea to blackberry leaves. The city of Brunswick filled with Confederate troops—two thousand by the fall of 1861. Women formed sewing circles to stitch uniforms.

Soon the area registered its first human losses: a soldier felled by measles in May 1861; months later a Saint Simons boy, James Hamilton Couper Jr., son of the richest man in Glynn County, dead of typhoid near Manassas, Virginia. "Literary by taste and culture," Couper's tombstone reads, "he became a soldier from a sense of duty." Picture the bookish thirty-two-year-old prostrate in his hospital bed, feigning valor as the end nears. They were, all of them, as Fanny's granddaughter hints, playing roles in a great drama. Fanny Scarlett wrote to Frances Ann Parland, on November 13, 1861,

> Oh Puss, I realize now that war is awful. Today's paper brings us the sad news of Hamilton Couper's death. . . . I have been thinking today of his poor mother. He was her first-born and promised fairly.

By November Union ships had seized parts of the South Carolina coast and were sailing toward Brunswick. From her home at Fancy Bluff, Fanny could hear cannons firing and late at night the whistle of locomotives as trains ferried evacuees from Brunswick to safer ground. "I have committed my way to the Lord," she wrote. "I believe I would be crazy if I could not trust in Him."

She ordered her enslaved workers to strip the house at Fancy Bluff and take the family's poultry farther inland—probably to Chicora, a summer residence she and Frank owned near Waynesville, sixteen miles west. Fancy Bluff became unrecognizable. "Bare walls and lonely deserted looking house." Fanny's vigorous, blue-eyed husband looked "dreadfully," she told her nieces. "You have no idea how he has fallen off." That month Frank had begun "removing" enslaved children from the family's vulnerable Colonel's Island plantation, separating little boys and girls from their parents and sending the children inland—hostages to keep their parents from running. The process, called "refugeeing," took place across the South, wherever Union troops threatened. Frank's father, Francis Muir, was doing the same at Oak Grove, moving his "little negroes" away from the coast to more secure locations. Not that the enslaved went willingly. North of Brunswick, Fanny Scarlett's brother Jesse was dispatched to a swamp, along with fellow members of his local militia, to "reduce to subjection [subjugation] and obedience" two hundred African Americans who had refused to follow their enslavers inland.

"You must try not to be miserable about us," Fanny told the Parlands. "Remember the promise 'All things shall work together for good, to them who love God.' Let us cling to that, my dear Jeannie and Puss."

At Christmas eight enslaved people escaped from a plantation owned by the Parland sisters. Two months later Confederate general Robert E. Lee ordered southern troops to abandon Saint Simons Island—ten miles northeast of Fancy Bluff—and head north to defend the more strategically important city of Savannah. On March 7, 1862, Georgia's governor called for a statewide day of fasting, humiliation, and prayer for deliverance "from the power of our enemies" and the restoration of "peace and prosperity." On March 9, a Sunday, Union ships captured Saint Simons and Jekyll Islands.

That night federal gunboats near Jekyll fired on Confederate soldiers stationed at Fancy Bluff and on Colonel's Island. "The gunboats just rained shot and shell," Fanny reported. There was only one injury (to a horse), and no buildings were damaged. "Thank God our dear old homes stand untouched." Fanny was writing from the relative safety of the family's plantation at Chicora, miles inland, where she and her children had fled. But Frank was still on the coast, working to "remove" the last of the family's enslaved workers from Fancy Bluff and Colonel's Island. Only a handful of trusted African Americans remained on either property. Frank and Fanny were acutely aware they might lose their coastal homes. Even Chicora was not safe, and Frank had begun making plans to move farther west, to yet another family property in neighboring Appling County.

On Monday, March 10, federal troops seized Brunswick and raised the Union flag over the deserted town. Fires burned in the surrounding woods where Confederate troops were encamped.

That same day Frank learned that two of the family's remaining slaves on Colonel's Island, Dick and John, had "broken open the office, helped themselves to liquor and tobacco, and made their escape to the Yankees," an indignant Fanny wrote the Parlands. Clearly Dick and John wanted to avoid being "removed" inland. Later that night four more enslaved men—Sandy, Tony Cornelius, Charlie, and Dave—escaped from Francis Muir Scarlett's plantation at Oak Grove and found their way as contrabands to the Union navy. The next day another four fled the Scarletts: Primus, Alex, Levi, and Robert—George Scarlett's "boy," who had recently accompanied his master to a Confederate army training camp.

"You can realize somewhat our feelings," Fanny told her nieces. "Independent of the loss"—financial, she meant—"the trust betrayed causes many a pang."

On Saint Simons Island, Union troops set up a temporary refugee settlement—a "colony," they called it—for fleeing Blacks. Within weeks scores of African Americans were living there. They created schools, held prayer meetings. At night lights flickered inside their tents, and you could hear music, remembered a Union commander stationed on the island. Drums, the faint trill of a flute, hands clapping, voices lifted in the quintessential African ring shout. Then dancing, people "circling like dervishes," and applause.

Miles away, on the mainland, Frank and Fanny tried to persuade Frank's parents to join them at Chicora. Across Glynn County and points west, white families were doubling up, two and three inhabiting the same house. But Francis Muir Scarlett and his wife stayed put. At seventy-seven Scarlett was too old and too stubborn to relinquish the small empire he had so painstakingly built. His daughter-in-law Fanny prayed for his safety. She prayed for strength to withstand her afflictions, from common colds and sore throats to the sudden deaths of loved ones ("Sallie's little Dave . . . was taken in the morning with a violent headache and died at 1 o'clock") and the mounting trials of war.

"God," Fanny reasoned, "has permitted these troubles for some wise purpose and they must be right for that reason." And again: "We needed this discipline or it would not have been sent and we will rejoice in it, if by it we are better prepared for that house of 'many mansions' which Christ has gone to prepare."

There is nothing in Fanny's existing correspondence to indicate that she is in any way attuned to the possibility that she—or anyone else in her extended family—has done anything to merit discipline. Merely, "I think my troubles have done me good, at least I hope so."

Beautiful Fanny Scarlett, staring out from her one surviving photograph: ringlets of chestnut hair, thick gold earrings, a jeweled brooch at her throat. Willow neck, ivory skin, pale eyes ringed in shadow. The face is oddly contemporary—young, unlined, fawnlike in its innocence.

She was at most thirty-two when this portrait was made. The image gives no hint of the enormous labor—unpaid, unending, pitilessly enforced—that went into its creation. If Fanny was aware of the human cost of the work required to feed and clothe and groom her, she left no record of it—the shrug of the white, moneyed American woman who simply looks away. Witness her contemporary Mary Chesnut, another daughter and wife of enslavers, whose diary captures the smug certainties of their kind. "Slavery has to go, of course," Chesnut predicted rosily in 1861, "and joy go with it." (Historian Elizabeth Fox-Genovese notes the widespread belief by many in the prewar South that "a more humane slavery or personal servitude would characterize the society of the future.") Chesnut blasts "holy New England women" (the reference is to Harriet Beecher Stowe), who do not know what it is like to have a "swarm of blacks about them as children under their care—not as Mrs. Stowe's fancy paints them, but the hard, unpleasant, unromantic, underdeveloped savage Africans."

Distance—psychic, if not physical—sheltered women like Chesnut and Fanny Scarlett from the realities of their household arrangements and bolstered their claims to goodness. Call the enslaved "children," and you become their benefactor. Give them an endearing nickname—Daddy, Uncle, Mammy, Maum—and you're family. Mention "our people," and your humanity is plain. Fanny to the Parland sisters, 1862:

> Meta wrote you about Maum Betty's death. I think she had pneumonia. Susan doesn't seem to mind it very much. Poor Susan, I'm afraid she is given up to some of her old ways.
>
> Peter is up here with us. . . . He is good and cheerful and faithful as he can be. Having him and Washington I have very little trouble.
>
> Maum Matilda seemed to feel awfully about Dick's going off. I should not be much surprised if he runs away and comes back.

By 1862 Fanny seems to have been almost wholly dependent on captive labor for her daily needs. Frank was away much of the time, tending to the family's many properties. Fanny's brothers and at least two of her brothers-in-law had joined the army. Her aging father was recovering from a broken leg, and her father-in-law was nearly deaf. Fanny herself had a weak back as well as some undiagnosed ailment that had begun to plague her, and at home she had a young niece and four daughters under nine to care for. The youngest, Jeannie, turned two that March. "It was the most quiet birthday we have ever spent."

And there was the war. Goods were scarce ("I am having homespun dresses woven for the children"), and soldiers were everywhere—more than a thousand Confederate troops in nearby Waynesville—and there was a growing chance Frank himself might be called up for service, so depleted was the Southern army. Frank and Fanny had already dismantled two coastal properties—their own home at Fancy Bluff and the Parland estate on Colonel's Island—and were bracing to empty more. Everyone was dealing with freedom seekers. Frank wanted to take the small number of Scarlett captives left on the coast and move them west by as much as a hundred miles. "Now that we have proven that the negroes cannot be trusted, it is time for them to go," Fanny coolly informed the Parlands. "It would make your heart ache to see Mr. S."

Left largely on her own with the loyal Peter and Washington, Fanny fretted about Frank and her girls and waited for news. "I try to teach my children but you know something of what my interruptions must be." She assured the Parlands their belongings were safe. When it had become clear the women might be trapped in Texas for the duration of the war, Fanny had had their dresses and bed linens and blankets packed into trunks and boxes and stored at another coastal Scarlett plantation, Glencoe, just south of Fancy Bluff and Colonel's Island. "It was so much nearer, the road better, so much more house room," she told her nieces. Every box was labeled. She had ordered Maum Matilda to keep an eye on the place—reliable Matilda, Fanny and Frank's devoted "mammy." Fanny told Matilda that if for some reason she did not live to see her nieces again, she wanted to be sure the women would find everything "all right" when they returned to Georgia.

If Matilda replied, Fanny did not record it.

10
REVOLT

In her history of the plantation household, *Out of the House of Bondage*, Thavolia Glymph details the ways enslaved women assailed southern white planters' homes. Even before the war, assaults small and large—from careless housework and slipshod childcare to outright defiance, even flight—were common. But war escalated the resistance. "The transformation of the plantation household (and sometimes its literal destruction) . . . was a major goal of freedom as slaves understood it," Glymph writes. This was especially true among women who labored inside planters' homes, many of whom worked quietly to ensure that those homes became "increasingly unmanageable" as the war progressed and that, long before combat ended, the plantation household itself would be "unrecognizable by its old terms."

That Maum Matilda was a strong woman is clear—the nature of her work (nursing, cleaning, laundering, lifting) demanded it. But she also possessed an inner strength, as her actions soon showed. While the particulars of her relationship with Fanny Scarlett are unknowable, it's well known that within the upholstered trappings of their private homes, white women regularly slapped and hit the African American women who cooked their food and washed their clothes and looked after their children. Many mistresses used whips. Frederick Douglass describes a "psalm-singing" planter's wife who used to sit in her rocking chair with a cowhide strap at her side. Whenever one of her enslaved servants walked by, the woman would lash the girl and snap, "Move faster, you Black jip!" and then go back to singing hymns.

Who can say what kind of discipline Fanny Scarlett imposed on her workers? In a world where women of all colors knew violence at the hands of men, and corporal punishment was the norm for kids, a strike to the face in the parlor would not have been that big a deal—at least not to the woman inflicting it. Fanny herself admitted that at times her toddler Jeannie got "so high strung I have to bring her to Measures." Precious Jeannie, who could "say her prayers so sweetly."

Perhaps at times Fanny also brought Matilda to "Measures." Certainly, in a society built on the pretense that someone like Matilda was a willing employee, the threat of abuse was ever-present. Whatever else took place between them, Matilda's relationship with Fanny was not safe. Nor was it honest. At a national gathering of Coming to the Table in 2016, a pair of African American women spelled out the lies that buttressed the slave system. Blacks, they said, feigned loyalty to survive. Whites pretended their enslaved workers were contented servants—and white women pretended the mixed-race children who ghosted their plantations had no connection to their husbands. These fictions masked powerful emotions: for African Americans, rage, terror, and shame; for white Americans, fear and shame. "This is the package we've been given," the women said. "Now think about how you feel about race today."

The first months of the war put a crack in slavery's wall of lies. "I think we know a little now of trouble," Fanny conceded after the first of the family's enslaved workers fled in 1861. By the start of 1862, the unmaking of the Scarlett plantation household was in full throttle.

Matilda was at the center of it. By 1862 she had smelled freedom and begun to plot. Like African Americans across the region, she knew the Union navy had captured the Georgia coasts and that enslaved people were fleeing to the Yankees. She'd seen how Frank Scarlett dealt with potential freedom seekers and knew the same fate likely awaited her. What Fanny Scarlett would primly term Matilda's "betrayed trust" was, in fact, an act of fierce and calculating will.

To run was life-threatening. Fleeing Blacks faced paramilitary patrols of the sort Frank captained, Confederate soldiers and deserters, extremes of cold and heat, a waterlogged coastline filled with snakes and alligators. African Americans drowned in swamps and rivers; children tumbled from boats and mules. For those caught trying to escape, planters devised chilling reprisals. "Terrible corporal punishment," proposed a Savannah enslaver, "accompanied with close and protracted confinement in the county jail, or public punishment followed by banishment from the county and sale in some distant part of the country, seem to me to be proper."

Blacks who made it to the Union side arrived "in every stage of disease or decrepitude, often nearly naked, with flesh torn by the terrible experiences of their escapes," said Union chaplain John Eaton, charged with creating a system of relief for the torrent of refugees. They arrived filled with hope and terror, Eaton remembered, and even then the dangers persisted. Women faced the threat of sexual violence. Men could be dragged into military service. (Some enlistment practices were so harsh "they were barely distinguishable from kidnapping," Andrew Delbanco writes in *The War before the War: Fugitive Slaves and the Struggle for America's Soul from the Revolution to the Civil War*.) Northern soldiers shared many of the same racial prejudices their southern counterparts embraced. Many of Lincoln's troops thought little of withholding rations from contrabands or confiscating what few items Blacks managed to bring with them when they ran.

Undeterred, Matilda professed fealty and began packing. A man named King—"Daddy King" to Fanny and Frank, an enslaved man they had put in charge "of every individual thing at Fancy Bluff"—joined her. When Union ships first fired on Scarlett property at the start of March, King was so scared he ran all the way from Fancy Bluff to Glencoe in his nightclothes, a distance of several miles. But three weeks later, this same gun-shy man summoned the courage to flee. He seized a pair of Scarlett boats and, on the night of March 26, 1862, hours after Frank Scarlett had visited Fancy Bluff to check on things, King, Matilda, and nearly two dozen other enslaved men, women, and children climbed into those boats and set sail. One of them, a young woman named Julia, was so pregnant she had to be carted to the boat in a wheelbarrow.

It was dark and cold, and there were armed Confederates in the area—a picket would be spotted the next day at Fancy Bluff—and the freedom seekers had no way of knowing if they would reach Union lines or, if they did, what kind of reception they would get. Who among them, laden with clothes and small children, could swim? The same waterways that by day held placid views of dolphins and egrets could be treacherous by night—errant tides, racing currents, temperatures as low as fifty degrees Fahrenheit. Anyone who fell overboard—especially a child—could die.

King and a second man, Elias, another prized Scarlett slave, piloted the boats. They sailed to neighboring Colonel's Island, it seems, for the next day at noon two Union steamships pulled up in front of John Parland's abandoned plantation home and found a group of "contrabands, who, in fact, had belonged mostly to [a] Mr. Scarlett," Union commander

S. W. Godon informed his superiors. Godon and his soldiers were in search of supplies, and the newly freed people led them to a cache of provisions Frank had stockpiled: corn, peas, sweet potatoes, cotton. Hoes and spades, a corn sheller and mill. The soldiers took everything, then fired "a shell or two" in the direction of Fancy Bluff and sailed off to Saint Simons.

It's likely the freedom seekers went with them and moved into the contraband colony Godon and his men had set up on the island. By late summer the settlement at Saint Simons held more than five hundred formerly enslaved individuals, many of whom had arrived on federal boats. Godon ran the place much like a plantation, sending Blacks out into the cotton fields to earn their keep. If they balked, he cut off food. "I have also placed men in irons for punishment," he boasted. "Thus far," Godon reported in late May 1862, "the government has not spent a dollar on those people." "Those people" were also forced into military service.

And still, the newly freed people thrived. Eyewitness accounts show African American men and boys working on Saint Simons as pilots and navigators, helping Northern troops patrol coastal waterways and haul supplies—rice, wood, salt, beef—from nearby plantations, among them Pierce Butler's deserted properties on Butler Island and Saint Simons. (Told of the Union occupation of Saint Simons, Butler's ex-wife, then in England, exulted. "I little thought to live to see the day when Northern ships would ride along that coast . . . bringing freedom to the land of bondage," Fanny Kemble wrote to a friend.)

By the fall of 1862, when Susie King Taylor, previously enslaved in Savannah, reached Saint Simons, she found women growing food for their families and selling excess vegetables and poultry to soldiers. Black women also took in washing and sewing at prices set by Union commanders ("coats, 75 cents each, where the materials are furnished"). Taylor, who had learned to read during her enslavement, opened a school for children. At night she taught adults, "all of them so eager to learn to read, to read above anything else." "Their love of the spelling-book is perfectly inexhaustible," recalled Union commander Thomas Wentworth Higginson, who oversaw a regiment of Black soldiers on Saint Simons. An ardent abolitionist (and friend to both John Brown and Emily Dickinson), Higginson was struck by the poverty of the African Americans he encountered on the island. "Never had I seen human beings so clad, or rather so un-clad, in such amazing squalidness and destitution of garments." But, he added, "their spirits are good."

Within the year Higginson would be issued a hefty supply of printed copies of Lincoln's Emancipation Proclamation. He distributed the document among the refugees. Few of them could read it, he saw. "But they all seemed to feel more secure when they held it in their hands."

Historian Kenneth Stampp, whose landmark *The Peculiar Institution*, published in 1956, dispelled any notion of slavery as a benign institution, quotes a formerly enslaved woman on her feelings after reaching freedom: "I feel lighter—the dread is gone. It is a great heaviness on a person's mind to be a slave."

For King, Matilda, Julia, Elias, and the twenty-some others who fled the Scarletts that cold March night, rowing past Confederate rifles, there was no looking back. The Scarlett plantations at Fancy Bluff and Colonel's Island and Glencoe would never again be slave-labor camps. Colonel's Island would remain mostly empty until 1889, when the Brunswick Harbor and Land Company bought the property from the Scarletts and set out to develop it into a commercial port. Today it is home to Georgia's second-largest seaport. The only people to live there after the war seem to have been free African Americans, who moved back into former slave cabins and went to work as seasonal laborers in the timber industry. They built new cabins as well—one-room dwellings whose tabby foundations archaeologist Carolyn Rock and her colleagues would excavate in 2015, then rebury, so that the Georgia Ports Authority could turn the land into a parking lot.

Frank and Fanny Scarlett's home at Fancy Bluff fell prey to soil erosion and was torn down in the first decades of the twentieth century. For a time the property was a popular local fishing area. Developers eventually purchased the land and turned it into residential sites, among them a neighborhood called Satilla Shores, which would make national news in 2020.

The Scarlett property at Glencoe was reportedly sold during World War II for use as an airfield to train blimp pilots. Except for the word "plantation" affixed to the occasional site around Brunswick, there's little sign that slavery once flourished along this stretch of the Georgia coast.

Matilda herself vanishes from the historical record for more than two decades after her escape, but it is clear she survived the experience—and possibly even flourished in its wake, taking shelter on Saint Simons or in another of the refugee settlements federal troops created along the coasts of Georgia, Florida, and South Carolina.

Of her life in the days immediately before the exodus, however, there is more. In July 1862, four months after Matilda and the others took flight, Fanny Scarlett at last ventured from the safety of her inland refuge at Chicora to inspect the plantation house at Glencoe, which she had asked Matilda to guard. Inside the vacant home, Fanny found a crime scene: the Parland sisters' belongings, so carefully packed away in boxes and trunks, had been plundered—dresses and bedclothes seized, blankets taken, boxes ransacked. A green chest belonging to Fanny's precious niece "Puss" had been ripped apart with an axe and emptied. Just "three old dresses and a new tarlton" were left, Fanny said. All of it Matilda's doing. Her "treachery."

"Dear Puss, please don't blame me. The overseer at Glencoe says there was much hammering in the house where the boxes were for several days before the negroes went off, but said he thought it was all right," Fanny wrote. Matilda was to blame. "We had given the things in her charge, and he says he would have as soon thought of watching Mr. S. as her. I wish I could talk to you but I don't think you will blame me, for we all trusted Maum Matilda with anything."

Eighty years before Margaret Mitchell enshrined the troubling image of a loyal Mammy—"shining black, pure African, devoted to her last drop of blood to the O'Haras"—the woman Fanny and Frank Scarlett called "Maum" made her audacious stand—she and countless other African American women across the South who had had enough of bathing and powdering their imperious owners and wet-nursing their children. Central to the making of American slavery, Glymph argues, the plantation household was also "central to its unmaking." When Fanny's beloved "Maum" picked up that axe and slammed it into "Puss" Parland's green trunk, she shattered more than a set of hinges, and her pampered young mistress was left to figure out why. In the most damning of her statements about Matilda, Fanny Scarlett wrote, "I wonder if it is possible that she can be so depraved as to be happy."

A short notice in the April 4, 1885, edition of the *Brunswick* [Georgia] *Advertiser and Appeal* describes "an aged colored man, King Heppard, Sr., by name, who is indeed a patriarch." The brief (and curiously admiring, given the year) article goes on to state that King Heppard "is 85 years old and still strong and vigorous. His wife, Matilda, is 59 years old."

I first read the article in 2011 on Amy Hedrick's website. I had shown Amy my copies of Fanny Scarlett's letters, and she had pounced on the names King and Matilda. "They were husband and wife, and their last name was actually Hippard, not Heppard. Their descendants live in the area. They'd love to know this story."

Amy gave me the phone number of a descendant—a nurse in her early fifties named Brenda Bailey—and I called. Brenda told me the Hippards were holding their annual family reunion in Brunswick that August, just a few weeks away. I said I had a story about their family I wanted to share and asked if I could possibly join them. Brenda hesitated, then said she would check. A few days later she called back to tell me I was welcome to come. Her voice was warm and generous—I caught hints of my grandmother's Brunswick drawl—and she said eagerly, "We *must* exchange stories. Oh, you'll hear stories." She described how the reunion would unfold: Lowcountry boil (she pronounced it "bowl") on Friday night, banquet on Saturday, communion on Sunday morning in a church dating back to slave times. "We're big churchgoers, you'll see."

On the flight down to Jacksonville, I rehearsed scenarios in my mind: awkward introductions, indifferent shrugs, bitter accusations. I knew these encounters could be tense. A friend of mine in Michigan—a retired Lutheran pastor keen to acknowledge his family's complicity in the slave system and its long aftermath—had reached out to the descendants of the people who had sharecropped his grandfather's Tennessee farm. One of them wanted to know, "Why did your family sell our land?"

My friend had no good answer.

Nor did I when, a few years earlier, at a national gathering of Coming to the Table—founded in 2006 and dedicated to "addressing the legacy of slavery"—an African American woman cornered me after dinner and proceeded to detail the ways well-meaning whites like me fail to use our privileged position to change this country's racial dynamic. "And don't just tell me you've got two Black friends and you voted for Obama," she said. "It's not enough."

What I did not envision, as I drove up the interstate from Jacksonville to Brunswick in the thick August heat, was the effusive welcome I would receive. The park where we gathered that first night wasn't far from my family's old property at Oak Grove—same sandy soil and dusty pines, scrub oaks and holly. The extended Hippard clan included two additional families, the Blues and the Bells, and there were people everywhere. Cars and vans kept pulling off the road, backing into graveled spots under the trees. Groups of men stood on either side of a long, cinder-block grill, steaming crabs. Women sat at picnic tables, fanning themselves. Inside the park's air-conditioned pavilion, I made my way to a table where a woman in a purple T-shirt sat with a cashbox. I gave my name, explained who I was, and paid my fifty-dollar fee. She wrote my name down in a notebook and clipped a yellow band around my wrist. "Proof that you've met your obligations," she smiled. "I'm Gertrude Maxwell. My father was Andrew Hippard." She handed me a tote bag. "Hippard Blue Bell," it read. "25th Family Reunion—Be Fruitful and Multiply."

A half mile down the road, at Francis Muir Scarlett's former plantation, Oak Grove, weeds choked the tombstones where my ancestors lay buried, and the foundations of the gray house I'd seen on that one childhood trip to Brunswick had vanished. (More than one Hippard descendant would tell me they remembered the battered Scarlett house just off Route 82 being dismantled so the highway could be widened.) That trip south in the 1960s was the only time I could recall my Scarlett relatives getting together en masse, and the size of that gathering did not begin to approach the commotion surrounding me now. At one end of the pavilion, men and women were heaving trays of food onto warming racks. Boiled shrimp, sausage, corn, potatoes, sliced bread, fried fish, grits, spaghetti and meatballs. Slabs of pound and blueberry cake, a three-tiered red velvet cake wreathed in buttercream.

The call went out for supper. People streamed in. Toddlers, teens, women with crosses looped around damp necks. Someone pressed a piece of sheet music into my hand. A woman in a bright-red apron—Gertrude's sister Margie—began to sing. "We've got a friend in Jesus." The crowd joined in. We swayed from side to side. The hymn soared to its conclusion, and a young man in a pale-blue vest stepped forward to recite a psalm. "Have mercy on me, O God . . . according to your abundant mercy / blot out my transgressions." Murmurs of "yes" and "amen."

Then a blessing, more "amens," and at last the invitation to eat. Margie reminded people to fix plates for family members who couldn't walk to the buffet themselves. Someone mentioned crabs. "Eat them outside!" Margie howled. "Don't bring them in here!"

By the time I sat down, Gertrude and Margie's niece Wanda was spinning CDs at an elaborate setup in the corner, and it was hard to hear. But we persevered. When I told one man why I was there, he broke into a smile and said he remembered my grandmother's polio-stricken Uncle Bobbie giving him rides in his automobile when he was a kid. The car had special hand controls, and the man grinned as he recalled all the levers and gearshifts around its steering wheel.

"Bobbie would give anyone a ride," another man broke in. He too had a soft, singsong voice. "Bobbie ran a fishing business on Fancy Bluff Creek. He liked to drive people back and forth from the dock."

Still another man—Gertrude and Margie's brother, Johnny Hippard—told me the Scarletts used to let him hunt racoons on their land with his dad.

"You eat racoon?" I asked.

"It's delicious," he laughed. "You have to remove the musk glands from the muscle, of course. If you once bite down on one, my dad always said, you'll never eat coon again." Johnny told me that as a boy he had been spooked by the Scarlett house—"tall and stuck back there in the woods"—but he had liked the Scarletts. One of the Scarlett women, he told me, was bowlegged. He couldn't remember her name.

And so it went for the rest of the night and most of the next two days. "Oh, you'll hear stories." At the banquet on Saturday evening, I was invited to take part in a ceremony honoring the ancestors. Candles were lit. A piano played quietly. Voices called out names. "We are truly standing on the shoulders of giants," the MC intoned. I thought of Matilda and King Hippard but could not bring myself to say their names out loud—it didn't feel right. I thought of my grandmother. "Mary King Pettigrew," I whispered. Earlier in the day I had phoned my eighty-nine-year-old mother in Pennsylvania to tell her where I was and how fondly people spoke of the Scarletts. "Oh, I wish I could be there," she said.

On the last day of the reunion, midway through a boisterous Sunday morning service in a packed Baptist church, I was asked to introduce myself. "Our cousin Leslie from Michigan has an interesting story,"

Johnny Hippard announced to the congregation. He was a deacon in the church. Faces swung in my direction. I stood and repeated my name. I said I lived in the North but was a descendant of the Scarlett family of Brunswick. Heads nodded. People knew the Scarletts—our name was on the federal building, after all. "I stumbled upon your extraordinary family while reading through my family's papers," I went on, wondering how long I was supposed to talk. "You've all been so incredibly welcoming to me this weekend. Thank you."

There must have been a hundred people in the sanctuary—women in white dresses and hats, men in suits, little girls in pastel crinolines—and they seemed to be waiting for me to say more. My face and arms were slick with sweat. "Back in the day," I stammered, "my family was not so welcoming to yours." The phrasing was clumsy, if not offensive. "Our stories are intertwined in difficult and sad ways, and I am sorry for what my family did." I looked out at the room. "God bless you all," I finished and sat down. I caught a few nods, then faces swiveled back to the front of the sanctuary, and the service resumed: hymns, a long sermon, communion. Cardboard fans fluttered. The back of each fan featured a photograph of President Barack Obama and his family.

In the parking lot after the service, a man asked for my address. "We're getting together next year in Orlando." Another man—Gertrude's tall, soft-spoken son Gregory—who lived in Atlanta, came up to me. "Welcome to the family," he said.

That afternoon, after another lavish meal, Margie invited me to share my story. By then several families had left, and the crowd was thinner. I took out my copies of Fanny Scarlett's letters and explained who she was and when and why she had written them. I talked about King and Matilda Hippard, how they had organized a revolt against the Scarletts during the war. I said Matilda had taken an axe to the Scarletts' trunks and collected supplies, and King had commandeered two boats and piloted his family and nearly two dozen others to freedom. I described how they had helped Union soldiers load up on food and farm equipment. I read excerpts from Fanny's correspondence and handed out copies of the letters for everyone to have.

Days later, in Michigan, I got an email from a descendant. She and her mother had read through all of Fanny's letters, she said. "We felt proud that my Heroic Great Great Grandfather, King Hippard, would risk his life to provide supplies to the Union Army, and help several slaves to freedom. This is something we will truly cherish."

On the first night of the reunion, as we'd waited inside the air-conditioned park pavilion for supper to start, I had met a woman named Avedell Grant. She had known my grandmother's aunts and uncles and wanted to talk to me, I was told. She was sitting by herself in a corner with a cane across her lap, a handsome woman in her late seventies, with gray hair and chestnut eyes that seemed somehow both happy and sad. She rose slowly and took my hands in hers. "I never thought I'd see a Scarlett again," she murmured. Her eyes were damp. She continued holding my hands. "I worked for the Scarletts as a girl." Her father had arranged the job through my grandmother's uncle Bobbie when Avedell was nine or ten, she told me. "I worked in the kitchen." Washing dishes, putting away plates. Then she squeezed my hands hard and said, "The Scarletts were always good to the Blacks."

I could not imagine what she meant, and I didn't have the courage to ask. But I thought about Avedell's remark on my flight home a few days later and for a long time afterward. In what context had we been "good to the Blacks"? Certainly not in King and Matilda Hippard's day and not in the decades leading up to their escape. If my grandmother's fitful memories of twentieth-century Scarlett violence were credible, we weren't so good in the twentieth century either. Even north of the Mason-Dixon Line, in the segregated Pennsylvania suburbs of my childhood, we weren't exempt. I've never forgotten the day my Philadelphia grandmother complained about a Black woman she had spotted walking down the street at two o'clock in the afternoon carrying a bag of groceries. "And I suppose she calls *that* a day's work!" my grandmother snapped. Or the night my mother, prompted by something she had seen on TV, asked casually over dinner how we'd feel if a Black family moved into our neighborhood. I remember my distinct discomfort at the idea. It was my father who broke the silence. "If it was a family who could afford to live here," he ventured, "they'd be the kind of people we'd want."

In the years after the 2011 Hippard family reunion, I stayed in touch with Avedell Grant. Whenever I visited Brunswick, I went to her church—the same Baptist sanctuary where we had gathered that Sunday morning during the reunion. Avedell always sat regally in the front pew and always greeted me as she had the first time we met, with outstretched hands and a warm smile. She and I sometimes went to the Golden Corral for a meal with her daughter and cousin Margie. One day over dinner I summoned the nerve to ask Avedell what she had meant all those years earlier when she said the Scarletts were "good to the Blacks." She raised her eyes from her plate. "They just were." Then she remembered something. "Except at meals," she went on. "We wouldn't . . . you know . . . eat together like this." She traced a circle around our table with her hands.

"What do you mean?"

"Well, I had to eat on the porch. They'd prepare the food in the kitchen and then sit down together in the dining room, and, if I was there, Miss Pauline"—my grandmother's Aunt Polly, a lifelong Methodist and church organist—"she'd hand me a plate with my food, and it was understood I'd go onto the porch to eat it." Avedell looked into my eyes. Her face was expressionless.

"I'm sorry," I said.

Avedell looked back at her plate. "It used to bother me," she frowned. "But then I got older and understood. That's just how it was."

11

LET THEM FLOW

Shortly before dawn on January 19, 1863, Fanny Scarlett had a dream. She was in her home at Chicora, miles inland, surrounded by Confederate troops, safe from marauding Yankees and free Blacks. The place was so quiet she could imagine there was no war. Two days earlier she had received a letter from her Parland nieces in San Antonio, and now, in the first wash of daylight, she dreamed they were back in Georgia again—Puss, Jeannie, Jeannie's husband, their darling children. For a moment Fanny believed it was possible. "God grant, if it is His will, that we may all be spared to meet again."

But God worked in unpredictable ways. That fall He had shown mercy and rescued Frank Scarlett from a fever so grave he and Fanny both feared he would die. ("One evening he commenced telling me what I must do if he were taken from us. I did not attempt to stop him.") Then, suddenly, Frank revived: "What have I not to bless the Lord for giving me such a husband and then in sparing him to me." Weeks later, even more suddenly, Fanny's young half sister Clara died from pneumonia. "She and Mother had been here on a visit and the dear child seemed so lively and happy." But now Clara was gone, and "I trust is living and praising God in a brighter world."

This was also His work.

Whooping cough had struck the neighborhood. Fanny's brother Jesse was fighting federal troops and rounding up Confederate deserters near the Florida border. A business associate of Frank's, a Mr. Holcomb, had killed himself. An acquaintance of Fanny's was grieving the death of her fiancé in battle. More African Americans were fleeing. Frank was making plans to go "far back in the woods and try to rent a place to carry our little negroes"—those few children and old people who remained with the family. If the war went on much longer, he wrote bitterly to his nieces in Texas, the whole coast would be deserted. "O how I hate the

Yankies. I am done with them. I hope when peace is made a law will be passed to kill every one who ever dares to put his foot on our soil, and the negroes—the old boy is in every one of them—they have all turned fools about the Yankies."

He had no time for his wife's sunrise dreams or mercurial God. Let Fanny bargain all she wanted, Frank would rage:

> I have been so much troubled that one half my time I hordly had my right mind—but I see it is no use to fret, it dont mend matters, and this war cant last always. All things must come to an end. And if we can all live to see the end and get back home once more it will all be right. It is true we have lost much may lose all. God only knows. Such times I never saw before.

Alexis de Tocqueville had caught the type decades earlier. The rube planter, "irascible, violent, ardent in his desires, impatient of obstacles." Consider the fury of those run-on sentences, the rustic twang implicit in Frank's misspelled words. (In her book-length study of *Gone with the Wind*, critic Molly Haskell says, "If Southern writers had given their white characters, instead of standard grammatical English, the accented speech that is often closer to Negro dialect than to Northern speech," we'd have a clearer picture today of the tangled relations between Blacks and whites during slavery.)

Not for Frank his wife's pretty words and Christian trust in divine plans. His was a farmer's faith, grounded in the cyclical sureties of the natural world: "These are our dark days brighter ones ahead I hope."

But brightness eluded them; Fanny was not well. The symptoms had come on the previous spring and gotten worse. There were days when she could scarcely move. In December 1862 she had gone to Savannah to consult with a doctor and was now under his treatment. "It is possible that I have some affliction of the womb," she told the Parland sisters. By early 1863 Fanny was resigned to the possibility of dying. She was thirty-two.

Who was left to nurse her? Charlotte was dead, Matilda gone. Peter remained—he "has proven himself one in a thousand"—and Maum Sary, who had promised Fanny and Frank she would not leave. But friends? Fanny was miles from her old neighborhood at Fancy Bluff. Family? The Parland sisters were in Texas. Frank was away for days at a time, tending to the estate of his late colleague, Mr. Holcomb. (This seems to have been the same Franklin Holcomb who had discharged his prewar debts to Jean Parland King and her husband by giving Frank 242 enslaved people.) Fanny's daughters were young—the oldest, Annie, not yet ten; the youngest, Jeannie, Fanny's "big fat smart spoiled pickle," a girl with a bossy disposition and dark-blue eyes like her father's, barely three. The burden of care seems to have fallen mostly on Meta—Fanny and Frank's sweet, loving, motherless, adolescent niece, on whom Fanny had grown so dependent she could not bear the thought of sending Meta off to school and was searching for a governess instead.

It had to be withering, so much loss. The war was at once eerily distant and just up the road, in the little town of Waynesville, where women younger than Fanny went about in widow's veils. Two hundred miles north, in Columbia, South Carolina, Mary Chesnut observed that when she met people on the street, "sad and sorrowful is the greeting; they press your hand; tears stand in their eyes or roll down their cheeks."

In late January 1863, at the same time Fanny Scarlett was dreaming of a family reunion in Georgia, Union commander Thomas Wentworth Higginson was inspecting the destruction on Saint Simons Island. While peering through the broken windows of an abandoned plantation house—as he described it in his journal—he envisioned the yard outside filled with children, and he mourned the devastations of war.

In parts of the South, planters' homes were being torched by federal soldiers, sometimes at the behest of former slaves. The newly free people wanted to make sure the sites of "so much devilment . . . whipping niggers most to death to make 'em work," as one African American woman put it, were never again inhabited.

When he got word of Lincoln's call to emancipate the enslaved, Georgia governor Joseph Brown ordered up extra supplies of gunpowder for the state. Emancipation, charged a Savannah planter, is "a direct bid for insurrection . . . a most infamous attempt to incite flight, murder, and rapine on the part of our slave population." The Emancipation Proclamation became federal policy on January 1, 1863. In South Carolina Mary Chesnut detected a new attitude in her mother's enslaved butler, Dick, and noted the change in her diary. "He won't look at me now; but looks over my head, scenting freedom in the air."

In England Fanny Kemble heard the news and decided it was time to publish the journal she had written in Georgia in 1838 and 1839. She had circulated the manuscript privately for years but kept it hidden from the public while she negotiated her divorce from Pierce Butler. Her daughters now grown and Kemble herself no longer prey to Butler's demands, she hurried the book into print in England that spring. An American edition appeared in the summer. Drafted on Butler Island and Saint Simons, Frances Anne Kemble's *Journal of a Residence on a Georgian Plantation* laid bare the atrocities of American slavery. She issued the book partly to help dissuade the British government from siding with the Confederacy. She thought it her "imperative duty, knowing what I know, and having seen what I have seen, to do all that lies in my power to show the dangers and the evils of this frightful institution."

My grandmother must have bought her copy of the book from a secondhand store in Virginia, for the inscription inside references the state capital: "Richmond 11th Mo. 13.1863." The volume is a first edition, bound in fabric, still intact a century and a half after its publication. In a short preface, Kemble explains when and where she composed the journal and adds:

> The slaves in whom I then had an unfortunate interest were sold some years ago. The islands themselves are at present in the power of the Northern troops. The record contained in the following pages is a picture of conditions of human existence which I hope and believe have passed away.
>
> LONDON, *January 16, 1863*

This first edition of the *Journal* culminates in several pages of ads for new books then available from Kemble's American publisher, Harper and Brothers: guides to wine making, arithmetic, Latin, French; a biography of Martin Luther; novels by Wilkie Collins and Anthony Trollope. It's jarring to think that in the third year of the war—the year of Gettysburg, Vicksburg, Chickamauga—Americans were also conjugating Latin verbs and puzzling over grape types, but perhaps the call of civilization is never more urgent than when civilization is under assault. (In the midst of the federal occupation of the Georgia coast, Fanny and Frank Scarlett arranged for their niece Meta to have music lessons.) The final item in

Harper's long list of 1863 titles is Richard Hildreth's six-volume *History of the United States of America*, a work whose "inflexible impartiality" (*Boston Journal*) and "immense amount of material" (*De Bow's Review of the Southern and Western States*) made the work palatable to readers on both sides of the conflict.

Hildreth, an ardent abolitionist, suppressed his antislavery views enough to produce a reassuring history of America. Kemble did the opposite, and her *Journal* caught fire. In England excerpts were read out loud in the British House of Commons and handed out by the Ladies' Emancipation Society. In the United States, the book drew comparisons to *Uncle Tom's Cabin*. The *Atlantic Monthly* called it "the first ample, lucid, faithful, detailed account, from the actual head-quarters of a slave plantation in this country, of the workings of the system—its persistent hopeless, helpless, crushing of humanity in the slave, and the more fearful moral and mental dry rot it generates in the master."

Revelatory dry rot, to be precise. "Almost every Southern planter has a family more or less numerous of illegitimate colored children," Kemble disclosed. She used dashes to veil the identities of the white men who committed serial rape on her husband's properties, but Georgia's planter elite would have recognized the accused—among them Pierce Butler himself, by implication, and his longtime overseers, Roswell King Sr. and son Roswell Jr. Kemble paid special attention to the younger Roswell, who reigned over Butler's estates on both Saint Simons and Butler Island. An enslaved woman named Judy told Kemble her firstborn son was Roswell Jr.'s child. The overseer had "forced her, flogged her severely for having resisted him, and then sent her off, as a farther punishment, to Five Pound—a horrible swamp in a remote corner of the estate, to which the slaves are sometimes banished for such offenses as are not sufficiently atoned for by the lash." Judy was left alone there for days. Later, after she had returned to the plantation and given birth, Roswell Jr.'s wife, Julia, had Judy "severely flogged," together with a second enslaved woman who had also given birth to a child fathered by the overseer. Julia King then sent both women back to the swamp at Five Pound with orders that they be flogged daily for a week.

I strain to imagine my grandmother reading passages like this. She never discussed them with me—yet another item "we don't talk about." But she wasn't naive. When I drove off to Florida in my early twenties to move in with a married man, then left after four days, Mamie said only, "Sorry your plans didn't work as well as you had expected."

It was, again, her own mother who admitted there were "dark secrets" in the Scarlett family, and Mamie herself who, in her last addled months, murmured the phrase "dark mistresses."

Others of my grandmother's generation—her cousin Judge Frank Scarlett, for one; Margaret Mitchell, for another—rejected Kemble's vision of a corrosive antebellum South. Glynn County historian Margaret Davis Cate, who attended the same Brunswick high school as my grandmother, spent years working to discredit Kemble. Cate's 1960 article "Mistakes in Fanny Kemble's Georgia Journal," published in the *Georgia Historical Quarterly*, enumerated Kemble's factual errors and asked, "Can anyone know *fact* from *fiction* in Mrs. Kemble's *Journal*?"

Cate hoped her critique would quash plans to reissue Kemble's *Journal*, long out of print, on the centenary of the Civil War. She feared a rerelease of the *Journal* would "fan the flames of hatred" at a time when Georgia's schools, restaurants, and other public places were on the verge of being integrated. "The plantation people of St. Simons need no defense," she told the book's editor at Knopf. "Their lives stand for what they were and there was no culture anywhere in the South that was superior."

Knopf ignored Cate's claim and reissued Kemble's *Journal* in 1961. Cate died later that year; Kemble's exposé remains in print.

They were Lost Cause proselytes, the Margarets Cate and Mitchell—and Judge Frank Scarlett, who in 1947, during a naturalization hearing in Brunswick, inquired of an applicant seeking U.S. citizenship, "Who do you think was the greatest of all Americans?"

"General Robert E. Lee," the man replied dutifully.

Judge Scarlett was pleased. "I'm convinced this man is qualified to become a citizen," he declared.

Kemble's pained account of life in the South would have infuriated Judge Scarlett, as it surely infuriated an earlier Frank Scarlett—Francis Muir Scarlett's oldest son—in the summer of 1863. Kemble chronicles the damage done to women forced back into the fields three weeks after giving birth. She describes a fourteen-year-old who had already borne her first child. She tells of a woman who had sixteen children—fourteen of whom were dead—and four miscarriages, one because she was strapped to a tree while pregnant, arms tied overhead, and whipped. A woman named Die ripped her "scanty clothing" apart so Kemble could see first-hand what constant childbearing had done to her body. Sickened, the actor promised to get Die the care she needed. "But these are natural results," Kemble writes, "inevitable and irremediable ones, of improper treatment of the female frame."

Northern readers vouched for the accuracy of such passages. Southerners accused Kemble of perverting the truth. In a long letter to the *Cincinnati Daily Enquirer*, a Louisiana planter's wife sought to correct the impression that slavery was an unqualified evil. This self-described "Southern Matron" listed the many kindnesses she and her husband had granted their own enslaved workers over the years: hot coffee brought to fieldhands in winter "to prevent chills from the dews on the cotton"; melons and peaches distributed in summer; four days off at Christmas; cozy dwellings, some "with front porches"; a spacious hospital with round-the-clock nursing. "I do not deny that there are abuses in slavery," the writer allowed, "but with all its evils I believe it has been the means of elevating the African by bringing him in contact with Christianity and civilization, under a wholesome restraint to break up his habits of indolence."

It's the sort of passage Frank Scarlett's wife, Fanny, could have written. (It's the sort of passage Fanny Scarlett did write in her exuberant, prewar years: "I hear them shouting from below that Sam is coming with a large *turkey*.")

Kemble most likely did exaggerate, of course. She was a woman of melodramatic proclivities—a fact not lost on her critics—and these were dramatic times. But as the African American scholar Edda Fields-Black has pointed out, Kemble's *Journal*, with all its bombast, is one of the few eyewitness records we have of plantation life as seen from the perspective of an enslaver, and as such it is indispensable. Kemble's book did what the actor hoped it would—lift the curtain on people like Frank and Fanny Scarlett and help steer Britain away from a morally indefensible alliance with the Confederacy. Parts of the *Journal* still shock.

Its American publication coincided more or less with the battle of Gettysburg—the war's turning point, or *peripeteia*, to invoke a term the histrionic Kemble might recognize. It's unclear how the Scarletts took the news from Pennsylvania—the famous scene outside the telegraph office in *Gone with the Wind* still haunts—because by the time the news from Gettysburg reached Brunswick, Fanny had stopped writing. No other Scarlett woman seems to have picked up her pen—correspondence being women's work, as my grandmother so amply demonstrated.

Frank's wife was dying. It seems she had cancer. Perhaps, after months of indeterminate suffering, Fanny felt the way Alice James felt in 1891 after learning that she had a fatal tumor in her breast. The news came as a relief, Alice said, "lifting us out of the formless vague and setting us within the very heart of the sustaining concrete." Knowledge of the end meant time to prepare. "What you are when you die, the same will you reappear in the great day of eternity," southern boys were reminded in a tract issued by the Presbyterian Church to Confederate soldiers heading into war. "The features of character with which you leave the world will be seen in you when you rise from the dead." Therefore shun attachment, resist despair, make ready to relinquish your soul gladly and willingly, pattern yourself on Christ.

As Fanny apparently did. Her obituary, published in the *Savannah Republican* on November 3, 1863, four months after Gettysburg, reads in part, "Lost to her friends on earth, let them seek to imitate her bright Christian example."

It's telling that, at a time when newspapers were filled with reports of dying on a scale never before seen (seven thousand dead at Gettysburg alone, with another twenty-two thousand wounded), the Scarlett family took the trouble to publicize their own, very private loss:

> She was the light and idol of her immediate family, and her noble Christian life shed a lustre on all around. How sad must be the home thus bereaved! How many the tears that will be shed over her early grave by the doting husband and little ones who feel that they have lost their best and truest friend! Let them flow, for she deserves them all.

In Fanny's last days, the battle for Chattanooga raged. Shortly after her death on October 29, 1863, Union victory came and Union troops began marching toward Georgia. Impossible to conjure the snarl of emotions that must have gripped Frank Scarlett at the conflation of these events.

A year earlier, barely recovered from his own life-threatening illness, he had told his Parland nieces, "All will be right again I hope." But the doubt in his voice is audible. And now Fanny was gone.

"We needed this discipline or it would not have been sent," she had written the previous summer. But this?

Frank would live out the rest of his life a widower and die on October 30, 1897, within one day of the thirty-fourth anniversary of Fanny's death. He seems to have genuinely loved her. Why else the long obit in a paper otherwise packed with stories of wartime carnage?

In another year Fanny's brother Jesse would be captured by Sherman's army outside Augusta and sent to prison near Philadelphia. Across Georgia ministers would warn their congregations that, as a Macon preacher counseled in the fall of 1864, "God may be changing his plan." Savannah fell in December 1864. The following spring Frank Scarlett's brother George surrendered to Union troops outside Tallahassee and signed a document stating, "I will not bear arms against the United States of America, or give any information, or do any military duty whatsoever until regularly exchanged as a prisoner of war." After nine days in jail, George Scarlett was paroled. Maybe he was telling the truth when he pledged loyalty to the U.S. government, maybe not. When Lee surrendered at Appomattox, he conceded only that the South had been "compelled to yield" to the superior strength of the Union military.

Without Fanny to document the end, there is little sense of how the Scarletts coped with defeat. War records and deeds give partial clues. In 1866 Frank sells the family's Glencoe plantation and mortgages Fancy Bluff to his brother David, who, like the industrious Frank Kennedy of Mitchell's novel, has gone into the lumber business. Notices in the local press show the widower Frank Scarlett working as an attorney and co-founding a railroad company and, in 1877, producing "the choicest plums of the season. We have tasted nothing to compare with them" (*Brunswick Advertiser and Appeal*). All of this he achieved in Fanny's absence. Her death must have been the nadir. *Suis stat viribus*, the motto on the Scarlett coat of arms instructs: "He stands by his own strength." Left to console four young daughters and a motherless niece, Frank may have told himself the same.

They buried her under a stone slab in the family cemetery at Oak Grove:

FANNY

Wife of

FRANCIS D. SCARLETT

died

October 29th 1863

Aged 33 Years

3 Months and 11 Days

"Thanks be to God which

giveth us the victory through

our Lord Jesus Christ."

In her single—and singular—extant photograph, Fanny sits beside a vase of white flowers. A funereal touch, never mind the black dress and deep shadows circling her eyes. Maybe Frank kept the image near him after Fanny's death: a vestige of his former life preserved inside a tiny case, ornately framed, as if he could trap happiness and pull it out when things got tough. When, for instance, he looked out at his unplanted fields or glimpsed those enemy warships anchored in Saint Simons Sound or remembered (as did so many others across this once-unified land) the horror of a loved one's too-soon death.

It is Fanny Kemble who went public with her anguish. With the release of her *Journal*, the actor so scandalized her youngest daughter that the girl ruptured ties with her mother and after the war joined her father in trying to revive their old plantation on Saint Simons Island. Kemble took no notice. She handled criticism as she handled bad weather, remembered her good friend Henry James, who met the actor in England in 1872 and quickly fell under her spell. The matronly Kemble was then in her early sixties and James nearly thirty. He began calling on her weekly at her London residence (Kemble even visited his ailing sister, Alice). "She is like a straight deep cistern without a cover, or even sometimes a bucket into which, as a mode of intercourse, one must tumble with a splash," he swooned. After Kemble's death in 1893, James published a remembrance in which he praised her *Journal of a Residence on a Georgian Plantation* as the most valuable and particular account of "impressions begotten by that old South life which we are too apt to see today as through a haze of Indian summer."

That haze still clings to the old Butler properties in Glynn County. In front of Butler Island, a pair of historical markers erected in 1957 identify the plantation as the mere site of a famous rice plantation renowned for its association with the British actor Fanny Kemble—and for its intricate system of dikes and canals "installed by engineers from Holland." No mention of enslaved labor.

Pierce Butler's second plantation, at the north end of Saint Simons, is today a gated community filled with columned homes and pastel condos of the sort Sotheby's peddles. I found my way there in 2016. Hampton River Villas at Plantation Point of Hampton Plantation, it's called, without context or apology. A sign at its entrance shows a jaunty outline of some bygone figure being driven in a carriage by a coachman in a top hat. The silhouetted image cleverly skirts the issue of race. (On my one visit to the neighborhood I spotted just two people of color, both of them yard workers.) The only apparent nod to what occurred here is a cluster of tabby walls—the ruins of three former slave dwellings—preserved behind a steel fence shielding a row of luxury homes. I asked a man who was out in his driveway washing his car if I could get in to see them. He told me to drive around the back, and I'd find an opening in the fence.

"But be careful," he cautioned and flashed a toothy grin. "At night you can hear those old slaves."

I asked him what he meant, and he said, "There's a kid here with some kind of autism who says he's heard them come out and dance and sing at night." The man shrugged. "I haven't seen them myself, but you never know."

It was a pretty spring day. Low sun, faint wind, light glinting on the water behind the houses. Three men in polo shirts drove by in a golf cart and waved. Inside the fenced enclosure, I walked around the remains of the old slave cabins, snapping pictures. The tabby walls were a chalky reminder of the ocean that played such a grim role in this terrible saga. The people who built and inhabited these dwellings lived, in effect, inside the sea on a tract of oceanfront property now valued in the millions.

(The land was equally prized in Butler's time.) Shorn of their original purpose, these fragile structures could have been an idyllic beachfront settlement from some quaint era, not the joyless penal colony Kemble saw. With enough money I could see myself wanting to buy one of the condos in this neighborhood—it's the sort of milieu I sometimes frequented as a child. But I would have to shut my mind to the history of the place. Otherwise I might be as addled as that boy with his nighttime apparitions.

A few miles away, in a humbler part of Saint Simons, there is another haunted site, Igbo (or Ebo) Landing, where in 1803 a group of thirteen Igbo captives shipped to America from West Africa drowned themselves rather than submit to slavery. An African American woman who grew up on Saint Simons told me, "When it's real, real quiet, you can hear the chains clanging and hear them chanting, 'The river brought me here, and the river will take me back.'"

And what of the 436 enslaved people Pierce Butler sold off in Savannah in 1859 to pay his debts? An account of that "Weeping Time" was published as a sequel to select editions of Kemble's *Journal* in 1863 under the title "What Became of the Slaves on a Georgia Plantation?" The piece, adapted from reporter Mortimer Thomson's eyewitness coverage in the *New York Tribune*, details the wrenching two-day auction and the "crushing grief [it] laid on loving hearts." (Thomson does not mention the possibility, alleged by Kemble biographer Catherine Clinton, that Butler's ex-wife "counted on the proceeds" of the auction to help lift their daughters from poverty.) On the last day of the sale, Thomson reports, "several baskets of champagne were produced, and all were invited to partake, the wine being at the expense of the broker," who had just cleared over $300,000. As trains and ships steamed out of Savannah that night carrying their desolate human cargo to points south and west, stars "shone out as brightly as if such things had never been."

Sunk under parking lots and malls, left to crumble inside ancestral trunks, reframed as florid novels and picturesque communities of the sort I beheld at Hampton River Villas at Plantation Point of Hampton Plantation—the real story of what we did to African Americans has, for the better part of four hundred years, been buried. The tabby display at Hampton River Villas seemed little more than a polite nod to a distant past. I wondered who had made the decision to mark the former cabins not with explanatory text but with signs instructing visitors to please "not walk in or climb on the ruins." When I asked one of the men in the golf cart that day if he had ever encountered a ghost in the neighborhood, he laughed. "But then I've only lived here a year," he beamed and, with a wave of his hand, drove off with his buddies.

12

NEW ORDER

My Dear Father, the note begins.

> Bad news! Bad news! God alone knows how I hate to tell it—*but our cause is lost*. It has been confirmed the awful news from Lee's Army—The army is to be disbanded—and sent home. God knows best and we must try to believe that *all will be well*. That all is right. With love affectionately your daughter S. B. Scarlett / April 24th 1865.

The original note is said to be glued inside the back cover of the Scarlett family Bible, now in the collection of the Georgia Historical Society. But I have paged through that Bible more than once and found no trace of it. My only source for the note is a typed transcript of the original—another urgently copied item in my grandmother's boxes. I don't know who "S. B. Scarlett" is. I'm tempted to think the whole thing is an invention, the rabid daydream of a would-be Margaret Mitchell who thought our family should document its allegiance to the Lost Cause. (The term dates not from war's end but from 1866, when Virginia journalist Edward A. Pollard published the first of his racist screeds, *The Lost Cause*.)

In my grandmother's telling, the Scarletts lost everything with Lee's surrender. Years of hardship followed. Evidence sprouts inside the family archive: letters to my great-great grandmother Virginia Scarlett about the "miserable *War*" and the ill health it bred in veterans. Requests for flour and baking soda. A long account of the difficulties of postwar farming (starving cattle, bad weather, taxes and debts with no means of payment, formerly enslaved people desperate for food). We're not far from Scarlett O'Hara in her radish patch.

"Dear Sister Jenny," reads an undated letter to Virginia Scarlett. "As you expect company on Tuesday, I will send you up on that day a little piece of pig for dinner, anything to help out these hard times." The sender appears to be Virginia's widowed brother-in-law, Frank Scarlett.

Virginia married George Scarlett, Frank's youngest brother, on Valentine's Day 1866. A happy occasion in uncertain times. Tall, strapping, red-haired, blue-eyed George, then twenty-seven, had been jailed by the Union army and made to sign papers of surrender. Virginia, a planter's daughter, had grown up on a nearby plantation, Bethel, noted for its fragrant gardens and "bountiful hospitality." She was nineteen on her wedding day—a tiny woman with dark hair pulled back into a bun, thin lips, a long nose, a heart-shaped face. Her brown eyes conveyed both kindness and the sort of brute acuity children learn to dread. Throughout her life she weighed no more than a hundred pounds. She wore plain cotton dresses—no crinolines or brooches for this Scarlett wife. She and George were farmers. They set up housekeeping in the old Scarlett homestead at Oak Grove and seem to have gotten by that first postwar year on what they could hunt and fish and grow. (In another decade George would be hailed as one of Glynn County's "champion sweet potato raisers.") In December 1866 Virginia gave birth to their first child, a daughter: Annie Belle—known as Minnie. My great-grandmother.

There would be thirteen children in all, twelve of whom survived childhood. Several would live well into my lifetime—the ancient Scarletts I met as a kid on that gray porch in the woods outside Brunswick. The countryside around little Annie Belle and her parents was occupied by federal troops and Confederate army stragglers and free Blacks, some of whom took up residence on former Scarlett plantations. Postwar records show African Americans living at Fancy Bluff and on Colonel's Island, where they moved into old slave cabins or scrounged materials to build new cabins. They furnished these meager dwellings with items left behind when the slaves ran: lamps, padlocks, spoons, fishing and gardening tools.

Colonel's Island itself was part of William Tecumseh Sherman's "Reservation"—the fabled "40 acres and a mule" the Union general promised to free Blacks along the South Carolina and Georgia coasts in early 1865 with his Field Order No. 15. Sherman aimed to redistribute approximately four hundred thousand acres of land, much of it abandoned sea-island plantations like Pierce Butler's and John Parland's, in forty-acre parcels to formerly enslaved African Americans. (A subsequent order stipulated that Blacks were to receive the loan of mules as well.) There was nothing high-minded about it. Sherman needed a way to deal with the thousands of refugees who had trailed his army across Georgia. A gaunt, steel-eyed man of restless drive and deep prejudice, Sherman believed Blacks were inferior to whites in all ways, and he backed Emancipation only because it would further disrupt the Confederacy. But the idea to redistribute land to Blacks, born of discussions with twenty free Black leaders in Savannah—most of them formerly enslaved—was radical, says historian Henry Louis Gates Jr.

Or, as the Reconstruction scholar Eric Foner puts it, "Over a century ago, prodded by the demands of four million men and women just emerging from slavery, Americans made their first attempt to live up to the noble professions of their political creed—something few societies have ever done."

Had this "first systematic attempt to provide a form of reparations to newly freed slaves" been thoroughly implemented and enforced—had formerly enslaved people truly been able to own land, realize economic self-sufficiency, and "build, accrue and pass on *wealth*"—Gates believes the history of race relations in this nation would be very different from what it is.

But less than two months after Lincoln's death, his successor, Tennessee native Andrew Johnson, a onetime enslaver and "thoroughgoing white supremacist," according to David W. Blight, rescinded Sherman's order. Johnson's Amnesty Proclamation of May 29, 1865, returned most of the land Sherman had seized to its former owners and shattered African American dreams of economic autonomy. "Within a few years the Black tenants were dispossessed or became laborers," sociologist W. E. B. Du Bois would note in his 1901 report for the U.S. Labor Department on "The Negro Landholder in Georgia." "Thus the efforts to provide the freedman with land and tools ended, and by 1870 he was left to shift for himself amid new and dangerous social surroundings." Many white Americans feared that government support of newly freed Black Americans would lead to infinite dependence.

In 1867 former Confederate president Jefferson Davis was released from jail. By then many northerners were calling for an end to the animosity between North and South. Lee's surrender, in short, was the start of what critic and historian Michael Gorra calls the "forever war over the place of Black people in American society, and of slavery in American history."

Georgia's poorly staffed Freedmen's Bureau—the federal agency charged with overseeing "all subjects relating to refugees and freedmen from rebel states"—could not check the chaos Union victory unloosed. Some Lowcountry planters refused to acknowledge defeat or even let their enslaved workers know they had been emancipated. Some burned, or threatened to burn, slave cabins on their property so free Blacks would not move in. The bureau itself soon halved the number of government rations designated for poor Blacks in Savannah and blocked the state's asylums, hospitals, and homes from providing long-term housing to destitute African Americans. Intent on reviving the South's economy, the bureau rounded up countless unemployed Blacks from Georgia's cities and shipped them to Mississippi, Alabama, and other places short on labor.

There are few hints as to how the Scarletts negotiated the shift to a new order. As Gorra writes, "We shouldn't discount the extraordinary difficulty of what the United States tried to do during that postwar decade." The shift from one political, economic, and social system to another is never easy. "It was made impossible here," says Gorra, "by the fact that those interlocking systems each rested on the white refusal to see Black people as fully human."

The Scarletts managed to hang onto their land, or much of it, and, to judge from the assortment of porcelain I inherited from my grandmother, many of their possessions. By 1867 Frank Scarlett was back at Fancy Bluff with his daughters. George and Virginia Scarlett were living two miles away at Oak Grove. Frail but thriving Francis Muir and Ann Crum Scarlett, the family patriarchs, were either at Oak Grove or Fancy Bluff, where, on January 2, 1869, Francis Muir died a "calm, peaceful and happy" death at age eighty-four. His wife survived him by ten years. Ann Crum Scarlett died in 1879 and lies beside her husband under a shared tombstone in the family plot at Oak Grove.

Six years after Francis Muir's death, his nearly three-thousand-acre property at Oak Grove was subdivided into six lots of roughly four hundred acres each and distributed among his immediate heirs, one of whom was George Scarlett, my great-great grandfather. George's share of the property held both the original Scarlett home (where an old slave bell still hung from the back porch) and a handful of slave cabins. Who occupied those cabins or what ultimately became of those people is a mystery.

Records show that on many southern properties, African Americans lived in conditions approaching slavery. Few were compensated with more than food and clothing. My grandmother would long remember the "little old retainers" who lived behind George and Virginia Scarlett's house at Oak Grove in the early years of the twentieth century. "We used to watch them eat their sweet potatoes which were roasted in the fire—'Daddy March and Daddy February,' Pinkie 'Blue' and others." The lot where my grandmother saw them eat held a millstone for grinding sugar cane and a vat for turning ground cane into syrup, and presumably it was the labor of these men and women that produced that cane and syrup. It's unclear how they were compensated. I'm troubled by the term "retainer"—as if Oak Grove were a feudal estate and the Scarletts some kind of nobility. Were people like "Daddy March" and "Daddy February" and "Pinkie Blue" paid in cash? Shares? Housing? Were they allowed time off to cultivate their own crops? A clipping in the Scarlett archive claims that Virginia Scarlett hired an elderly Black woman named "Mum Sarah" to accompany the Scarlett children on their two-mile walk to school every day and beat off the alligators that congregated at a low point in the road. Sarah's pay, according to the clipping, was a biscuit.

A sepia photograph in the same archive shows an African American man by the name of Alec Massie drawing water from a well at Virginia Scarlett's girlhood home, Bethel, around 1888. He is dressed crisply in a white shirt, spotless gray trousers and vest, a broad-brimmed hat. The handwritten caption on the back of the image states, "This faithful old slave at the well died a short while since after having lived for 98 years. He never left after the war." The trope of the "faithful old slave" was then common (*Gone with the Wind* depends on it). Former masters and mistresses gave rapturous accounts of the men and women who had labored for them without pay before Emancipation and remained loyal afterward. The story in my family was that Alec Massie had single-handedly extinguished a house fire set on Scarlett land by Union soldiers during the war. It's the kind of wishful thinking that "tells us more about tensions in the Jim Crow South than it does about antebellum history," says historian David W. Blight.

Maybe Alec Massie was faithful—though certainly, in 1888, he was no slave. And maybe he lived to be ninety-eight—the implication being that people could survive slavery and live decades beyond the average lifespan, which in the 1880s was forty-three. I can more easily believe his decision to stay at Bethel was a matter of expediency. In Georgia alone nearly five hundred thousand people moved from bondage to freedom in the spring of 1865, and few had land or money. (Land was plentiful in the South after the war, but little of it was given to Blacks. As W. E. B. Du Bois discovered, the North had little taste for government seizure of private property—even rebel property—and the South wanted "to keep the bulk of Negroes as landless laborers.") Little wonder many African Americans traded their one commodity, labor, for shelter and food on properties where they were known. There's evidence of an African American named Daniel Parland—very possibly one of John Parland's mixed-race children—living for a time after the war on Colonel's Island. Black families took up residence at Fancy Bluff as well. Among them were King and Matilda Hippard and several of their children and grandchildren. (The 1880 census identifies King as a farmer and notes that neither he nor Matilda nor their son Abraham can read or write—but their grandson Becket, aged nine, can read and is attending school. Progress.)

I think of Avedell Grant's remark—"the Scarletts were always good to the Blacks"—and wonder how my family treated the people they had once regarded as property. As wealthy, slaveholding white Georgians lurched from the shock of Sherman's March to self-governance under the eye of the Freedmen's Bureau to military reconstruction—the federal government had to step in to "reconstruct" the state three times between 1865 and 1870—and ultimately to the post-Reconstruction white supremacist counterrevolution known as Redemption, how did my ancestors behave? What kinds of agreements did Frank Scarlett and his brothers forge with people like King and Matilda Hippard, who had turned against the family during the war? Across Georgia—across the South—white landowners drafted labor contracts designed to cheat and exploit their Black workers. Ten-hour workdays, Sundays excepted, were common. On some properties bells rang, as in slavery, to mark the start and end of the day's work, and employers brandished pistols and whips.

I find it both difficult and all too easy to imagine Frank Scarlett doing the same. Frank, with his contempt for the way his "little negroes" had "all turned fools about the Yankies," his presumptions about status and autonomy. "I hope when peace is made a law will be passed to kill every one who ever dares to put his foot on our soil." How did he respond when Congress, prodded by men like Thaddeus Stevens from my Pennsylvania hometown, passed the Fourteenth and Fifteenth Amendments guaranteeing Black men the right to vote? What did Frank Scarlett do in the summer of 1867, when Georgia, under military orders, launched a statewide drive to register African American voters? Or the following spring, 1868, when thirty-two African Americans were elected to the state legislature, where his own father had once served? Did Frank take part in the statewide campaign to unseat them? Did he contribute to the violence and intimidation that kept Black men and white Republicans away from the polls the following November, sweeping Georgia Democrats into office and sparking another short-lived period of federally mandated military reconstruction?

And so it went from 1865 until the "final betrayal," as Gates terms it, of 1877, when U.S. president Rutherford B. Hayes pulled the last federal troops from the South, and any hope of a biracial democracy in the former Confederacy died. Mitchell's novel, reliably one-sided, tracks Georgia's deliverance from "the scourge of Reconstruction" to the blessings of Redemption, when white men reclaimed their rightful place in the social and political pecking order, and an ascendant Ku Klux Klan preserved white women from the menace of Black men, "many of them scarcely one generation out of the African jungles," Mitchell asserts.

"It was the large number of outrages on women and the ever-present fear for the safety of their wives and daughters that drove Southern men to cold and trembling fury and caused the Ku Klux Klan to spring up overnight," Mitchell elaborates, as if citing historical fact and not white supremacist dogma—the same dogma that begat more than 4,400 documented terrorist lynchings across the United States between Reconstruction and World War II. "And it was against this nocturnal organization," Mitchell goes on, "that the newspapers of the North cried out most loudly, never realizing the tragic necessity that brought it into being."

Mitchell's hyperbole stems not just from white supremacist dogma but from her own traumatic past. She herself had been raped by her first husband, Red Upshaw, a volatile white man on whom she modeled Rhett Butler. In her book Mitchell dwells so insistently on sexual violence that critic Leslie Fiedler labeled *Gone with the Wind* a "fantasy of interethnic rape." There's little mention of the realities Fanny Kemble witnessed—the commonplace predations of white enslavers like Frank Scarlett and his brother-in-law John Parland—just a lighthearted exchange about the ubiquity of "mulattoes" in the South and a barbed nod to the "yellow babies" sure to emerge from the coupling of Yankee soldiers with their "black fools."

In his electrifying 1903 plea for racial justice, *The Souls of Black Folk*, Du Bois pointed to the hypocrisy of white "Southern gentlemen" who accuse Black men of violating white women while ignoring "two centuries of systematic legal defilement of Negro women." Du Bois, like Mitchell, notes the ubiquity of mixed-race Americans, but he does so without the novelist's tacit *boys-will-be-boys* wink. "The rape which your gentlemen have done against helpless Black women in defiance of your own laws is written on the foreheads of two millions of mulattoes, and written in ineffaceable blood," he charges.

Two years after Du Bois published his cry for Americans to "listen to the strivings in the souls of Black folk," the North Carolina novelist Thomas Dixon issued the second volume of his "Race Conflict" trilogy, *The Clansman*. The book's key event, as anyone who's seen *Birth of a Nation* knows, is the sexual assault of a young white woman by a Black man—and her postsuicide vindication, thanks to a posse of white-hooded, cross-burning vigilantes who terrorize the African American community. Mitchell so adored Dixon's work that as a child she staged one of his "Race Conflict" books as a play. Dixon, equally enthralled by Mitchell's febrile vision of a degenerate, Africanized South, told her that with *Gone with the Wind* she had "not only written the greatest story of the South ever put down on paper, you have given the world the Great American Novel."

"I was practically raised on your books and love them very much," Mitchell fawned.

In *Gone with the Wind*, Dixon's acolyte served up her own portrait of a redemptive KKK—one whose members dutifully hang Black men rather than subject their alleged victims to the shame of "having to testify in open court." So routine is the murder of African American men in Mitchell's novel that when Rhett Butler (the book's only actual rapist—a man who shares Pierce Butler's surname) shoots a Black man to death and goes unpunished for his crime, no one questions it, least of all the book's author. Butler's excuse for the killing—"he was uppity to a lady, and what else could a Southern gentleman do?"—passes without comment.

By 1899, the year my grandmother Mamie turned one, Georgia led the nation in terrorist lynchings, a distinction the state would retain until 1918. In 1899 alone, over twenty-seven lynchings took place in the state. Between 1882 and 1930, a reported 453 African Americans were lynched in Georgia. Shortly before Mamie's eighth birthday, white mobs, inflamed by rumors of an "epidemic of rape," went on a five-day spree of violence against Blacks in Atlanta. In Mamie's ninth year, the Georgia Assembly disenfranchised Black voters. In her twentieth year, nearly a dozen African Americans were murdered near Valdosta, Georgia—roughly a hundred miles from Brunswick—in retaliation for the killing of a white man. Among the dead were a man named Hayes Turner and his pregnant wife, Mary, who was hanged, burned, and shot after publicly decrying her husband's murder. Their unborn infant was torn from Mary's body and its skull crushed.

By the time Mamie married my grandfather in 1920, in an afternoon ceremony in Brunswick's First Methodist church, with "soft rays of the afternoon sun . . . beaming through the stained windows," Blacks across Georgia were fleeing north, and the KKK was holding annual parades in downtown Brunswick.

How much of this seeped through the walls of that gray house in the woods and into my grandmother's consciousness, I don't know. But she caught something. Along with stories of postwar poverty and loss (the same kinds of tales Mitchell was imbibing in Atlanta as a child), Mamie picked up some inkling of another reality, and it stuck. She couldn't voice it except in private in her later years; her loyalties were too fierce, and the pressures of a Jim Crow South (or what Bryan Stevenson calls the "era of racial terror")—where to question the status quo was to risk social and familial exile or worse—too great. But she could imagine. "I always felt that the reason that there were so many Southern women writers was because they were always a part of the family, and while they had to be quiet [as children] while with adults, they could listen and wonder," she once wrote to me. "Children are often lonely but they have their own dreams and can sense what is being said by the manner it is said. Then they can make up the rest."

My grandmother was not a writer. She was a visual artist, and I have always wanted to believe those bleak cameos of African American women she painted in her upstairs studio were her way of acknowledging the cruelties white Americans have so relentlessly inflicted on people of color. Mamie spoke and behaved in the coded language of the segregated South. I wince to recall her whispered allusions to "colored people" as we sat in the living room in the evening or the racial divide we observed inside her house. But my grandmother never, so far as I know, embraced or endorsed the sort of violence Mitchell extols in her book.

If her nightmare memory is to be believed, Mamie understood what it meant to sit inside the safety of a white home while people she loved went off in the dark to terrorize human beings they reviled because of their skin color. That scene, so reminiscent of the passage in Mitchell's novel—Scarlett and those women gathered around the parlor table, reading out loud—is as much a part of my inheritance as Fanny Scarlett's letters and that apocryphal note admitting our "cause is lost." Mamie did what she could to pass on the facts.

FIG. 19. The Scarlett family in front of their home at Oak Grove, outside Brunswick, circa 1899. The house was then under construction after a fire. The infant in the carriage, being tended by an unnamed nurse, is the author's grandmother Mary King Hilsman. Scarlett-Tison family collection, Georgia Historical Society.

FIG. 20. The Scarlett house at Oak Grove, post-1899. (There are no surviving images of Oak Grove before 1899.) Scarlett-Tison family collection, Georgia Historical Society.

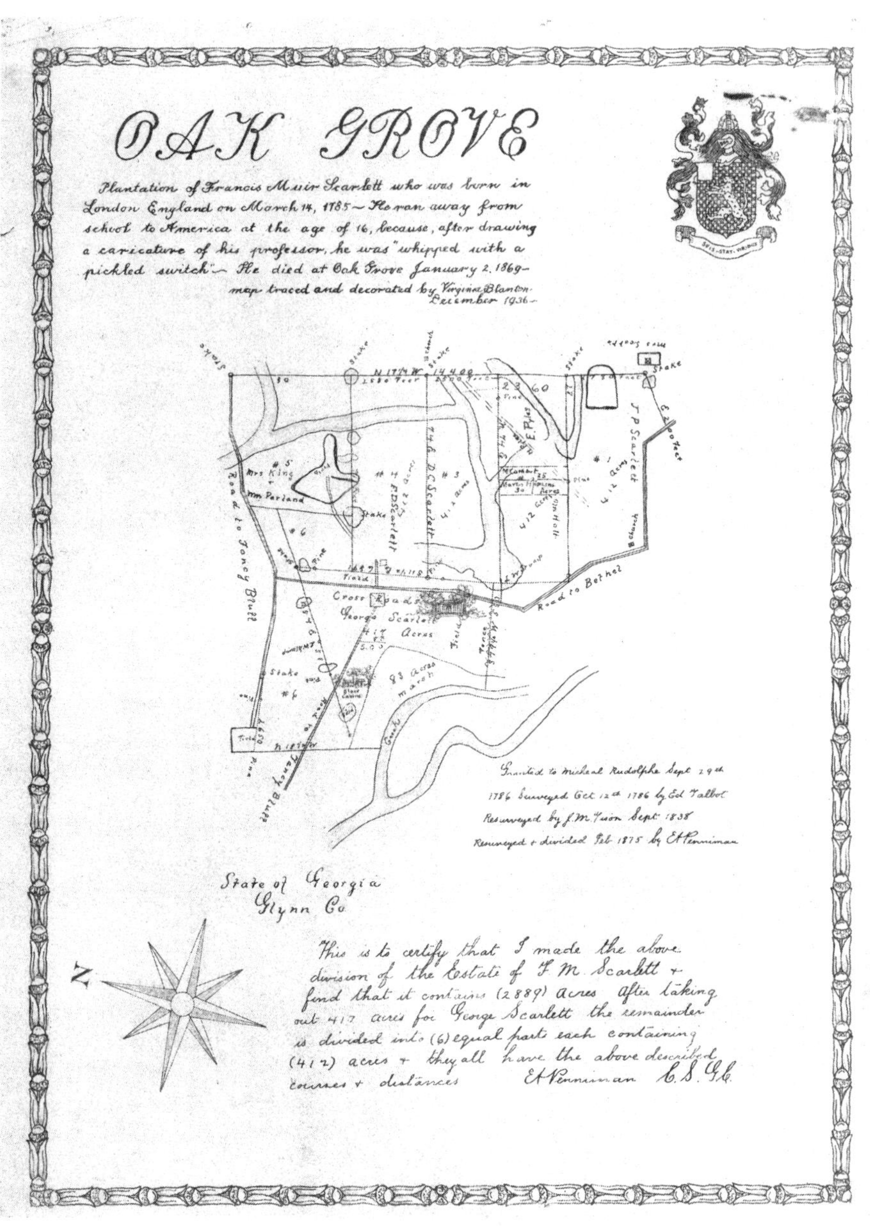

FIG. 21. Map of Oak Grove, 1936. Drawn by Virginia (Ginger) Hilsman Blanton (1897–1983). Scarlett-Tison family collection, Georgia Historical Society.

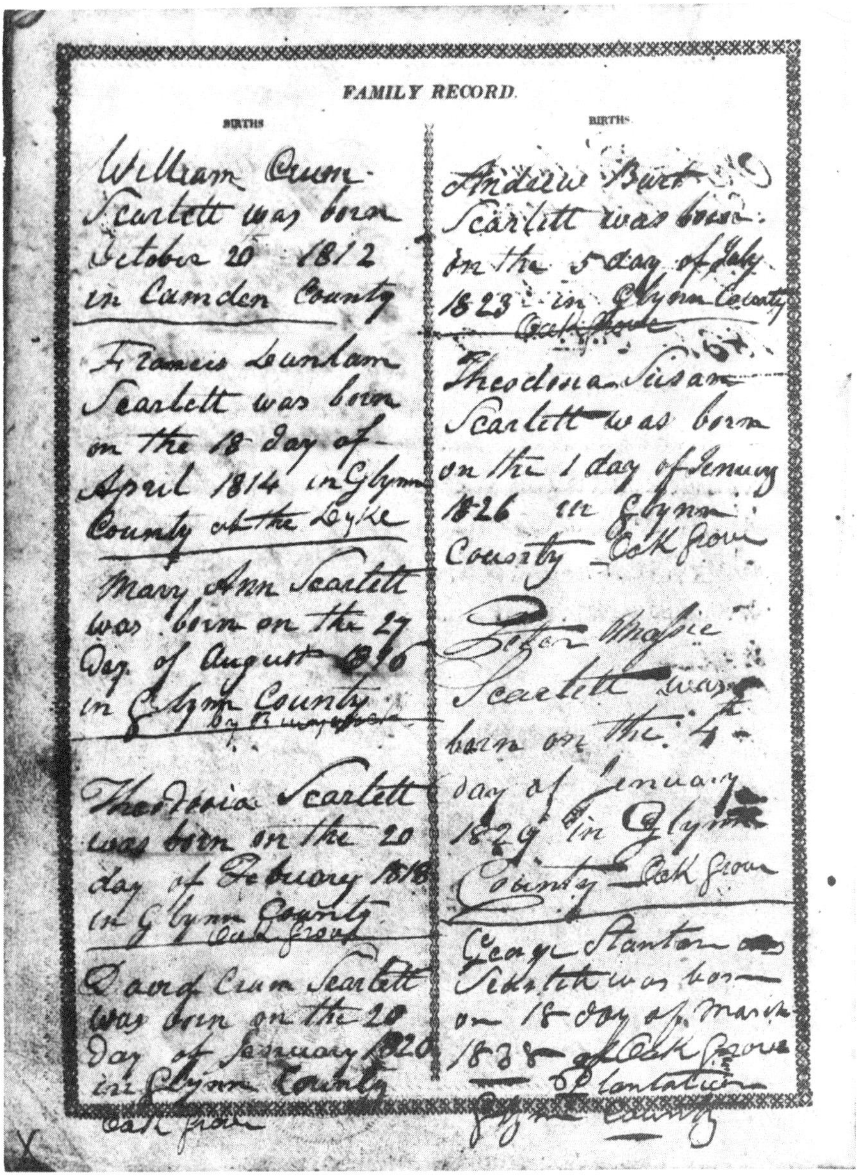

FAMILY RECORD.

BIRTHS

William Owen
Scarlett was born
October 20 1812
in Camden County

Francis Dunham
Scarlett was born
on the 18 day of
April 1814 in Glynn
County at the Dyke

Mary Ann Scarlett
was born on the 27
Day of August 1816
in Glynn County

Theodosia Scarlett
was born on the 20
day of February 1818
in Glynn County
Oak Grove

David Owen Scarlett
was born on the 20
Day of January 1820
in Glynn County
Oak Grove

BIRTHS

Andrew Burt
Scarlett was born
on the 5 day of July
1823 in Glynn County
Oak Grove

Theodosia Susan
Scarlett was born
on the 1 day of January
1826 in Glynn
County Oak Grove

Peter Massie
Scarlett was
born on the 4
day of January
1829 in Glynn
County Oak Grove

George Stanton
Scarlett was born
on 18 day of March
1838 at Oak Grove
Plantation
Glynn County

FIG. 22. Scarlett family Bible entries, 1812–88. Scarlett-Tison family collection, Georgia Historical Society. The original Scarlett Bible is now in the collection of the Georgia Historical Society in Savannah.

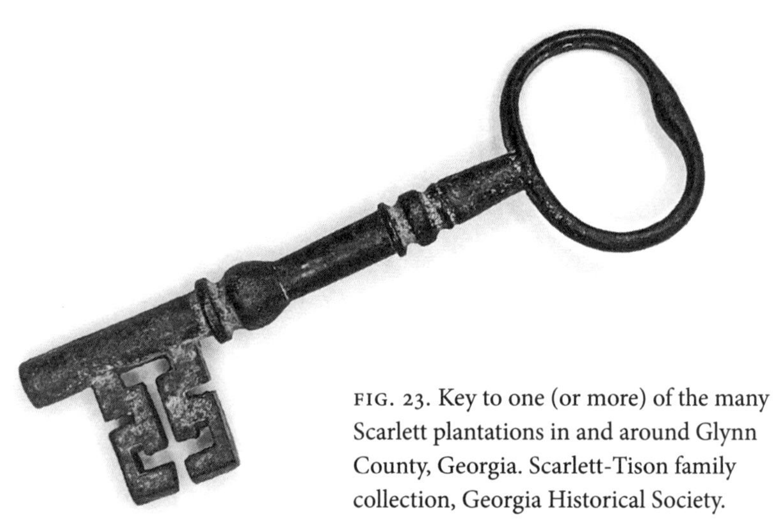

FIG. 23. Key to one (or more) of the many Scarlett plantations in and around Glynn County, Georgia. Scarlett-Tison family collection, Georgia Historical Society.

FIG. 24. Cover and interior of a Scarlett archival box sent to the author by her uncle Robert Pettigrew in the 1990s. Photograph by Don Hammond; Scarlett-Tison family collection, Georgia Historical Society.

PART 4

Inheritance

13

INDUSTRY

Whether George Scarlett or his brother Frank joined the Klan, as even the saintly Ashley Wilkes does, is hard to know. ("They are men, aren't they? And white men and Southerners," India Wilkes tells Scarlett when it becomes clear that both Ashley and the bumbling Frank Kennedy are members.)

But shortly before Christmas 1868, George Scarlett helped draft an agreement among the "Freeholders" of the Twenty-Seventh District of Glynn County, Georgia, aimed at "regulating" Black labor in the coming year. A coy word, *freeholder*—as if you could *hold* a free person as you once *held* a slave. But then that was the point. Terrified by the prospect of armed Black rebellion, former enslavers across the South were drafting documents like this, spelling out the terms under which emancipated African Americans could live and work on white-owned land. Such agreements were a key part of the infamous Black Codes, encouraged by Andrew Johnson and widely implemented, which spelled out both the conditions of Black labor (all but impossible to meet) and the punishments (financial as well as physical) to which those in violation of these agreements would be subjected.

George Scarlett's brothers Frank and John and his brother-in-law Robert Tison all signed the document. The men agreed, collectively,

> That we will not allow any Freedman to live on our lands unless they have made a Contract with us for full time or for some portion of the time while on our lands. That none of those who do so live on said lands on said terms shall be permitted to be scattered over said lands but shall *all* live in one settlement subject to the direct control of the Landlord.
>
> That we will hold ourselves responsible for any depredations that said Freedman may commit.

> That we will hold anyone in this the 27th District, whether agreeing here to or not, responsible for any depredations committed by Freedmen living in these lands contrary to these terms.
>
> That we would strongly recommend that no Freedman or Freedmen should be allowed to live on any land on which no responsible white person resides.

The agreement does not define the word "depredations" or indicate how those depredations were to be addressed, although it doesn't take much to imagine. Bryan Stevenson's Legacy Museum and National Memorial for Peace and Justice in Montgomery, Alabama, are filled with examples.

The freeholders' agreement signed by the Scarlett brothers in 1868 was another of the items my grandmother saved in her archive. Inside that archive I also found a note to George Scarlett, written in early 1871 by one James Houston, asking George to verify the ages of two African Americans then working for the Scarlett family. Houston, who years earlier had served as mayor of Brunswick, was keen to establish "the fact of their not being 21." He also wanted George and his brother Frank to procure the birth records for a list of Black men living on Scarlett lands. "It will be doing our County and State a great service, perhaps. I think we will succeed in contesting this election and turning out Mr. Blue."

As they did. With the implicit help of George and Frank Scarlett, Houston and his cronies purged countless African Americans from Georgia's electoral rolls in 1871. Pro-Confederacy Democrats took control of the state government later that year, and in what Eric Foner calls the "most comprehensive effort to undo Reconstruction" by any southern state, helped send Union occupiers packing. The despised "Mr. Blue" gone—a prewar racial hierarchy restored.

At times it must have felt like old days. George Scarlett busied himself with farming. ("A citizen of this county, Mr. Geo. Scarlett, we learn, has raised 57 bushels of corn on one acre of land. A small farm well cultivated is what is needed now-a-days."—*Brunswick Advertiser and Appeal*, 1876.) George's brother Frank served as an attorney on real estate transactions, as he'd done before the war. In 1868 Frank Scarlett secured an appointment from the Georgia General Assembly to the Glynn County Board of Education, where his duties included helping to choose textbooks and arranging "for the instruction of the white and colored youths in separate schools." ("In no case," the assembly specified, "shall white and colored children be taught together in the same school.") In time Frank became a postmaster—another government appointment reserved exclusively for white men. (Georgia's first Black postmaster, Isaiah H. Lofton, appointed in 1897, was run out of town after his post office was burned and he was shot in a racially motivated assault.)

Both Frank and George Scarlett engaged in the state's burgeoning rail business. Railroads were fast becoming the most lucrative business investment throughout the postwar South, supplanting agriculture and propelling the idea that North and South had patched up their differences and resolved slavery. Frank Scarlett helped incorporate two railroad companies in Brunswick, one connecting Glynn and Appling Counties and a second linking Brunswick with Augusta. Hoping to cash in on a scheme to build a profitable commercial port just south of his property at Oak Grove, George Scarlett granted rights to the South Brunswick Terminal Railroad Company to lay tracks across his land. The old Scarlett plantation would see the transfer of goods from inland sites to a new terminus called South Brunswick. Among the materials to be transported through Oak Grove was coal—much of it mined in Alabama by African Americans convicted of such "crimes" as vagrancy, burdened with impossible fines, and jailed. Leased by corporations like the Tennessee Coal, Iron and Railroad Company (a subsidiary of U.S. Steel), these men—whose only offense was that they could not prove themselves employed—labored underground for years, often decades if they survived, at no pay. Peonage, the system was called. A practice even Margaret Mitchell disparages:

"You didn't have any objections to working slaves!" Scarlett cries when her husband Frank Kennedy chides her for hiring convict labor.

"Ah, but that was different," Mitchell steps in. "Slaves were neither miserable nor unfortunate. The negroes were far better off under slavery than they were now under freedom, and if she didn't believe it, just look about her."

The great South Brunswick seaport south of George Scarlett's property ultimately failed to materialize, and he did not get rich. But the slave-labor system by which unjustly imprisoned Black Americans enriched an industrializing South run by white capitalists endured well into the twentieth century.

I was born three months after my great-grandmother Minnie died (in September 1955). Minnie (George and Virginia Scarlett's first child, Annie Belle) was herself born the year the U.S. Congress proposed a fourteenth constitutional amendment granting equal protection of the laws to all people born or naturalized in the United States. Minnie was two when the amendment was ratified in 1868. Her father, George, was a war veteran; her mother, Virginia, grew up tended by enslaved people. Minnie's childhood nurse was a young African American woman named Laula, daughter of the pregnant Julia who had fled the Scarlett plantation at Fancy Bluff together with King and Matilda Hippard and more than a dozen others in 1862. Laula was rolled to her freedom in a wheelbarrow.

How close this history is, just a couple of generations. There she is, my great-grandmother Minnie, tucked inside my grandmother's albums: bright-eyed, vigorous, a working woman stylishly clad in a veiled hat and starched shirtwaist. ("We used to tie the ribbons around her short sleeves, and she would put a rose in her hair for the evenings," Mamie remembered.) Minnie's handsome face was stiffened by loss: an only son, Tom, dead at age three of meningitis. A picture of him sits on my dresser—blond pageboy hair, winsome smile. I like having the ghost child nearby. His stricken mother buried him in the Scarlett cemetery at Oak Grove in 1896. Inside a trunk beneath her bed, Minnie kept mementoes of the little boy: books and a small rubber donkey, battered from use. "She never could talk about him and later destroyed the donkey," my grandmother said.

Less than a decade after Tom's death, Minnie's forty-three-year-old husband—my grandmother's father, Albert Hilsman, a businessman from Macon—died of tuberculosis. He seems to have been a compassionate man. A note in Mamie's hand tells me that when Albert Hilsman's half sister married a Jewish man and was consequently shunned by her "horrified" family, "Mother and our Papa felt differently."

Widowed, with three small daughters to support, Minnie Scarlett Hilsman sought work outside Atlanta as a housekeeper. She left her children in the Scarlett family's care at Oak Grove. "I sometimes wonder how she managed to raise us," Mamie reminisced. "Of course, I know—because the family stood behind her with what little they had and with all their love." Eventually Minnie moved closer to home and opened a boardinghouse and home-based bakery. I have her recipes for spice cake and tea cakes and "Plantation Berry Cake"—the last a dense mass of berries, eggs, butter, sugar, flour, nutmeg, and lemon. For a period in my twenties, my mother and I baked the berry cake annually. Decades later I tried making it again. But when I unmolded the thing it collapsed under its own weight, a metaphor not lost on me. (Who gave it that name? And where did the recipe come from—another family keepsake born of African American industry?)

My great-grandmother Minnie grew up surrounded by the apparatus of slavery: slave bells, cabins, overseer's house, cotton fields. And people: Laula; Tony, the man who wheeled pregnant Julia to the boat that carried her and her unborn child to freedom (as an old man, Tony loved telling the story of how he was subsequently caught by the Confederates and then pardoned); King and Matilda Hippard, farmers near Fancy Bluff; Alec Massie, the "faithful old slave" at Bethel, Virginia Scarlett's childhood home, who stayed on with the family after the war. (Alec was reportedly married to a survivor of the *Wanderer*, the illegal slave ship from which Francis Muir Scarlett purchased a kidnapped African in 1858.)

As she moved about her childhood home at Oak Grove or visited family at Bethel or Fancy Bluff, Minnie would have crossed paths with some of these people and would have heard snatches of their Lowcountry creole, with its distinctive West African phrasing—words like *buckruh*, *cawnfiel*, *hongry*, *suppuh*, *gawd*. (At least four thousand Gullah-Geechee words have African roots; once derided, Gullah-Geechee is today recognized as the only uniquely African American creole language.)

Minnie's brother Bobbie, born in 1882, loved to recite Gullah-Geechee lore. My grandmother heard him repeat one exchange so often she memorized it:

> Jahnee!!!
> Yes maam
> You hongree??
> Yes maam
> Go down yonder in de cawn field look in de jam o de fence
> You hear me??
> Yes maam
> You find some swampy seed and some mashie barrow

You hear me??
Yes maam
Tuk some and leave some for tarry time
You hear me??
Buckety buckety buckety.

("Swampy seed," Mamie explained when she typed out the lyrics for me, "was rice. Mashie barrow was coon.") She also remembered her Uncle Bobbie telling Brer Rabbit stories.

What was it like to grow up in a place so saturated with the recent past—a vanquished, traumatic past whose wounds persisted? Minnie and Bobbie and their siblings were the first of my direct Scarlett ancestors to be born into a non-slaveholding South. Surely, in addition to faithful retainers and doting nursemaids, they encountered African Americans desperate to find food and housing and work, African Americans searching for loved ones lost in slavery (ads for the missing ran well into the twentieth century). The scars of bondage, psychic and physical, were raw. You didn't mention them, but you knew. As Wendell Berry says of his enslaving forebears, "They were burdened with a malignant inheritance, and they endeavored to protect themselves by a carefully contrived myth, preserving them against any acknowledgement, spoken or unspoken, of their involvement."

I never asked Mamie for the truth. I suspect if I had, she would have pursed her lips and given an icy stare and reminded me of the "things we don't talk about." (A friend from Georgia recalls "that ancient, ironclad rule that women must keep the family secrets.")

It's odd to me that the Scarletts went so abruptly from pride in their "little negroes" to what I can only call shame. But then shame is at the heart of this. As Berry found when he at last decided to probe his ancestry, "Once you begin to awaken to the realities of what you know, you are subject to staggering recognitions of your complicity in history and in the events of your own life."

Complicity is not a word I associate with my grandmother—or with her mother or grandmother. Forgiveness, love, devotion, yes: that was the Scarlett lexicon of choice. And yet Mamie grasped that she and I shared more than blue eyes and fair skin. "We all have roots, and our heritage no doubt makes us what we are," she wrote me in 1978, around the time Alex Haley's family saga was airing on TV. "These genes are powerful things."

For years whenever I told someone about my Scarlett roots, I'd bat my eyes and raise my fist like Scarlett O'Hara, and in my best Georgia drawl declaim, "I will never be hungry again!" Reared on Mamie's tales and Mitchell's iconography, I fell for the lie that we had been "good slaveholders," like the O'Haras, or at least innocuous ones, with our waltzing belles and obliging Mammies, our tragic fall and brave afterlife.

I cannot fathom today how Mitchell managed to reach into slavery's malevolent well and come up with the fictions she did. Even my grandmother, born two years before Mitchell and brought up on identical racial tropes, shunned the kinds of caricatures and assumptions that fill *Gone with the Wind*. Although she stuck to the boundaries that segregation mapped in her life, Mamie brought a touch of nuance to her dealings with African Americans—or at least that's the impression I get from her correspondence. Neither my grandmother nor Mitchell had the audacity of someone like William Faulkner, obviously, or even the Tennessee author T. S. Stribling, whose Pulitzer Prize–winning novel, *The Forge* (1931), presents a meticulous portrait of slavery's arbitrary and awful powers over Black lives. But Mitchell, who defended her novel by claiming its African American characters had higher scruples than their white counterparts, twisted the realities of the slave system and the terrors of postwar Black life into "an encyclopedia of the plantation legend," critic Malcolm Cowley asserted in his 1936 review of the book. "It is all here, every last bale of cotton and bushel of moonlight, every last full measure of Southern female devotion working its lily-white fingers uncomplainingly to the lily-white bone." (Faulkner was blunter: "No story takes a thousand pages to tell.")

Mitchell gave families like mine a history to be proud of. That her mythology lasted into the twenty-first century has much to do, I suspect, with the idea that Americans are uniquely incapable of evil. In 2016 I spent a weekend in Atlanta with a group of *Gone with the Wind* fans who call themselves the Windies. It was the eightieth anniversary of the book's publication, and we toured the relevant sites: Mitchell's house in downtown Atlanta, the library that holds her archive, the *Gone with the Wind* Museum in Marietta (where, to my surprise, I saw a pair of African

American women eagerly poring over memorabilia). Several Windies carried bags emblazoned with scenes from the film. One man wore a necktie stamped with an image of Scarlett and Rhett embracing; he told me he'd modeled his house outside Atlanta after Tara. Another Windie confided over lunch that she admired the novel because "it's this country's history. It's what happened during the war." I was astonished to hear a Windie from rural Georgia tell me she loved the book but was troubled by its racism. By the end of the weekend, I had concluded that most Windies were fans not because they embraced Mitchell's vision of a copacetic antebellum South but because they loved Vivien Leigh's costumes.

Mitchell's storytelling plays its part. Despite knowing what I know, I fell smack into the book's quicksand plot when I picked it up again during my time with the Windies. Molly Haskell, writing in 2009, captures the seven stages of audience attachment to *Gone with the Wind*: "Love, Identification, Dependency, Resentment, Embarrassment, Indifference, and then something like Half-Love again." Haskell is talking about the movie, but the novel exerts a similar grip. "There's a primary pull, then a recoil, a secondary period of shame at having been so thoroughly captivated." Yes, and yes.

And yet Mitchell herself turns out to be more complicated than you might expect. In the early 1940s, Benjamin E. Mays, a son of former slaves and then president of Atlanta's historically Black Morehouse College, asked Mitchell if she would help fund his school. The novelist promptly sent Mays a check but requested that the gift remain anonymous: "I am sure you understand the reasons behind this." White southerners of her status didn't fraternize with Blacks. A few years later, Mitchell gave another $2,000 to fund scholarships for medical and dental students at Morehouse, and she arranged for an additional $3,000 to go to the college after her death. In 2002 her estate gave the school $1.5 million to endow a chair in Mitchell's name. Her gifts to Morehouse—and to Atlanta's Fulton DeKalb Hospital, where she helped fund a public medical unit for African Americans—stemmed in part from direct experience. In 1946 Mitchell's African American laundress, Carrie Holbrook, was unable to find a paying hospital to take her in when she was dying of cancer. Mitchell prevailed on the sisters of Our Lady of Perpetual Help to admit Carrie, and Holbrook died there three days later. "I do not think people who have not experienced so heartbreaking a time can realize the need for more beds for our colored population who are able to pay something for medical and hospital care," Mitchell told the chair of Fulton DeKalb's board. "Atlanta is big enough now to have colored people in the white-collar class, and I wonder how many of them have been in the situation of our Carrie, willing to pay but being unable to buy a bed in which to die."

Does Mitchell's generosity make up for the stereotypes she perpetuated in her novel? "No Black man or woman can read this book and be sorry that this particular wind has gone," novelist Pat Conroy wrote in his otherwise laudatory preface to the fiftieth-anniversary edition of *Gone with the Wind* in 1986. It's hard to get a read on Mitchell's chameleon behavior: loyal to the Klan-loving Thomas Dixon one minute, funneling clandestine checks to Black causes the next. But as former Atlanta mayor Andrew Young acknowledged in his 2010 documentary about Mitchell's friendship with Mays—and with Hattie McDaniel, with whom the novelist maintained a warm correspondence—real friendship between Blacks and whites in 1940s Atlanta was unthinkable.

My grandmother's housekeeper of forty-plus years, Carrie Johnson, also died of cancer, in 1983. I have never known the extent to which my grandparents helped with Carrie's care. They seem to have contributed to her funeral expenses. Stoic to the core, my grandmother wrote me the day after Carrie's death to let me know she was gone and to tell me, "None of us can be sorry," for Carrie had suffered horribly. My mother and I had gone to Virginia to see Carrie a month before she died—my one and only visit to the house Carrie shared with her husband, Louis. We found her sitting in a recliner in her living room, cradling a golf ball–sized tumor below her left ear. "I don't know what to do," she rasped. "Don't know what to do."

My mother knelt beside Carrie and took her hands.

"Have they given you something for the pain?" my mother asked softly.

Carrie nodded.

"Is it working?"

Carrie said nothing. My mother stroked her hands. I sat across from them both, silent. I was twenty-seven and unpracticed at offering comfort to the dying. It was my mother who knew what to do—my mother, Scarlett Ann Stainton, Mamie's firstborn, who scolded me when I was five for staring at a Black woman, Katie, who had come to clean our house.

"Don't you ever do that again," my mother hissed after she and I were alone.

"What?"

"Stare at Katie the way you did. You know perfectly well the only reason you did it is because she's Black, and that's rude, and don't you ever do it again." (My sister would recall that whenever Katie came to clean, my mother served lunch to all of us together, Katie included, in the dining room, on fine china and cloth place mats.)

I watched as my mother whispered to Carrie and continued to stroke her hands. I saw Carrie's head nod, her lips close. I saw her clutch at my mother's fingers. Louis sat off in a corner, speechless. On the wall above him was a portrait of John F. Kennedy. I had no idea he had meant anything to Carrie, none at all. I hadn't known her, I realized, not in ways that matter. I had known her in a role, and I had loved her in that role, and I wanted to believe she loved me. But I will never be sure.

My mother and I stayed for a few more minutes, until it became clear our presence was exhausting Carrie. We said our goodbyes, hugged Louis, and climbed into our car. As we were backing down the driveway, I remember thinking we could leave this place and Carrie could not, and that image stays with me.

I pick at the threads of my family's two-hundred-year entanglement with people of African descent and come up empty. Even our good deeds feel patronizing. Never mind the bad, which for the most part I am left to conjure, as my grandmother presumably was. The records go only so far.

What to do with this history? Old family scrapbooks, for example, filled with photographs of African Americans: my grandmother's sister Ginger compiled one album with several pages of snapshots of Black men and women, none of them captioned. One day I showed the book to Avedell Grant, who had worked for the Scarletts, and she recognized many of the faces. People from around Brunswick, some of them Avedell's relatives. They all seemed to have worked for the Scarletts at some point; one man tended our cemetery well into my lifetime. That they were all here, in my Great Aunt Ginger's scrapbook, meant she had cared enough about them to want to hold onto their images, didn't it? (And yet this same great-aunt refused to let her grandkids swim in an integrated pool in the 1960s. *Why?* I asked my cousin when she told me the story. *Was she afraid of disease?* My cousin, a lifelong Atlanta resident, eyed me thoughtfully and said, "You didn't grow up in the South.")

The Georgia Historical Society holds a late nineteenth-century picture album that belonged to Frank and George Scarlett's brother David, who lived from 1820 to 1887. This book too has pictures of African Americans—carefully composed studio portraits of boys, girls, and one grown man posing before a painted backdrop. Not a white person in sight—not so much as a white baby cradled in a Black woman's arms. The boys wear rumpled suits; one seems to have flowers pinned to his jacket and another to his hat. An adolescent girl in a patterned frock stares up pensively from her seat with great, glowing eyes. A young girl in a bright-white dress holds two small children, probably siblings, also in white dresses. The faces in these unidentified portraits feel vulnerable to me—all but those small children, who I suspect were too little to grasp the oddity of their situation: arranged before a camera at the behest of a white man keen to pay for them to be memorialized. Not one of them smiles (but then David Scarlett and his wife don't smile in their pictures either). I ask myself when and where these images were made—and why. Their presence in David Scarlett's album suggests some measure of attachment, but what do I know?

Another curiosity, one that arrived by email in 2011, just as I was beginning to delve seriously into this history: Michael McDonald, a white descendant of Fanny McDonald Scarlett's family, wrote to say he had been trawling the National Archives in search of information about his ancestors and had stumbled on records showing that in 1868 this same David Scarlett, brother to Frank and George, donated wood from his lumber company for the construction of a Freedmen's school and church not far from Brunswick. David Scarlett eventually gave those buildings and the land around them to the African American community. Whether he did so for altruistic reasons or for financial gain is anyone's guess. (In a letter dated October 29, 1868, David Scarlett reminds Douglas Risley, then head of the Freedmen's Bureau in southeast Georgia, that he has furnished nearly all the lumber to build the combined school and church and "only charged $20 not *half what* I would have charged any other institution. I will be obliged if you will enclose the above amount to me *$20*.")

Like others in his immediate family, David Scarlett worshipped at Brunswick's Emanuel United Methodist church, which the Scarletts had helped found in the early nineteenth century. For a time after the war, David Scarlett served as a church trustee and delegate to its quarterly conferences. He also took part in Georgia's constitutional convention in 1865, where, under federal orders, delegates voted to acknowledge the authority of the U.S. Constitution and the abolition of slavery.

Perhaps this David Scarlett was a good man, whatever that means in such a context. Yet he too, like his father and brothers, owned human beings before the war and in 1844 helped his brother Frank capture and jail a pair of African Americans who had fled the Scarletts. In 1857 David Scarlett served as a witness to a deed by which a white woman, Mary Barnard, bequeathed seven enslaved individuals to her niece and nephew. The names of those enslaved individuals were Raymond (age twenty-three), Hager (age twenty-two), Jim (no age given), Leah (age twenty-six), and Leah's three children: Lavinia, Aleck, and Jenny. Mary Barnard bequeathed these people to her niece and nephew in consideration of the "natural love and affection" she believed her niece and nephew bore these seven enslaved individuals.

14

MATILDA

In the first years after the war, all four of Francis Muir Scarlett's surviving sons—Frank, George, David, and John—scrambled to make ends meet. They were "land poor," my grandmother used to say—meaning they had more land than cash. But unlike Margaret Mitchell's postwar Scarlett, who refuses to give up Tara, the Scarletts were willing to trade land for cash. In a process that lasted more than a century, they chiseled away at Francis Muir's one-time cotton empire until the only thing left was a four-hundred-acre wooded lot surrounding the old Scarlett cemetery at Oak Grove. Much of that acreage went to real estate developers in the 1980s, after my grandmother's last surviving aunt, Polly, died. Money from the sale of the so-called Scarlett Estate was distributed among the descendants of George and Virginia Scarlett's thirteen offspring; as their great-great granddaughter, I received $150. There was talk of turning the land into a subdivision to be called "Oak Grove Plantation," with a buffer zone around the family graveyard. For a while an entity called the Scarlett Plantation Limited Partnership toyed with converting the property into a mixed-use residential and shopping district, but nothing came of it. As of the early 2020s, the spot where Francis Muir first ordered his enslaved laborers to clear land and build a house, around 1812, had reverted to forest.

Even before the war, my ancestors were selling off land. In 1856 the Scarletts sold one of the late John Parland's old Brunswick plantations, Blythe Island, to the U.S. government for use as a naval base. After the Civil War, Frank Scarlett began dispatching tracts of Parland's Colonel's Island plantation to help pay for the care of Parland's disabled daughter, Frances Ann. Frank sold the first parcel in 1867; by 1890 he had sold the entire island.

Frances Ann Parland, the much-loved "Puss" of Fanny Scarlett's letters, had returned to Brunswick after the war and for a time lived with her widowed Uncle Frank and his daughters. Frances Ann's sister, Jean Parland King, stayed on in Texas with her husband and children. (My grandmother's first name, Mary King, was chosen in tribute to this branch of the family.) I have never figured out what was wrong with Frances Ann. Perhaps, as I've said, it had to do with the insanity of slavery itself. (Think of the vengeful planter's wife in Solomon Northrup's *Twelve Years a Slave* or of the overseer's wife in Kemble's *Journal*, who flayed the women her husband raped.)

According to a cousin, who would not reveal her sources, Frances Ann contracted a fever in Texas, and it led to violent outbursts the family could not manage. Whatever the reason, in 1874, shortly before federal troops withdrew for good from the former Confederacy, plunging southerners into the madness of so-called "Redemption" and Jim Crow, Frances Ann was legally declared a "hopeless lunatic" and sent to the state asylum in Milledgeville—for a time the world's largest hospital for the mentally ill. She remained there until her death somewhere around 1909. Another lost cause.

Unlike most women of her time and place, this Frances Ann had known a world beyond her immediate home. With her sister she had attended an elite boarding school outside Atlanta; she had also been to Texas and back. She was free in ways many of her peers were not: moneyed, unmarried, unburdened by the constraints of pregnancy and children. She seems to have had no actual responsibility for the hundreds of enslaved people who legally belonged to her before the war. And yet she grew up under circumstances that can only be called deranged—one in which rape and other forms of violence were both legal and commonplace.

And when those circumstances change—when they are declared criminal by an invading army—what then? Ask the Germans, suggests Susan Neiman, a Jewish American who grew up in Atlanta in the 1950s and 1960s and has lived in Berlin for decades. Neiman's *Learning from the Germans: Race and the Memory of Evil*, published in 2019, examines the ways our two nations have simultaneously addressed and skirted our vicious ancestries. "It's crucial to have a broken relationship to your past, to be ready to see your own history with shame and horror," one German tells Neiman. "Germany didn't do it willingly." (Given more recent developments in both Germany and America, Neiman now believes Germany can serve not as a *model* for countries seeking to address our past failures but as a *warning*. The notion of progress, she writes, "rarely proceeds in a straight line.")

Postwar, Americans did not willingly confront their history, especially in the South. Those eight years of Reconstruction led to a century of racial terror and not just in the former Confederacy. Neiman contends that we should date the end of slavery's trauma not from 1865 but from 1964 and the passage of the Civil Rights Act. "For however many forms of racism still continue, that was the moment racist policy was banned by law," she submits. By this calculation "we are only fifty years from zero hour." Which may explain why it has taken us well into the twenty-first century to begin collectively breaking the silence. Women like the Parland sisters and my great-great-grandmother Virginia Scarlett and even my grandmother Mamie did not speak out, because to do so—to question your husband's prewar behavior or your grandfather's wartime actions—would be to threaten your own social and financial well-being. Best to obscure reality—including realities like mental illness. Frances Ann Parland's condition may have been nothing more than the awful outcome of a terrible fever, but at the same time it seems emblematic of the post-Emancipation American impulse to shroud what really happened—lock it away in a trunk or an asylum until it is forgotten, as Frances Ann eventually was. It's still not clear when exactly John Parland's youngest daughter died or where she is buried, except that it is somewhere near the grounds of the old state hospital in Milledgeville, where twenty-five thousand others who perished inside that asylum lie in unmarked graves.

The same things that conspired to make my forebears go along with slavery and its aftermath—that led so many Germans to acquiesce to Hitler—are no less present today: fear, family, treasure. The status and opportunity that come with inherited wealth. Frances Ann and Jean Parland grew up in a cocoon of prosperity. Sterling spoons in their teacups, bottles of imported cologne on their vanities. Their father made annual trips to Scotland from Brunswick, and chartered ships to bring home the lucre he'd bought overseas. At his death in 1836, Parland's personal goods were valued at nearly $40,000, his enslaved workers at over $90,000 (sums collectively exceeding $3.5 million in twenty-first-century currency).

Among those workers listed on his estate inventory was the girl Matilda. I've long assumed this is the same woman who later rebelled against Frank and Fanny Scarlett—the much-loved "Maum Matilda" who broke into the Parland sisters' trunks with an axe.

But there is more to her story. One snowy morning in Michigan, as I was rummaging through Amy Hedrick's ever-expanding website, I came across information about Matilda's husband, King Hippard. A link led to the 1880 U.S. census, which I had glimpsed before but not studied carefully. This time I looked more closely. I saw that King had been born around 1800 and that his parents were from Africa, which meant they must have endured the Middle Passage—a fact I hadn't registered. I scrolled down to Matilda's entry. She was fifty-nine in 1880, nearly twenty years younger than her husband. Her birth year, estimated, was 1821. Her mother was from Georgia, and her father—I paused; the cursor blinked—her father was from Scotland. I scrolled up to the line marked "race" and saw that Matilda was *mulatto*. Not *Black*, like her husband, or *white*, like the two women I now suspected were Matilda's half sisters, but *mulatto*.

For the first time I put it all together. John Parland—son-in-law of Francis Muir Scarlett; brother-in-law of Frank and George Scarlett; father of Frances Ann and Jean Parland—was in all probability the father of Matilda Hippard. "He is a native of Scotland," his tombstone reads. In 1821, the approximate year of Matilda's birth, John Parland would have been forty-two—a bachelor planter in possession of four properties and over 150 enslaved people. His eventual wife, Mary Ann Scarlett, was then five years old. Parland was doing what white men of his ilk did—biding his time while he waited for his bride to grow up.

I dashed off an email to Carolyn Rock, the archaeologist who had helped excavate John Parland's former property on Colonel's Island. She wrote back quickly to say that she and her colleagues had reached the same conclusion: Matilda was almost certainly John Parland's daughter, one of countless mixed-race children conceived and born on his plantations. Carolyn too had noted the appearance of Matilda's name, along with eighty-one others, in the 1836 inventory of assets *belonging to the estate of J. Parland on Colonel's Island*. With the 1837 transfer of that estate to Parland's father-in-law, Francis Scarlett, Matilda, then in her teens, would have become the property of the Scarletts. And when

John Parland's two orphaned daughters moved in with Frank and Fanny McDonald Scarlett after their mother's death in 1850, Matilda, then almost thirty, would have gone with them.

According to the census, Matilda was by then herself a mother of two: daughter Mary, born around 1848, and son Columbus, born about 1850. King Hippard appears to have been their father, but whether he and Matilda were married by then is unknowable; maybe the Scarletts gave permission for something approaching a wedding ceremony, maybe not.

There is an eight-year gap between her son Columbus and Matilda's next child, Hamilton, born somewhere around 1858, so it's possible she suffered a miscarriage, maybe more than one. Who knows how soon she was back at work, feeding and diapering and rocking Fanny Scarlett's babies? Who knows how long she was given to recover from the births of her own infants or who took care of those newborns once Matilda resumed her duties in the Scarlett household? She and King would have at least eight children in all. Among them, as I discovered in the 1880 census, was a son, Stockton, born around 1862. This suggests that when Matilda took an axe to her half sisters' trunks that March and later climbed onto the boat her husband had seized from the Scarletts and allowed herself to be piloted into the cold, uncertain night, she was quite possibly pregnant or had just given birth. Either way, her son Stockton would grow up free.

I wondered if the Parland sisters—or any of the rest of the Scarletts, for that matter—knew who Matilda was. Whether her skin color or facial features or the shape of her hands or tilt of her chin pointed to her patrimony. Think of the decades she spent pretending to be someone other than herself (one of slavery's fundamental conditions). Just another Scarlett "Maum," like Charlotte, shorn of identity. Except that this "Mammy" survived to claim her birthright. *Scotland*, she told the census taker in 1880. *I am the daughter of a man who was born in Scotland.*

On the night after I put all this together, I dreamed about Matilda and her Parland blood, her half-white skin. I dreamed about her husband, King, and the Middle Passage his parents had withstood. What part of Africa did they come from? That identity, too, stolen—though perhaps a vestige of it persisted in the occasional turn of phrase (*buckety buckety*) or plate of food (*gumbo*; *yams*) or in the kind of spiritual ecstasy I came to expect inside the small Baptist church I attended whenever I visited King and Matilda Hippard's descendants in Brunswick.

I've seen no photos of Matilda or King. The family doesn't seem to own any, and the short sketch of King the "patriarch"—grandfather of forty-eight, great-grandfather of twenty-seven—that appeared in the Brunswick press in 1885 is not illustrated. I try to envision King and Matilda in the refugee camp on Saint Simons, outfitting a makeshift home, planting vegetables, inhaling the ocean air for the first time as free people. Years later, in Brunswick, King would open a Freedmen's Bank account for his daughter Mary and somehow, by 1880, acquire twelve acres of tillable land and sixty-eight acres of woodland not far from Frank Scarlett's old house at Fancy Bluff. The 1880 census reports that King's small farm was worth $250 that year, his farming tools $15, his livestock $100. He owned one horse. He had recently spent $12 to build and repair fences. Behold the free man.

Government records for King and Matilda's oldest son, Columbus, tell more. After the family's escape from the Scarletts in 1862, the young man found his way to Philadelphia, where, on March 6, 1864, he enlisted in the U.S. Navy. A fifteen-year-old mulatto, five feet tall. By month's end Columbus was a "1st Class Boy" on the Union transport *Massachusetts*. (The navy stipulated that all African American "contrabands," regardless of age, be called "boy.") That August the *Massachusetts* helped capture a Confederate blockade runner off the coast of North Carolina. Northern reporters hailed the seizure of the boat and its cargo—more than seven hundred pounds of cotton, fifty of which were hurled overboard. After the war Columbus filed a claim with the navy for his share of the reward for the boat's capture, and he apparently got it. He signed his name with an X.

Nearly eighteen thousand men of color enlisted in the navy during the war, and more than one hundred thousand African Americans served in the army. Frank Scarlett's mixed-race son Madison was among them. His ship, too, nabbed a blockade runner. I take pleasure in imagining the pride these two men must have felt in helping to free their families, although it's highly likely neither Columbus nor Madison served willingly. In 1863 the federal government began mandating the forced conscription of formerly enslaved men on the Georgia coast. A Scarlett contraband named Robert, who fled Oak Grove in 1862, later complained that he was shuttled without notice from one navy ship to another over a period of several months. He swabbed decks and unloaded cargo and toiled at a sawmill and served as an attendant to a Union officer and saw battle, all of it without pay. The story may have been a fabrication, published in the southern press to boost Confederate morale. But it is a fact that racial prejudice was rampant in the U.S. Navy, and formerly enslaved men bore the brunt of it.

After the war Columbus Hippard married and fathered a pair of twins, Hettie Ann and Andrew. Andrew Hippard went on to marry and have children of his own, who had children of their own, some of whom turned out to be the Hippards I first met in Brunswick in 2011—among them Avedell Grant and her cousins Gertrude Hippard Maxwell, Margie Hippard Clinch, and Nancy Hippard Cahoon. From the get-go, these four women insisted on calling me *family*.

"And it turns out we are," I told Gertrude when I next saw her after discovering Matilda's parentage. I did my best to explain the genealogy, but it didn't much matter. The story was a familiar one, and while Gertrude seemed pleased to know we were related, she wasn't surprised.

The original Columbus Hippard—King and Matilda's oldest son—died in 1879. He was barely thirty. Frank Scarlett's son Madison lived into his seventies. He died in Brunswick in September 1923, the month my mother turned two. Madison Scarlett had worked as a railroad porter in Brunswick well into his sixties and owned property in the city. After the death of his first wife, Janie, he had married a woman named Julia Tison, formerly enslaved on the same plantation where my great-great grandmother Virginia Tison Scarlett grew up: Bethel, with its pomegranate shrubs and sweet orange trees, its eight rose beds laid out on either side of a tranquil garden walk. Madison and Julia had five children. They named one Frank, after Madison's father, and another George, after Madison's uncle and Virginia Tison's husband—my great-great grandfather George Scarlett. I don't know what's behind the choice of names—homage or declaration? Or simply familiarity?

Like Matilda Hippard, Julia Tison Scarlett was mixed-race. Her great-great grandson Ed Wood and I both believe she was the daughter of Virginia Tison Scarlett's father, John Mason Berrien Tison—and thus Virginia Scarlett's half sister. Another of the "dark secrets" that sent my great-grandmother Minnie into a giggling fit. I keep a daguerreotype of John Tison on a shelf in my office, one more Scarlett inheritance. It sits inside a small leather case that locks with a tiny latch. The spine is nearly worn through. The image inside, rimmed in gold, has grown so faint I seldom look at it for fear of further erasing this man who, like Francis Muir Scarlett, happens to be my great-great-great grandfather. John Tison is maybe thirty or forty years old in this likeness, handsome and vigorous. Glossy black hair, pale skin, chiseled features, piercing eyes. A portrait of power and wealth in his satin vest and cravat, ivory shirt and black morning coat.

If Madison Scarlett's wife, Julia, was indeed born in 1863 or 1864, as Ed Wood maintains, John Tison would have been forty-six at the time. His white daughter Virginia was then fifteen. Julia Tison experienced so little of slavery she may have had no memory of the system at all, but surely she heard stories. It's possible she and her family stayed on at Bethel after the war, like the "faithful old slave" Alec Massie. Maybe Alec told Julia about the time the Yankees tried to burn the place down, and Alec hid below the steps until they left and then put out the fire—a story my grandmother liked to repeat.

According to a rapturous sketch of Bethel plantation published in 1913 by a Georgia archivist named Lucian Lamar Knight, after the war most of the enslaved people on John Tison's property "refused to quit the service of a kind master to avail themselves of an unwelcome release from bondage, preferring to remain on the estate . . . where there was more of real happiness to be enjoyed in the freedom of slavery than they could possibly find in the slavery of freedom."

Knight—a fervid Lost Causer—adds that John Tison's Bethel "was the only estate in Glynn County which preserved amid changing conditions the semi-regal life of the old southern regime." (It's worth noting that in 1913, the year of Knight's essay, the African American poet James Weldon Johnson published "Fifty Years," in which he declared, "This land is ours by right of birth, / This land is ours by right of toil." The year 1913 was also the year D. W. Griffith and Thomas Dixon began collaborating on *Birth of a Nation.*)

Somehow John Mason Berrien Tison, the probable father of Julia Tison Scarlett, held onto his riches for the rest of his life. At his death in 1883, he left $10,000 to his widow, Ann; $7,000 to his son John; $4,000 in bonds to his daughter Mary; $3,000 to his grandson Pinckney; and thousands of acres of land to his remaining children, among them Virginia Tison

Scarlett, my great-great grandmother. Decades after his death, as Knight reports, stories of John Tison's kindness and generosity endured "like a lingering incense around the hearthstones of Glynn [County]. No one ever appealed to him in vain."

Except, perhaps, his unacknowledged daughter Julia, married to Frank Scarlett's unacknowledged son Madison. In 2010 Ed Wood emailed me a JPG of the picture of Julia he had first shown me when we met in Atlanta. The image dates from the 1920s. Julia is decked head to toe in magenta: hat, dress, coat, gloves, boots, purse. "Semi-regal," to borrow Lucian Knight's phrasing. In Julia's handsome, near-white face and high cheekbones, her fierce gaze, I detect more than a trace of the man whose likeness sits on my bookshelf.

15

SONGS

My grandfather Robert Leslie Pettigrew was also a navy man. Born in Missouri and raised in Montana, he enlisted during World War I because he wanted to see the ocean. Given a choice between an inland posting and one in Brunswick, Georgia, he chose the latter and got his sea.

In Brunswick he met my grandmother, Mary King Hilsman—Mamie—a fetching ingenue known for her "unusually strong character and winning personality." They married in 1920 and, after a short honeymoon in New York City, sailed to the island of Saint Thomas, my grandfather's new posting. One day at lunch during her first week on the island, twenty-one-year-old Mary King Hilsman Pettigrew—who had never been outside Georgia before—ordered a hearts-of-palm salad.

"They had to cut down a whole tree for you to have that one little heart," my grandfather joked.

She did not see the humor. "I'd have sailed back to Brunswick that minute if I could have," Mamie told me decades later. But the next boat didn't come for a week, and by then she had changed her mind. They were married for sixty-seven years.

Their first child, my mother, Ann Scarlett Pettigrew, was born on Saint Thomas Island in 1921, in the midst of a hurricane watch. Their second child, Florence, arrived a year later. By the time their third and last child, Bob, was born in 1923, my grandfather had been promoted to lieutenant commander and reassigned to Haiti as the navy's assistant chief engineer of public works. In Haiti he met a Wall Street investor who wanted to start a sisal plantation in the country's north. He asked my grandfather to manage the enterprise, which became known as Dauphin Plantation. My grandparents spent the next twenty years living in a remote quadrant of Haiti, some twenty miles east of Cap Haitien. It was the great adventure of their lives.

I bring this up not to probe the connotations of the word *plantation* in twentieth-century Haiti or the pernicious U.S. Marine occupation of that country from 1916 to 1934 (an occupation that allowed Wall Street investors to get rich on Haitian labor and land)—though both topics warrant examination—but to note, simply, that my Georgia-born grandmother spent a third of her adult life living happily in a Black-majority country founded by formerly enslaved people. I don't actually know how she felt about Haitians—the relationship was unequal, after all, servant and master, essentially—but my grandmother never seemed to tire of talking devotedly about Haiti: the fruits and flowering trees, the sun rising over the bay, and the women who would emerge from their houses with tin cups of thick black coffee whenever Mamie went out into the countryside with her husband on one of his business trips, which was often. Mamie would tilt the scalding brew to sterilize the rim of the cup—she was terrified of tropical diseases—and drink the coffee as she talked with the women in her tenuous creole. Later she would go off by herself on a walk while she waited for her husband's meeting to end.

Robert Leslie Pettigrew eventually wrote a book about his time in Haiti, which he self-published in 1958. By then he and Mamie were retired and living in a segregated Virginia grappling with an incipient civil rights movement. Given the context, his attitudes toward Haiti and Haitians, as voiced in his book, seem noteworthy. He calls slavery a "vicious industry" and describes the Black resistance leader Toussaint L'Ouverture as a man "of magnetic personality and extraordinary ability." He mentions the "heedless greed" of white men and the "iron heel" of the U.S. Marine occupation. He even mocks, gently, the very enterprise in which he was engaged, noting the American mania for spreading progress "to a backward world not hitherto blessed with American knowhow."

Of the murderous revolt by which enslaved persons of African origin overthrew their French oppressors at the end of the eighteenth century and then built a new nation, having no model but the "cruel code of bondage" to guide them, Pettigrew writes, "The feat has few parallels in history. It is one of which the Haitian and the Black man should be proud. The wonder is that Haiti survived at all."

Not once does my grandfather invoke the tired trope of Haiti as the "poorest country in the Western Hemisphere." Instead, he repeatedly reminds readers that this is "the second independent nation in the New World."

By 1939 the plantation he had helped launch in 1927 housed some ten thousand families and employed between three and four thousand Haitians. The sisal business ultimately collapsed with the rise of synthetic rope, but, at its peak in the early 1950s, Dauphin Plantation produced thirty million pounds of sisal fiber annually and in some years generated 10 percent of Haiti's tax revenues. Its legacy today is less clear. I've had one Haitian tell me the sisal years devastated his country's small farms and ultimately pushed thousands of rural Haitians into the nation's crowded capital. Scholars Laurence Dubois and Deborah Jenson agree, noting that the U.S. occupation led to violence, economic and environmental degradation, and population exodus. But a Haitian I met in 2015 in Cap Haitien told me that at its height Dauphin Plantation accounted for 25 percent of Haiti's GDP. This Haitian man was hoping to revive sisal production on the same acreage.

My grandfather came away from his years in Haiti with a deep affection for its people and a contempt for "cynical estimates of Haitian weaknesses." This did not make him immune to the pleasures of racist banter. In the 1960s and 1970s he used to joke that in the South the nasty bugs he called chiggers weren't "chiggers" but "Chegroes." In a scrapbook he compiled in 1917, during a trip across the Deep South, he assembled not only souvenir shots of state capitals and fellow travelers but photos he had taken of African Americans he met along the way. He captioned one such image, of a Black man holding a slice of watermelon, "Joy."

He captioned another image—of an African American splitting logs—"Rain? Caint say suh. De ole Massa tends to dat." Next to a picture of a Black family seated beside their dog in front of a cabin, he wrote, "And the indispensable dawg." And above a two-page spread showing African American children in various poses (a toddler on a dirt road, a boy hauling a wagon, two girls sitting on a porch), twenty-four-year-old Robert Leslie Pettigrew wrote just three words: *Niggers—Dat's—All.*

At some point during their years in Haiti, my grandparents invited Lydia Parrish to spend a month with them on the island. Mamie traveled regularly to Georgia during those years, so I assume that's where she met Parrish—a Philadelphia-born Quaker ethnomusicologist married to the painter Maxfield. In 1921 Lydia Parrish had bought an old slave cabin on Saint Simons Island, across the water from Brunswick, and begun paying African Americans in the area to sing the tunes they remembered from slavery. At the time many Blacks thought their music was worthless because it did not conform to white definitions of culture, and many whites dismissed Black spirituals, in particular, as mere derivations of white hymns. Parrish sought to debunk both myths.

"These primitive songs—like the carvings of Africa—had been ridiculed, and the Negroes were ashamed to sing them in the presence of strangers," she writes in her 1942 anthology, *Slave Songs of the Georgia Sea Islands*. "It took considerable brain-cudgeling to find a way to overcome their feeling that the traditional mode of expression was peculiar and old-fashioned, and to show the singers that many white people recognized its beauty."

Among those white people were Robert and Mary King Pettigrew, who gave Parrish what she described as "the opportunity in a never-to-be-forgotten month to hear repeatedly the primitive drum rhythms of Haiti." Parrish showed up at Dauphin Plantation with a recording machine the size of a refrigerator and set it up in the yard and brought in local musicians. My Uncle Bob remembered a group of English-speaking singers from Turks Island crooning "Juba dis and Juba dat and Juba killed a yeller cat." His mother, Mamie, would have been right there with them, listening: hair pinned up in a thick rope, the way she always wore it, face perspiring, tapping her feet and humming. "I seem to have only a range of four notes," Mamie once told me. "I used to sing to your mother when she was an infant." Mamie claimed to know just one song, an African American spiritual she must have imbibed as an infant herself, rocked to sleep by a Black nurse. "Oh Mary doan you weep doan you moan cause Pharoahs chillun got drowned—Oh, Mary doan you weep." Family members begged her to sing something more cheerful, but she persisted—something about the mournful lullaby resonated.

She admired, perhaps even envied, Parrish, a woman who in her fifties had staked out a place of her own on Saint Simons Island and gone to work preserving what she could of a fragile oral tradition. Parrish soon added a new room to the cabin on her property and papered its walls with sheets of newspaper—a touch of African American sorcery meant to ward off evil. (Parrish chose the financial section of the *New York*

Times—"for good measure," she said.) Inside the one-room structure, Parrish convened "sings" by Black musicians from Saint Simons and nearby communities. Shout songs, ring-play, fiddle songs, work songs, spirituals—songs barely distinguishable from dancing. The boisterous gatherings must have been something to behold; women in kerchiefs and aprons, men with red bandanas around their necks. And white-haired Parrish herself, in her long skirts and practical shoes, notebook in hand.

She spent twenty-five years documenting slave songs. Her 1942 book contains sixty of them, with musical notations and accounts of Gullah-Geechee language and culture as well as stories and photographs of the African Americans Parrish got to know during her Georgia sojourns. Among them were Alec Massie, who lived with my Tison ancestors at Bethel, and Millie Polecat, a "goof doctor," or conjurer, once enslaved by the Scarletts, whose husband worked for the family at Oak Grove after the war. Parrish got her information about Millie from my great-grandmother Minnie ("Mrs. A. S. Hilsman" in the book), who seems to have delighted in passing on all the lurid Polecat gossip she knew. Parrish dutifully took it down: how Millie made "goof bags" and lived in a windowless cabin ("door's enough to watch"); how she turned her back on you whenever she spoke; how other Blacks feared her, and well they might, for "in addition to being looked upon as a witch, she was the mother of murderers." Word had it Millie's children had pushed their father into a fireplace and burned him to ashes after he got too old to be useful. Those same children were now all dead or in jail, Parrish said, and the walls of Millie's cabin were lined with their trunks. Did Mrs. A. S. (Minnie) Hilsman see that cabin interior with her own eyes or was she merely repeating what others told her? No matter—Parrish wrote it down.

My grandmother also knew Millie Polecat. "She never wore shoes and bought her first pair to go to Brunswick when her son Prince killed Big Brown," Mamie remembered. "She had a daughter in prison for life for killing—rather, drowning—a neighbor's child. We loved Millie—called Maum Millie." Pictures of Millie, turbaned and shoeless, turn up in several of my grandmother's albums. "She used to take us crabbing when the tide was low, and we could walk through the marsh," Mamie told me. "We took forked sticks to hold the crabs while she picked them up and put them in the croker sack on her head. When the sack was full we would walk back to Grandmother's and they would be cooked—a huge black pot of them."

Lydia Parrish welcomed guests to her sings—carloads of whites from Brunswick and neighboring Sea Island, with its posh accommodations for vacationing northerners. There's no proof my great-grandmother or grandmother ever attended a sing, though it's hard to believe they didn't. Mamie had the instincts of an anthropologist. On her walks in Haiti she used to carry a stick to dig for shards of Indigenous pottery. She had more than a passing interest in Parrish's research. In a chapter of her book on the survival of African practices and beliefs in coastal Georgia, Parrish mentions having received "a letter from Dauphin Plantation" detailing similar practices in Haiti. The author of that letter had to have been my grandmother, the family's tireless scribe.

"The resources available to us for benign access to each other, for vaulting the mere blue air that separates us," Toni Morrison has written, "are few but powerful: language, image, and experience." Inside the kerosene-lit confines of Parrish's cabin on Saint Simons, Black and white Americans came together to hear African American music. It's not clear what kinds of negotiations went on behind the scenes—how much Parrish paid the singers and dancers who came to her makeshift studio, whether those people welcomed the opportunity to perform or were apprehensive about the white song collector from Philadelphia and her Georgia friends. Formerly enslaved men and women who gave their stories to interviewers from the federal Works Progress Administration in the 1930s often withheld information they thought might offend or upset their white interlocutors (who represented the U.S. government, after all). One elderly Black woman told her WPA questioner, "We ole 'uns still knows dat we is got ter be perlite to you white ladies."

Parrish noticed a reluctance among her African American sources to reveal the full scope of what they knew. She attributed this both to a prevailing African suspicion "that it is unwise for a man to tell anyone more than half of what he knows about anything" and to a fear of derision for embracing African customs. Historically, Parrish knew, white Americans had pushed the lie that people of African descent "were barbarians in need of our 'civilizing' influence. It seems to me that the attitude of the whites toward the Blacks has never been calculated to encourage the latter to parade their Africanisms."

She was in many ways ahead of her time. In the depths of the Jim Crow South, Parrish created a space where the children and grandchildren of former enslavers could come together with the children and grandchildren of formerly enslaved people in a spirit of camaraderie and respect: King's table of brotherhood, Morrison's "vault" through blue air. Though it lacks today's methodological rigor, Parrish's work is foundational. "I don't know of any significant source on African American music that does not include a reference to Parrish's book," the ethnomusicologist Lester Monts told me. Like Fanny Kemble, whom she admired, Lydia Parrish sought to upend white prejudices about Blacks and their culture.

Parrish says little in her book about the realities of everyday life for Black Georgians in the 1920s and 1930s. She doesn't mention, for instance, that the individuals whose songs she recorded may have had other, weightier reasons for being tight-lipped about how they lived and what and whom they held dear. She makes no reference to the tens of thousands of African Americans who fled Georgia for the North during those years and beyond or to the annual KKK parade in downtown Brunswick or to the election, in 1932, of the white supremacist Eugene Talmadge to the Georgia governorship—a post he held until his death in 1946. (Talmadge's son Herman, who succeeded his father as governor and later served in the U.S. Senate, called for Congress to name Brunswick's federal building after the prosegregation Judge Frank M. Scarlett.)

There's little hint in her book that during the same years Parrish was convening her integrated *sings*—complete with barbecues and fatwood fires—a child like Avedell Grant was being told to eat her dinner alone on the porch of the Scarlett home rather than at the table with the family. I once asked Avedell and her cousin Margie Clinch what Brunswick was like during segregation. Margie rolled her eyes and ticked off the memories: separate schools, a separate ticket window at the Greyhound bus station, rules forbidding Blacks to eat at restaurants—including the ones where they worked. "We had to buy our meals through a special window, and then we were expected to take them somewhere else to eat," Margie said. "And we were the ones cooking the food!" "We knew it wasn't right," she went on. Elders, practiced in the way things had to be in those days, coaxed the young along. "We knew we were loved, and that's all that mattered."

The church, Springfield Baptist, that Margie and Avedell joined as children—the church they still attended in the twenty-first century—was founded in 1858 by enslaved people. The first time I attended Springfield, I thought I could hear, in the mournful cadences of certain hymns, a vestige of slave times. Turns out it's true. Margie's brother Johnny told me the call-and-response system by which he and his fellow parishioners worshipped was rooted in slavery. "It's what they sang to each other in the fields, to communicate."

"Oh Mary doan you weep doan you moan cause Pharoahs chillun got drowned." Words sung by my grandmother to her infant daughter. My grandmother herself was born on November 11, 1898, at a time when African American culture and experience were a source of ridicule and when the possibilities for benign communication between Blacks and whites were steadily being erased. In her vast history of the Great Migration, Isabel Wilkerson notes that it was around the year 1900 when southern states began devising new laws to regulate every aspect of Black life and "prohibit even the most casual and incidental contact between the races."

On November 10, 1898, one day before my grandmother's birth, a mob of some two thousand whites overthrew a legitimately elected multiracial government in Wilmington, North Carolina, in what would become known as the Wilmington Massacre. They attacked Black businesses in the city and murdered more than sixty African Americans. The pattern would continue well into the new century, in places like Slocum, Texas, and Tulsa, Oklahoma—to name only two. "Not unlike European Jews who watched the world close in on them slowly, perhaps barely perceptibly, at the start of Nazism," Wilkerson relates, "colored people in the South would first react in denial and disbelief to the rising hysteria, then, helpless to stop it, attempt a belated resistance, not knowing and not able to imagine how far the supremacists would go."

Was Mamie aware of the origins of the sorrow song she used to soothe her firstborn? Of its utility to African American women who intoned those same words over their children's cradles or groaned them aloud as they hauled cotton on their backs under a pitiless sun? For the cotton picking went on far into my grandmother's lifetime—and with it the exploitation. A sharecropper in Mississippi told a WPA interviewer that she could not afford to wear clothing made of the cotton she picked but instead pieced together her dresses from flour sacks boiled for hours to soften the burlap and bleach the flour company's logo. In a letter to the *Montgomery Advertiser* in 1917, a Black minister in Alabama pointed out that "the Negro farm hand gets for his compensation hardly more than the mule he plows, that is, his board and shelter. Some mules fare better than Negroes."

Or as W. E. B. Du Bois wrote, "The master's grand-nephew or cousin or creditor stretches out of the gray distance to collect the rack-rent remorselessly."

"The fact that Black people keep making music means that we as a people refuse to be destroyed," the Reverend James Cone writes in *The Spirituals and the Blues*, a book first published in 1972, another moment when songs were stoking the furnace of African American resistance. "We refuse to allow the people who oppress us to have the last word about our humanity. The last word belongs to us and music is our way of saying it."

Pictures of Mamie as a little girl show her being tended by African American nurses. In one image the nurse is identified as Mattie, in another as Laura, in yet another as Flora—never a surname. In a fourth photograph the nurse has no name at all, but she is a young, pretty woman in a tailored shirtwaist with a stiff white collar, and she is laughing, as are my grandmother and her two sisters, impish blonds in cotton frocks and dark stockings. I presume at least one of these nurses was the source of the spiritual Mamie later sang to my mother in her four-note warble. She must have heard other spirituals as well, growing up as she did around the old Scarlett properties, not far from those men and women who boiled sugar and ate possum in the lot behind the Scarlett house at Oak Grove. I think of how closely they all lived to one another and how impossible it was to bridge the divide between them except in circumscribed ways. Nurse and child, cook and employer. Little Avedell mopping the Scarlett kitchen but banned from the dining room—and yet the curiously deep attachments that grew from such arrangements. Scarlett albums filled with portraits of African American men and women posing for the camera as dignified individuals, not servants; Avedell's startling words to me the first time we met, her hands tethered to mine: "I never thought I'd see a Scarlett again."

It's the world I knew as a kid in Virginia every summer, standing beside Carrie Johnson in my grandparents' kitchen while she taught me to churn butter and boil crabs but not how to talk to each other, because it couldn't happen. We communicated through food. One year Carrie told me she loved calves' brains scrambled with eggs. I was fifteen and frisky, and I asked her to make me some. The next morning at breakfast Carrie strode into the dining room with a plate of steaming gray matter that looked and smelled like something the Rappahannock had disgorged. She set it down on my place mat. I ate it all.

"Mix together fruit, sugar, flour, eggs, lemon juice, and salt. Turn into a pastry-lined pie pan," reads Carrie's recipe for rhubarb pie, which I copied onto an index card in my teens. Five decades later I still make the dessert yearly, often two or three times, as if somewhere inside its confusion of sweet and sour I can find the secret to digesting the past.

I'm being sentimental. The foods Carrie loved—catfish, brains—had their start in deprivation. The song my grandmother sang to quiet her babies is grounded in suffering. Those summers I spent in Tappahannock as a child coincided with the violence in Little Rock and Birmingham and Selma. Clear to me today are the textures and smells of my grandparents' house, the sound of bobwhites in the backyard, the slam of the porch door—all the ingredients of nostalgia—but not the woman who kept the place running, the one person who never seemed to mind my interruptions (did she have a choice?). One morning Carrie and I went down to the river to check on the crab pot and found it filled with more than a dozen blue crabs. We emptied them into a basket and headed back to the kitchen. As we neared the end of the dock, Carrie took the basket and swung it into the air over her head and laughed out loud. Or at least that's how I remember it. Maybe I've made up the moment because I so want her to have been happy, this woman whose presence made my happiness possible.

16

JUSTICE

Born in Kentucky in 1934, just as Margaret Mitchell was drafting the last chapters of *Gone with the Wind* in her Atlanta apartment, Wendell Berry grew up with a keen sense that he was "doomed by my history to be, if not always a racist, then a man always limited by the inheritance of racism." In childhood Berry grew fond of an African American man, Nick Watkins, who worked for his grandfather. Nick was a Joe Louis fan and liked to listen to the fights on the radio. But he did not own a radio himself and was not comfortable joining Berry's grandparents in their house, so he walked across the fields to another white household with a radio. Young Wendell found this embarrassing. And yet, like Avedell Grant and her cousins, like Mamie and her sisters—like Mitchell herself—he did not question it. "It was one of those complex operations of race consciousness that a small child will comprehend with his feelings, and yet perhaps never live long enough to unravel with his mind." The boy Wendell took to joining Nick at the other house on fight nights, and afterward they would walk home hand in hand.

One of many "racial contrivances of the society we lived in," Berry writes of the tacit pact by which he and Nick Watkins kept to their respective spheres. An avoidance tactic disguised as politeness. For a few years, children get a pass. They dart blindly back and forth across the divide, as Berry did on fight nights and as my grandmother and her sisters did when they strayed into the yard behind Virginia Scarlett's house in Brunswick and plopped down to watch Daddy March and Daddy February and the others eat their possum and sweet potatoes. "They loved us because we were Miss Jinny's grandchildren and could not tell us to go away," Mamie remembered. So instead of asking the girls to leave them alone to eat in peace, those men and women told a story:

> Little Miss de rattlesnake pilot pass by right at the corner of the fence three days ago. Now the rattlesnake gone to pass by real soon. If en you go sit there and wait you will see him. Doan get too close and he won bother you.

"And so we did," Mamie remembered. "We watched and watched and waited and waited shivering at every sound. Never a snake."

Eventually, as Berry learned, the day comes when a child's candor threatens the system. Then the rules kick in. I knew early on that when I turned sixteen, Carrie would begin calling me Miss Leslie, and I would be expected to take up residence with the grown-ups on the other side of the kitchen door. What I did not anticipate was that by the time it happened things had changed enough so that when I kept hanging out with Carrie in the kitchen no one said anything.

Mamie received no such dispensation. She soon grasped where and with whom she belonged, what she could and should not say. Her default look, even at eighty, spoke reams: sealed lips, rigid jaw.

"Your grandmother did tell me of 'men riding off in the night, mysteriously, and returning without explanation,' of that I'm quite sure," my Uncle Bob told me in 2016, after I pressed him for more about his mother's childhood memories of racial violence potentially involving the Scarletts. "She didn't mention any names nor did she directly suggest any reasons."

For years I tried to find an event that might correspond to my grandmother's memory, some act of early twentieth-century brutality perpetrated by a member of the Scarlett clan. It's not hard to find accounts of racially motivated lynchings in the press. The local Brunswick paper issued regular dispatches from across the country. ("Negro Burned at Stake in Colorado"; "Lake City [Florida] Scene of Lynching Bee.") But the identities of those who committed these atrocities were kept secret.

In 1902, the year Mamie turned four, a columnist for the *Atlanta Constitution* said of the murder of Black Americans in Georgia, "Let the good work go on. Lynch em! Hang em! Shoot em! Burn em!" Gangs of white men, as few as five or upward of fifty, blew up Black churches, raided Black communities, tore down Black schools. They called themselves *whitecappers*, *Ku Kluxers*, *night riders*, *regulators*—echoes of Frank

Scarlett's 1861 Satilla Wild Cats. Their reasons were predictable: alleged attacks on whites, alleged assaults on white women, alleged theft of livestock or cash (as little as seventy-five cents), alleged breach of labor contract. "The Same Old Story—The Same Old Crime," reads one headline in a Brunswick paper. You could be killed for being a migrant worker of color: a "vagabond," unsupervised by whites and therefore a threat. You could be killed for "trying to act like a white person." You could be seized and hanged for demanding your basic human rights. And lest you forget your place, there were monuments to remind you—including one of a Confederate soldier that went up in downtown Brunswick in 1902 and stayed there until 2022. "Lest we forget—lest we forget," the inscription read.

In my grandmother's seventeenth year, members of a resurgent KKK, inspired by the release of *Birth of a Nation*, climbed Stone Mountain outside Atlanta and burned a giant cross. A year later thousands convened in Waco, Texas, to watch an eighteen-year-old African American, Jesse Washington, be torched alive. "My son can't learn too young," said a spectator as he hoisted his toddler onto his shoulders to get a better view. In South Carolina two-term governor Coleman Blease bragged publicly that he had planted the finger of a lynching victim in his garden. Blease was later elected to the U.S. Senate.

It does not take much to see how this kind of imagery and talk could slip into an adult conversation easily overheard by a child parked in a corner minding her own business. In Margaret Mitchell's case, the rhetoric of Jim Crow was reinforced by a five-day wave of white-on-Black violence that gripped Atlanta in 1906. Spurred by rumors of rape—gladly spread by white officials—gangs of gun-bearing white men tore through Black neighborhoods. At least ten African Americans perished. Mitchell was six at the time. She never forgot how she and her family cowered inside their locked Atlanta house, convinced that "negro mobs"—not white—were about to burn the city. She would revisit that childhood trauma, and flip the history, in a postwar scene in *Gone with the Wind*, where Klan members hang a suspected rapist in Atlanta rather than subject him to public trial and risk "a concerted uprising against the whites by the negroes."

My grandmother's hometown of Brunswick was quieter. Overall, coastal Georgia saw fewer incidents of white-on-Black terror than other parts of the state. That's not to say it didn't happen. As of early 2024, Bryan Stevenson's Equal Justice Initiative had documented at least 17 lynchings on the Georgia coast between 1877 and 1950—three of them in Glynn County. That's 17 of 594 racial terror lynchings statewide during these years. (EJI distinguishes between "racial terror lynchings" and other hangings and acts of mob violence, as well as crimes committed against nonminorities without threat of terror.) Georgia ranks second in the nation—exceeded only by Mississippi—for racial terror lynchings between the end of Reconstruction and the middle of the twentieth century, when lynchings largely gave way to state-mandated executions.

Among the reasons for coastal Georgia's relative tranquility during my grandmother's childhood was the legacy of the task system of slavery, by which enslaved workers in the region were granted time to themselves once they had finished a day's allotted tasks. This led to more autonomy in the decades before the war—particularly for those African Americans enslaved by absentee planters—and higher levels of Black property ownership afterward. It also led to a vigorous, if vulnerable, postwar Black middle class, with strong leadership, in cities like Brunswick, Savannah, and Darien. Demographics played a part too. Outnumbered by African Americans, coastal whites recognized the dangers of "agitation on the race question" and issued calls for civility. Typical was a patronizing plea in the 1889 *Savannah Morning News* urging whites to "cultivate the best of feeling between the races, and the best way to do that is for the stronger race to treat the weaker one with absolute fairness and justice."

Maybe some of this explains my grandmother's less vocal embrace of the Lost Cause mythology Mitchell relished. Not that Mamie didn't resent Yankees. I learned my lines accordingly. "I'm just so proud to have a grandmother like you," I gushed the year she turned eighty-nine. "I suppose it's that Georgia blood that keeps you going. I'm grateful I've inherited some of it—keeps the boring Yankee side of me in check."

"Georgia Blood!" she enthused. "Sometimes it's just a trickle, but it is there."

In the summer of 1899, Mamie's uncle Mason Scarlett sped north with six other men from Brunswick to help subdue "negro rioters" in nearby Darien, the county seat of neighboring McIntosh County ("riot" being the preferred term in the white South for any mass action involving Blacks). "In response to calls for re-enforcements," the *Atlanta Consti-*

tution reported, the detachment sailed by night from Brunswick on a special boat "and have been doing splendid service as special deputy sheriffs." The paper listed the names of the seven deputies; one of them was thirty-year-old Mason Scarlett.

"He was the drinker, much to my grandmother's sorrow," Mamie said of her Uncle Mason. "Once, he started to wash my hair under the pump on the back porch. I was rescued and sent to sit under the mulberry tree with Helen"—one of Mason's sisters—"until he was himself again." At twenty-seven Mason confessed to his mother, "I know that you and Papa are good and all of the children are good (except myself)."

Mason Scarlett worked as a tax commissioner in Brunswick and liked to fish on Sundays and on one occasion caught a huge steelhead but was too drunk to haul it in. His behavior as a "special deputy sheriff" in Darien, Georgia, in August 1899 can only be guessed. Mason and his fellow deputies were summoned to help the Georgia militia quell a "riot" by African Americans who had rallied to protect one of their own, a man named Henry Delegale, from being lynched. Delegale, a prominent member of Darien's Black community, had been accused of raping a white woman and put in jail. As many as a hundred Black citizens, many of them armed, surrounded the building. They held their ground for two days. Authorities wired the governor for help. Fueled by fears of a race war, more than two hundred state troops, bayonets fixed, swept into town. There was a shootout at the Delegale home; one white man was killed and a second injured. Heavily armed white posses, "well equipped for trouble," scoured the marshy countryside by night.

Henry Delegale was ultimately transported safely to Savannah, tried, and acquitted. Two of his sons received life sentences for their part in the shootout. Dozens of African American "rioters" were arrested. More than twenty were sentenced to hard labor on chain gangs. This is what justice looked like in coastal Georgia in 1899. But no one was lynched—thanks mostly to a joint effort by Black leaders and white militia commanders to foster calm.

"All the negroes appear to be thoroughly overawed by the determined action of citizens and the military," the *Atlanta Constitution* observed coolly in the wake of the turmoil. "They now realize that the whites will not tolerate their lawlessness and that the whites remain masters of the situation. They have viewed the arrival of many rifles and much ammunition and noted the armed men scattered throughout the country until they have come to understand that all negroes must be peaceful."

Back in Brunswick, Mason Scarlett seems to have resumed his tipsy existence on the old Scarlett plantations. Darien was probably not the last of his efforts to help white authorities in the region maintain "calm." "In his early life he was active in local affairs and was always ready and willing to lend an aiding hand to the community in which he had spent his life," his obituary reads. Mason Tison Scarlett was a member of the Brunswick Riflemen, who used to march through downtown Brunswick in full military regalia on Confederate Memorial Day. Another reminder.

"The things that influenced my conduct as a Negro did not have to happen to me directly," said the Mississippi-born author Richard Wright. "I needed but to hear of them to feel their full effects in the deepest layers of my consciousness."

The unmarried oldest son of George and Virginia Scarlett, Mason Scarlett suffered a stroke in 1932 at age sixty-three and spent his last months in bed, paralyzed. On their visits to Brunswick during that time, my mother and her brother and sister were made to climb the steps of the old Scarlett house and go into the small room where Mason lay swaddled in bedclothes and hold his hand. They happened to be there the night he died. Someone rushed into my mother's bedroom in the dark and snatched a sheet from her bed. She could hear sounds of muffled voices in the hallway, the tearing of fabric, the clatter of a body being carried down the staircase. Sounds and images a child doesn't forget—the kind of memories that can make you wonder about your people, about what they cherish and why, and whether someday you too might be called on, as my grandmother Mamie was that night, to help wash and wrap the body of one of your kin and carry him to the family cemetery next door to the house and lower him into the earth beside all the other Scarletts and bury him with his secrets.

My grandmother was right to suspect the worst. Mason was not the only of Mamie's Scarlett uncles to head out in the night in the name of law and order. In early 1899 Mason's younger brother George Stanton Scarlett Jr., a police officer in Brunswick, helped arrest an African American charged with hurling a brick at a white man in a downtown Brunswick bar. "Officers Lamb and Scarlett located the negro on a vessel, nabbed him and placed him in jail," the *Brunswick Times-Call* reported. "He will probably be severely dealt with and should be." It's unclear what became of the man.

Two years later this same George Stanton Scarlett Jr.—whom Mamie called "Uncle Stanton" and remembered as having "the most penetrating eyes I ever saw"—helped capture and convict a Black man with the apparent name of Tricy Griffin, who had been accused of murdering a railroad conductor near Brunswick. A notice in the *Atlanta Constitution*, transcribed on Amy Hedrick's website, reported that Detective George Stanton Scarlett was present at Griffin's execution in the Brunswick jail on June 14, 1901.

Claiming this was the first legal hanging in Glynn County in seventy years, the paper provided a detailed timeline of that day's lurid events: the prisoner's short walk from his cell to the gallows; his last-minute admission that his "present troubles" stemmed from "women, cards and whiskey"; his farewell to the crowd pressed against the jail fence "anxious to catch a glimpse of the condemned man"; and his "unflinching demeanor" as the sheriff fastened a black cap over his head and a noose around his neck. "The drop was sprung and Griffin's body shot downward to recoil from the jerk," the *Constitution* stated. "It was seen that the knot had slipped from under the jawbone to the back of his neck. This prolonged his death evidently by strangulation." Five minutes went by before doctors pronounced Tricy Griffin dead. "The body was cut down and placed in a coffin for burial."

George Stanton Scarlett Jr.—or Stanton—was present throughout all this. His reaction to the spectacle is, of course, absent from the *Atlanta Constitution*'s account. Was the twenty-nine-year-old police officer simply doing his job—happy to have one at a time when pretty much the only other option was to be a small farmer like his father? Or was Stanton Scarlett actively perpetuating slavery's legacy? As a friend whose own Georgia family engaged in postwar racial violence said to me, "If you have enslavers as ancestors, you also likely have lynchers too."

Or, in the case of Stanton Scarlett, cops: white men legally authorized to hunt and prosecute African Americans.

Either way, here was a partial answer to the riddle of my grandmother's lifelong suspicion: Scarlett men—specifically Mason Scarlett and his brother Stanton—did indeed ride "off in the night, mysteriously," as Mamie feared, and return "without explanation." The excerpts on Amy Hedrick's website all but proved it.

And then one day I impulsively Googled "Tricy Griffin 1901."

PART 5

A Grandmother's Nightmare

17

STATE V. FRICIE GRIFFIN

Before I sent the phrase "Tricy Griffin 1901" into cyberspace, I had no inkling there was a newspaper called the *Brunswick Times-Call* or that two critical years of it—years during which Brunswick conducted its first reportedly "legal" hanging in seventy years—were online and searchable. I had not seen the verbatim text of Tricy Griffin's declaration to the press days before his death, nor had I downloaded a PDF of his trial transcript. I wasn't aware of Griffin's explosive last-minute statement to the court as to why Stanton Scarlett wanted him dead. I knew only what I had gleaned from that passage in the *Atlanta Constitution*: that Griffin's execution was the legally sanctioned outcome of a cut-and-dry murder case and that my grandmother's uncle Stanton was involved.

Before I Googled "Tricy Griffin 1901" I had decided I would never fully be able to confirm Mamie's suspicions about the men in her immediate family. Too many years, too few sources, too much absent information. I planned instead to write around the void—to say that for all their imprecision, the excerpts I had found on Amy Hedrick's glynngen.com were evidence enough that two of my grandmother's uncles engaged in racial violence—that she was right to be haunted.

One bleak Michigan morning in late February 2020, days before COVID-19 upended life, it occurred to me to try to find out how old Tricy Griffin was when he died. I typed in his name and the year of his death, and up came an article from the *Savannah Morning News*, from June 13, 1901: "Tricy Griffin Confession," the headline read. "Negro Who Is to Hang Tomorrow Claims Self-Defense."

A brief intro led into a three-paragraph statement by Griffin, made days before his execution on June 14. "I killed Conductor Latimer," the statement began, "but I did it in self-defense." Something about the voice caught me—a rawness, I would call it, that made me feel as if he was in the room with me. ("He wanted you to find him," more than one person would tell me in weeks to come.) I stopped reading, picked up the phone, called a friend.

"Do you have a sec? I've found something."

I started reading again, this time out loud. By the time I got to the end of Tricy Griffin's statement, my friend was crying and I could not speak. It was clear, peering not so deeply between the lines, that this young man was hanged not because of what he had done but because a particular combination of pigments had made him a threat to people with skin the color of mine.

"I simply wanted to have them stop," Tricy Griffin said of the brutal assault he had endured on a moving train outside Brunswick in early October 1900, at the hands of a white conductor and a white baggage master—an assault that led to a shooting that led to a death sentence. In his words I heard so many others.

Two more links turned up on that first impulsive Google search: one to a copy of the same statement by Griffin published in the *Waycross Journal* on the day after his death and a second to an article about Griffin in a paper called the *Brunswick Times-Call.* I found a digitized run of the paper online through the Library of Congress—a short run, barely three years, with plenty of gaps, but the crucial period between Griffin's hanging and the crime for which he had been convicted was intact. ("He wanted you to find him.") I spent much of the next week searching the *Times-Call.* With each new discovery, my gut clutched. Here was Mamie's nightmare come alive: a lynching masquerading as a judicially warranted hanging, with one of her uncles at the center of it.

"If you searched every county in Georgia in the late 1890s and early 1900s, you'd find the same pattern," Karen Branan told me when I emailed to ask if she could help me sort through what I was finding. I knew Karen through Coming to the Table. She had spent twenty years researching her own family's role in a Georgia lynching and had published a book, *The Family Tree,* about it in 2016. She spoke with a soft twang that reminded me of Mamie.

"They called them legal hangings, but they were lynchings," Karen said. "The trials were horrible farces. Get the court transcript," she urged.

I told her some of what I had learned about Griffin from my initial reading—that he'd wowed reporters with his "wonderful nerve" and big smile, his steadfast bravery in the face of stacked odds.

"Sounds like this kid had some moxie," Karen said.

He went by two first names: Tricy and Fricie. The latter seems to have been his legal name, for it appears in the official transcripts of both his trial in the Glynn County Superior Court in December 1900 and his subsequent appeal to the Georgia Supreme Court. I tracked down both documents soon after talking to Karen. "It's so interesting to look at these old trials," the clerk in the Glynn County courthouse murmured when she phoned to tell me she had found the transcript for Griffin's Superior Court trial, and at fifty cents a page it would cost me ninety-six dollars to get a PDF of the 192-page document. I sent a check that afternoon.

The trial of Fricie Griffin, as I'll now call him, took place in Brunswick and lasted just two days—a charade of the sort Karen had warned me about. "Jury Was Out Only Half Hour," the *Times-Call* crowed in its front-page coverage of the verdict. "Prisoner's Nerve Stays with Him / Did Not Flinch When Verdict Was Read / He Is a Cool Customer / Will of Course Have to Pay the Death Penalty." Griffin was pronounced guilty of murder and sentenced to die a few weeks after Christmas. But his lawyers appealed, and the case went to the state Supreme Court. Three weeks after Easter, the court ruled that the earlier conviction stood, and a new hanging date was set: June 14, 1901.

My search of the *Times-Call* uncovered the general outlines of Griffin's eight-month ordeal from arrest to execution. Here was a world where white people—lawyers, victims, witnesses, sheriffs, judges, cops, including my grandmother's uncle Stanton—all had names, and Black people none (unless, like Griffin, they were accused of a crime). There was no presumption of innocence. From the start, Griffin was *the murderer*, *the slayer*, *the prisoner*, *the desperate man*, *the negro*—almost never the *defendant*. On the day eyewitnesses first identified him in jail, hours after his arrest and nearly two months before his trial, the *Brunswick Times-Call* declared, "Tricy Griffin has been identified and there is now no question as to his guilt." Griffin protested that the witnesses had been coerced.

He had been accused of killing a white conductor while trying to hitch a ride on a train to Brunswick on the evening of October 7, 1900. The dead man, Marion Lattimore (alternately spelled Latimer), was a "popular" man, the paper stated. "Well known and universally liked." And, at the time of his death, "defenseless." (White victims were always popular and always virtuous, Karen Branan told me.)

On the night of Lattimore's death, hundreds of white men from Brunswick had rushed off on horseback in search of the killer. At their helm was a sheriff's posse of four that included George Stanton Scarlett—Mamie's twenty-eight-year-old uncle Stanton. He and his companions came back emptyhanded that night (without bloodhounds, a reporter lamented, "nothing could be done"). But Stanton Scarlett kept up the search.

For the next three weeks, my grandmother's uncle tracked "the murderer's trail. . . . It seems now that he was quite close to him all the time," the *Times-Call* reported, after Scarlett and a railway detective named Connelly at last caught their prey. Immediately after Lattimore's killing, Fricie Griffin had hidden among friends in Brunswick. "He changed clothes here and Mr. Scarlett got possession of the discarded apparel. . . . Mr. Scarlett knew the man and was also aware of the fact that he had a sister living here." At one point Detectives Scarlett and Connelly came within fifteen feet of Griffin but let him go for fear he would run, and "we'd have been compelled to have shot him," Scarlett affirmed. They wanted their man alive.

"The direct clue which led to the capture of the man was received by Mr. Scarlett when he secured a letter the murderer had written to a friend here," the *Times-Call* revealed. The newspaper did not say how Scarlett secured the letter or who the friend was—those salacious details would have to wait for the trial. "There is no doubt but that Messrs. Scarlett and Connelly have the right man. The *Times-Call* is in possession of facts which cannot be printed at present but this evidence will show conclusively that they have the murderer." The paper added this tease: "The detectives have a bombshell they will explode when the case is heard by the Superior Court. In fact it is something which will convict him beyond any doubt."

Stanton Scarlett was central to Griffin's case. He knew the accused man personally, knew his sister, and had gathered evidence to trap Griffin—those discarded clothes, the letter to a friend, that cryptic "bombshell." "Too much cannot be said in praise of the excellent work done by Messrs. Scarlett of this city and Connelly of the Southern Railway," the paper said. "They had only a slight clue on which to work, but they traced their man and ran him to earth with all the great odds against him."

"They traced their man and ran him to earth." I knew next to nothing about Mamie's uncle Stanton, but I knew his kind, and I could picture the swagger in his stride as he walked about town after Griffin's arrest—the curl of his lips as people congratulated him. Stanton Scarlett was a driven man. The Southern Railway was offering $500 (a "fat reward," the press called it) for the arrest and conviction of Lattimore's killer, and Scarlett and his fellow cop Connelly stood to split the money "as soon as the guilt of the negro is proven." Hence the push to catch and frame Griffin, to keep him alive so he could be put on trial and convicted. Nearly fifty years after the end of slavery, members of my family were still profiting from the pursuit and capture of African Americans on the run.

Except for his penetrating eyes, I have little idea what Stanton Scarlett looked like. So forthcoming on Fricie Griffin, the internet is tight-lipped when it comes to Mamie's uncle. He died in North Carolina in 1961, but I found no obit or photo of the man. Perhaps he took after his father, my great-great grandfather George Scarlett, who stood over six feet tall and was "handsome," with fair skin and blue eyes.

I do know what Fricie Griffin looked like. In his last weeks of life, he begged the sheriff to have his photograph "took" so he could give it to his family. The sheriff obliged. Officials had grown to like Griffin (this was often the case among white authorities—once a Black man was condemned to die for his crimes). "Jailer Rudolph says the murderer is the best prisoner he ever had and further states that he gives him absolutely no trouble."

Griffin's picture appeared on the front page of the *Brunswick Times-Call* on June 15, 1901, one day after his execution. I wasn't prepared for it. The face is handsome, gentle, more citizen-of-the-year than vicious killer. Short hair neatly parted to one side. A young, heavyset man, fair-skinned. (Where a shaft of light grazes his right cheek, Fricie Griffin could nearly be white. A railroad employee who saw him on the day of Lattimore's killing described Griffin as "a ginger cake mulatto.") The expression is strong but tender, somehow pensive and sad and trusting all at once, and I can only wonder how it struck readers, both those who knew and loved him—among them his mother in Waycross, too poor to travel the sixty miles to Brunswick to see her son in jail—and those few strangers who may have questioned the propriety of his hanging.

"Griffin Pays the Penalty," the headline above the portrait blared.

In his last week of life, the paper disclosed, as the gallows were being hammered into place in the yard outside his jail cell, Griffin had received daily visits from an African American preacher. On the day before his death, with crowds gathered outside the jail, he had been baptized.

That same day, June 13, Fricie Griffin was questioned for the last time by a reporter for the *Times-Call* who had dogged him all week, keen to sniff out his every thought. Was he afraid? Did his mother plan to come to Brunswick? What did he think of the scaffold going up outside his cell? On that last day, as the unnamed writer continued his interrogation, Griffin's eyes periodically teared up. "Are you ready?" his questioner wanted to know.

"I am ready to die when they are ready," Griffin answered. "I've prayed for God to forgive me. He knows that I did not intend to kill Mr. Lattimore."

"Do you think you will sleep any tonight?"

"I sleeps every night, slept good last night and I think I will be able to do the same tonight. I've lost my appetite, however, haven't eaten a thing today. I don't feel worried much, and am going to try and get on the gallows tomorrow without breaking down."

"When you see the rope and trap ready and you know you will be a dead man in a few minutes afterward, don't you think you will break down?"

"Not if I feel like I do now. Tell you the truth, boss," he said to his inquisitor—and here I imagine Fricie Griffin looking proudly into the journalist's startled eyes—"I ain't no more afraid than you are, not as much, because I can tell by your face that you are sorry for me, and if you come here tomorrow, I bet you will come nearer breaking down than I."

The imprisoned man reached two fingers through the bars of his cell. "Shake hands good-bye," he said. "Tomorrow at this time I'll be dead."

He was eighteen years old. A poor kid from the outskirts of Brunswick who had tried to steal a ride on a short-run train into town. Earlier that October day, a Sunday, he had played cards with friends, and, fearing one of the other players might come after him, he had bought a pistol. He had then snuck onto the Brunswick train and concealed himself on the platform between the engine and the baggage car. Conductor Marion Lattimore and the train's flagman and baggage master, William

Brock, had found him and ordered him to pay or get off. Griffin balked. The train was going between thirty-five and forty miles an hour, and he feared if he jumped he would die.

Lattimore and Brock kept at him. The prosecution charged that Lattimore's death was a plain case of first-degree murder. The conductor and flagman had treated Fricie Griffin in a "peaceable," "friendly," and "courteous" manner. At one point Conductor Lattimore "very kindly called to the negro two or three times to come into the car." Lattimore then picked up a broom and "gently tapped" Griffin on the shoulders. Moments later the conductor "slung" a coupling link "over where the negro was." When Fricie Griffin at last pulled out his pistol—in what he insisted was a last-ditch effort to warn off his attackers—Lattimore had "nothing in his hands." Griffin fired. The conductor died of his wounds later that evening at his home in Brunswick. Griffin leaped from the train and disappeared. Three weeks later Detectives Scarlett and Connelly caught him.

At a time when forensics were primitive and Black people lived in terror of white authority, when cops and lawyers routinely forced witnesses to alter their testimony, it wasn't hard to build a case against the teenager. The State of Georgia accused Griffin of having boarded the train with the express aim of killing anyone who tried to stop him. Prosecutors served up details guaranteed to sway an all-white jury. Griffin was "not dressed so nice." He wore a "slouch hat" over his "vicious looking face." While hanging around a train station earlier in the day, Griffin had gone "into the white waiting room and got a drink of ice water out of the water cooler," a white rail agent testified, "and that being a rather impudent thing for him to do, I ran him out of there."

The defense asked if the agent might be confusing Griffin with another Black man.

"All coons don't look alike to me," the witness shot back. "I have them around me so much, that I have become quite an expert in identifying one from another."

Griffin's lawyers—two white men from Brunswick appointed a couple of days before his trial—endeavored to establish an alibi. Fricie had been with them all day long, four of Griffin's friends in Brunswick swore. Prosecutors shredded the story. Under cross-examination Fricie's childhood friend Peter Meadows confessed he had been pressured by the defense to lie about the time of day he had seen Griffin.

The defendant had no chance. He had shot a white man—never mind that it had happened on a moving train at night inside a baggage car lit only by moonlight during a chaotic confrontation about which there was conflicting evidence. Griffin was a dead man. He knew it himself. It was preferable to die at a state-mandated time and date, he said on the morning of his execution, than to be "cut off in the twinkling of an eye and destroyed." Better to perish legally inside the Brunswick jail yard with as much dignity as a man could muster than be chased like a hog in the woods outside town and butchered by a pack of assailants on horseback determined to punish the *murderer*, the *slayer*, the *negro*.

In their appeal for a new trial, Griffin's lawyers argued that this was a case of self-defense, and the Superior Court of Glynn County had erred in not telling the jury there were three possible verdicts: murder, manslaughter, and justifiable homicide.

"You don't contend that voluntary manslaughter is in the case?" a justice asked.

"No sir," Griffin's attorneys replied. "We do not take that position. We say he was absolutely justified."

The Georgia Supreme Court took up the appeal on April 15, 1901. Not two weeks later the court rendered its decision. "Griffin Will Have to Hang," the *Brunswick Times-Call* announced. Only an act of clemency from the governor could spare him now. None came.

I could not help seeing elements of Christ's death in Griffin's story. The stoic march to execution, the wisdom imparted along the way, the condemned man's growing insistence that this was part of a divine plan. To people following the saga, the script would have been familiar. In what historian Michael Trotti terms the "theater of the gallows," Black men fated for hanging in the South routinely confessed their sins (blame typically fell on women and liquor), professed repentance, and declared their assurance of a heavenly home. Comparisons to Christ were commonplace. In his 1903 *The Souls of Black Folk*, W. E. B. Du Bois referred to the ritual killing of African Americans by whites as "crucifixions."

On one of his last nights of life, Griffin told reporters, an angel had appeared to him. Griffin was lying on his bunk inside his jail cell, eyes open.

"Fricie, God has forgiven your sins," the angel said.

He had been praying daily for forgiveness for "every idle thing and every wickedness I have done," and now suddenly he had received it. God knew he was innocent. The vision gave him strength. When he fell through the trapdoor that Friday afternoon, God would be there "to catch me up and carry me to my home beyond the skies." To Beulah land, where "I will be happy."

The *Times-Call* published an account of the angel's visit on the morning after Griffin's death. Readers hooked on the teen's drama could savor the last, delicious tale of his deathbed deliverance—another station on Griffin's way to the cross—as though the citizens of Brunswick needed this young man to teach them, by his pliant submission to the punishment they had decreed, how to die.

"Though I walk through the valley of the shadow of death I will fear no evil," he said on his way to the gallows. "How can I fear? Jesus Christ is with me. They say Fricie Griffin has nerve. It aint nerve. It's Jesus Christ with me. My soul is happy in His word. I am no murderer; I am no slayer. I am ready to die."

He said these things to people who had scorned him—to cops, prosecutors, reporters. From the start the local press had lampooned Griffin's looks and mocked his behavior:

> When Judge Bennet called his name the murderer arose with a smile on his face, which resembled a half-open clam. "Have you a lawyer," said the judge. Griffin replied in the negative, enlarging his smile several inches. (December 8, 1900)

A representative of the *Times-Call* had been at the jail the day before, looking at the gallows. He saw Griffin and asked the "negro" what he thought of it.

> "That looks cute," said Griffin, "and the only thing wrong about it is, I wanted it painted white, don't you think that would look better?" (June 11, 1901)

The same readers who relished the blackface minstrel shows that played at the local Brunswick opera house could feast on piquant accounts of

Griffin's courtroom antics—behavior befitting the farce in which the defendant realized he had been cast:

> But the nerve of this negro is nothing short of wonderful. A minute before the verdict was read he sat with his arms folded, a smile on his face, and even after the solemn words of the jury were read he laughed and joked with a person near him. (December 15, 1900)

It was Brunswick's own passion story, and it went on for months—through Thanksgiving and Christmas and Easter, into the long, hot days of early June. The murder, the chase, the alibi, the betrayals, the abrupt reversal and inevitable denouement, the last-minute conversion story: it was all there, in heart-gripping detail, on the front pages of the *Times-Call*.

> Griffin was then led to the gallows, and mounted the trap without a quiver. As the rope was being tied around his neck, the negro sang, and as the black cap was placed over his head, he said: "Good-bye friends, I'll meet you all in Beulah land." The trap was sprung at 12:20½ and he was pronounced dead at 12:31½. . . . The negro showed remarkable nerve and never shed a tear or trembled a particle during the entire execution. (June 15, 1901)

He never said a mumblin' word.

On its editorial page, the *Times-Call* congratulated Brunswick on what it claimed was the city's first legal hanging in seven decades. "Had Griffin been caught the night of the murder no doubt he would have been lynched by the mob that was in search of him." Lynchings were bad for business; legal executions, by contrast, reassured skittish northern investors and boosted newspaper sales. Fricie Griffin had committed one of the "worst, most cowardly" crimes in the history of Glynn County (a history that included a century of human enslavement). Let his example serve to warn others, the paper advised. "Especially the black man." Let Fricie Griffin's fate "stare them in the face."

18

MR. SCARLETT

What the *Times-Call* did not disclose, but what I discovered in the transcripts of Fricie Griffin's trial and subsequent appeal, was that the tale had its Judas: my grandmother's twenty-eight-year-old uncle Stanton. During Griffin's trial two separate witnesses, both white men, alleged that Detective Scarlett was, in effect, after his thirty pieces of silver. Brunswick police officer George Asbell accused Scarlett and his fellow detective, Connelly, of having meddled with Asbell's own investigation into the case. Asbell claimed he would have caught Griffin himself—and received his share of the $500 bounty—if Scarlett and Connelly had not intervened. "I did not think that Mr. Scarlett and Mr. Connelly had treated me right in the way they got my man away from me."

Ernest Dart, one of Griffin's two lawyers, also testified that Stanton Scarlett was motivated by greed. "He simply wanted him hung so that he could get the reward," Dart said of Scarlett's single-minded pursuit of his client. Not only had Officer Scarlett spent three weeks shadowing Griffin but he had eavesdropped on a meeting between Dart and four witnesses for the defense and had later forced those witnesses to testify for the state. Dart came from an old Brunswick family and knew the Scarletts. "I think Mr. Scarlett and myself are very good friends," he volunteered. "I have nothing against him."

It was Stanton Scarlett who had come up with the pivotal letter that led to Fricie Griffin's arrest and Scarlett who had procured the "bombshell" testimony that, as the trial transcript revealed, eviscerated Griffin's alibi. Both the letter and the testimony came from the same source: a woman of color named Bella Law, who took the stand near the very end of Griffin's trial. It is not hard to imagine the whispers that swept the room and rattled the otherwise cool Fricie as Bella placed her hand on the Bible and vowed to tell the truth. How young Stanton Scarlett must have glowed.

The usually tongue-wagging *Times-Call* is silent on Bella Law—her story was not the sort of thing Brunswick readers wanted to digest with their morning coffee. According to her testimony, Bella lived near the "gas house" in downtown Brunswick, in a part of town long disparaged. Fricie Griffin showed up at her place a few hours after Lattimore's death on Sunday, October 7, and found Bella in her room, resting. He took a chair at the foot of her bed and sat down.

"Hello, Fricie," Bella said. "When did you come?" [to Brunswick, she meant].

"Friday night," he lied.

"You've been in town ever since then and just come to see me?"

"Yes," he told her.

"Then he came up closer to where I was lying," Bella told the court.

"Miss Bella," Fricie said, "I've got something to tell you that I wouldn't tell my mother."

Griffin then made his confession—the one that would guarantee Stanton Scarlett his reward money. While trying to hitch a ride on the train to Brunswick earlier that day, Fricie allegedly told Bella as he sat on a chair at the foot of her bed, he had gotten into a fight with the conductor and baggage master. The conductor attacked him with a broom. Fricie shot at him. The conductor picked up a piece of iron and tried to hit him. Fricie fired another shot. The conductor shot back. Griffin fired once more and fell from the train.

"He didn't know whether he killed him or not," Bella testified. Under cross-examination Bella Law informed the court that she was a married woman but that her husband lived in another county. "I have been intimate with Fricie Griffin off and on for the past twelve months," she stated. "He slept with me that Sunday night that Conductor Lattimore was killed." The next morning, Bella went on, after Fricie had left, she told her housemate Mollie Muse about his confession. Mollie in turn told the story to Stanton Scarlett. How Mollie knew Scarlett or why she confided in him, Bella did not say.

Not long afterward, Stanton Scarlett had come to see Bella and gotten her to confirm the story. "I told it to Mr. Scarlett at my house one day," Bella said. Scarlett clearly knew where Bella lived and had the means to persuade her to denounce her friend. Bella herself told the court that all of Fricie's friends "had been talked to" by the prosecution—in particular

Griffin's pal Peter Meadows, who had turned state's witness. "Mr. Scarlett had got Peter Meadows and scared him up," Bella revealed.

After Fricie's arrest, Bella had gone to see him in jail—desperate to find out what he wanted her to say at the trial. But they could not talk, so Bella had written him a letter instead, which the jailer, a man named Rudolph, refused to deliver. "Mr. Rudolph wouldn't let me in," Bella remembered—and here her plot took another new turn—"and I went around to Mr. Scarlett's room, and he was coming downstairs, and I asked him if he wouldn't tell Mr. Rudolph to let me see Fricie, and he told me to go around there and tell him that it was alright and to let me see him."

She did not explain how she knew where Stanton Scarlett lived or why she chose to turn to him for help. That was for the jury to deduce. But she did disclose the contents of her letter, and they were incriminating. "I did advise Fricie in that letter to plead guilty and say that he killed the conductor in self-defense." She had one more detail to impart. "Mr. Scarlett did not know anything about the letter, he never saw it," she said. "It was in my bosom when I went to see him."

Under questioning from Griffin's lawyers, Bella Law swore that she and Scarlett were not in cahoots. "There was no understanding between me and Mr. Scarlett in regard to that letter." Bella repeated herself. "Mr. Scarlett did not have anything at all to do with my writing that letter. He didn't know anything about the letter, and never suggested to me that I write it, or what to write."

Fricie Griffin had the last word. He took the witness stand and, to Bella's sensational accusation, appended his own "Defendant's Supplemental Statement." First, he denied that he had ever confessed anything to Bella. She wanted him dead, Griffin charged, because he was jealous of another of her lovers—a Black man named Junie Campbell—and Bella wanted Fricie "out of the way" so he wouldn't harm Junie. Then Griffin turned to the judge and made a request. "If I had protection," he ventured, "I would like to tell the jury about the talk I had with Mr. Scarlett."

"You can say whatever you think necessary in your defense, and you will be fully protected," the judge replied.

The transcript does not say what Griffin did at this juncture—whether he paused to breathe deeply or wipe the sweat from his forehead or whether he was his usual calm, jaunty self. ("I have been as cheerful as I ever was," he'd said to the court moments earlier.) The transcript of *State v. Fricie Griffin* merely records the defendant's next words:

> After I was put in jail Mr. Scarlett came to the cell and asked me if I loved Bella and I said yes, I used to like her. And then he said, "Bella will never do you any more good. I have her now and I will fuck her, and I am going to have her for my woman, and I am going to hang you, for I like Bella myself."

With this declaration the trial of Fricie Griffin in the Superior Court of Glynn County ends. The transcript that was subsequently sent to the Georgia Supreme Court contains one further statement. Signed by Judge Joseph W. Bennet of Glynn County, who would twice sentence eighteen-year-old Fricie Griffin to death, the statement reads, "The foregoing brief of evidence is hereby approved as correct and true."

When I told Karen Branan about Griffin's statement, she said, "Oh. So that was in your family too. I'm sorry." Miscegenation—the seamy business of white men, in a white supremacist South, having not-so-secret relations with Black women—had been part of Karen's story too: as rampant in the first years of the twentieth century as it was in the days of Frank Scarlett and John Parland and John Berrien Tison and Pierce Butler. One more topic "we don't talk about."

Stanton Scarlett came from a distinguished Glynn County family. His grandfather had served in the Georgia legislature; his uncles had owned huge tracts of land and hundreds of servants. Impoverished, yes, by the losses of war but still prominent. ("I of course knew of the Scarlett family on our Georgia coast," Margaret Mitchell would tell Stanton Scarlett's sister in the fall of 1936.) Small wonder the *Times-Call* suppressed any mention of Fricie Griffin's incendiary charge.

My grandmother Mamie was two and a half years old when Fricie Griffin was hanged. At the time she and her family were living in her father's hometown of Macon, Georgia, some two hundred miles away. But letters traveled, relatives visited, and Mamie and her sisters spent nearly every summer in Brunswick "with our grandmother, aunts and uncles."

Those uncles were five: Mason, Stanton, Frank (who operated a boat line between Brunswick and Fancy Bluff), Bobbie (stricken with polio in boyhood), and Julian, the youngest, lost at sea in his twenties on a freight ship that sank in the Caribbean in 1918. Two years later their sister Helen, the youngest of my grandmother's Scarlett aunts, died from a sudden illness. The following year, 1921, the mother of these six children, Virginia, died from heart trouble. Virginia Tison Scarlett was seventy-three at the time of her death and long widowed.

"What a wonderful combination her character was," wrote a close relative. "Such absolute truth and justice that flooded her entire being, such great love for all humanity, such wonderful charity, such tenderness and gentle sympathy."

I have to wonder what Virginia Tison Scarlett made of her two sons Mason and Stanton, both of whom rode off into the night in pursuit of a brand of justice that would haunt my grandmother throughout her life. Did any part of Fricie Griffin's damning testimony find its way into the Scarlett home in Brunswick? Was Virginia Scarlett at all aware of the accusations Griffin had levied against her son Stanton?

The young police officer had his "room" downtown, of course, but Mamie's uncle Stanton was also part of the constellation of men and women in whose orbit my grandmother came of age. Mamie remembered her uncle Stanton—or at least his eyes—well into her eighties. Curiously, Stanton Scarlett's picture does not turn up in any of the Scarlett albums, although those albums contain images of every other Scarlett aunt and uncle Mamie knew. Maybe it's coincidence, maybe not.

For some reason Uncle Stanton left Brunswick for good not long after Fricie Griffin's death. By 1920 he was living in Alabama with a wife and two children. Stanton Scarlett was forty-eight and had a sixth-grade education. He worked for the railroad. By 1940 he and his wife were living in Winston-Salem, North Carolina, where he continued to work for the railroad. He died in 1961 at age eighty-nine and is buried in Winston-Salem—not in the family cemetery in Brunswick, as most of his siblings are.

Perhaps during an evening in the early years of the twentieth century, as Mamie and her sisters sat playing on the front porch of the Scarlett house at Oak Grove, Uncle Stanton made an appearance. Perhaps he came over to the little girls and peered down at them with his penetrating gaze and reached out with a hand to gently tickle their chins and to warn them, with a twinkle of his eyes, to be *good or else*. And everyone around them laughed—for although Uncle Stanton was a cop and knew all about what could happen to people who misbehaved, he didn't mean it, of course. Of course he did not mean it.

What really happened between Fricie Griffin and Conductor Marion Lattimore inside that train car on the night of October 7, 1900? In his final days, with reporters gathered around him, Griffin made one last attempt to set the record straight. The *Brunswick Times-Call* published a synopsis of what he said but did not quote him verbatim. The *Atlanta Constitution* did even less, telling readers only that Griffin claimed he had not intended to kill Lattimore and that he "attributed all his present trouble to women, cards and whiskey"—a cliché of the sort commonly ascribed to Black men on their way to the gallows.

But the *Savannah Morning News* and the *Waycross Journal*—the paper of record in Griffin's hometown—printed his remarks word for word, and, when I saw them on that first serendipitous online search for "Tricy Griffin 1901," I knew whose story I believed. The Waycross paper released his statement one day after Griffin's death. But the Savannah paper published it the day before he died—time enough, had anyone wished, to reconsider his sentence. No one did. They hanged him that summer day, and Stanton Scarlett was there to see the awful fruits of his many labors. For this Mr. Scarlett, as for so many others, it was all legal.

Here is what Fricie Griffin said:

> I killed Conductor Latimer, but I did it in self-defense. I got on the train at Everett City, and when they came out to ask me where I was going they said I must "get off here."
>
> "All right, Cap," said I, and before I could do anything, Mr. Brock, the flagman, hit me over the head with a stick, and I got dizzy like. Mr. Brock then went in, and Mr. Lattimore hit me with a broom three times over the head, and I was feeling faint and falling like, and I was holding on to the train and almost falling when they threw coal at me, and the conductor threw a coupling link; and all had some iron.
>
> I then thought I had better jump off or get killed. I knew I would get killed if I jumped off immediately after Mr. Lattimore threw the coupling link. I saw it was a case of either being killed by being

knocked off the train or getting hurt, so I fired to protect myself and to keep them from hurting me and to make them stop. I could have killed them all if I had wanted to murder anybody. I simply wanted to have them stop, as they did after I fired. I then waited until the train slowed down, jumped off and came to town. I told them if they didn't stop I would fire.

I have had a fair trial, and I want to thank the judge, for he gave me every chance and treated me fair and square. I want to thank Mr. Rudolph, the jailer, and Mr. Berrie, the sheriff, and to say that I have no fear in the world of death. I am only 18 years old, and it is hard to die that young, but it ain't in me to flinch. I am going to walk up Friday like a man, and you won't hear anyone say that Fricie Griffin lost his nerve. If I hadn't prayed and read my Bible I might have worried, but as it is I am not, and I am going to ask God to take me at once.

AFTER

On February 23, 2020, at around the time I unearthed the story of Fricie Griffin, twenty-five-year-old Ahmaud Arbery went for a run in Brunswick, Georgia. He had played football in high school—he was an all-state linebacker—and running was his "meditation," a former coach said. Arbery left his home on Fancy Bluff Road early that afternoon, a Sunday; crossed the highway; and jogged into a subdivision called Satilla Shores, on the west edge of Brunswick.

The presence of Arbery, a Black man, in his neighborhood aroused the suspicions of Gregory McMichael, a retired Brunswick police officer who lived in Satilla Shores. McMichael and his son Travis armed themselves with a pair of guns and climbed into Travis's pickup and set off in pursuit of Arbery. According to Georgia law at the time—a series of statutes going back to 1863—they had the right to conduct a citizen's arrest of anyone they suspected of criminal activity in their presence. Gregory McMichael thought Arbery had broken into a house.

The details of the story are knotty, as were the facts in Fricie Griffin's case. Backers of the McMichaels would insist Arbery threatened them. Arbery's defendants would contend he did everything he could to avoid a confrontation. What is indisputable—thanks to a video that surfaced ten weeks after these events—is that when Ahmaud Arbery met up that day with the McMichaels on a sun-dappled street in Satilla Shores, sixty-four-year-old Gregory McMichael was standing in the bed of the truck with a revolver, and thirty-four-year-old Travis McMichael was positioned in front of the vehicle with a shotgun. Arbery ran to the right of the truck and encountered Travis. The video records a gunshot, a struggle, a second gunshot. Arbery lurches at Travis; Travis fires a third time. Arbery staggers forward a few steps and collapses face down, on the street.

The police told his mother, Wanda Cooper, that Ahmaud had been trying to rob a house and was killed by "the homeowner." Weeks passed before she learned the truth. Shut down by the outbreak of COVID-19, people in Brunswick did not immediately take to the streets as they had in Ferguson and Baltimore and Chicago and all the other places in this country where African Americans have died for reasons too plain to belabor—and as people would take to the streets three months later, across the country, in response to yet another death of a Black man, this time in Minneapolis.

"Each time it begins in the same way, it doesn't begin the same way, each time it begins it's the same," Claudia Rankine writes in *Citizen*, her searing examination of what it means to be Black in America in the twenty-first century.

It was not until early May, after the video of Arbery's fatal run went viral, that Gregory and Travis McMichael were arrested. William (Roddy) Bryan Jr., the white man who filmed the video and whose own vehicle had trailed Arbery from behind, trapping him, was arrested two weeks later. The arrests came as late as they did because the Brunswick Police Department, long troubled by accusations of cronyism and corruption, had for weeks accepted as truth the McMichaels' version of what happened on February 23, 2020.

"Each time it begins it's the same." The week the McMichaels were arrested, I took out my maps of Brunswick. Satilla Shores was easy to find, a compact neighborhood west of town, between the Little Satilla River and Fancy Bluff Creek. I must have driven by it a dozen times over the preceding decade—even sailed past its docks one morning when I tried to chart Matilda and King Hippard's escape from Fancy Bluff. I layered an older map, showing the disposition of Glynn County's nineteenth-century cotton and rice plantations, over the first and saw that Satilla Shores, as I had suspected, was on former Scarlett land. Fancy Bluff, to be precise: Frank and Fanny Scarlett's old plantation. One of the many slave-labor camps my great-great-great grandfather Francis Muir Scarlett had built on his ravenous climb from impoverished immigrant to landed gentry. Fancy Bluff, where King and Matilda Hippard hatched their run to freedom; Fancy Bluff, where a bewildered Fanny Scarlett heard cannon fire from Union gunboats, and a hellbent Frank Scarlett organized his wartime militia, the Satilla Wild Cats. "We have uniformed ourselves and armed with *double barrel guns*," Frank had informed the governor, "and [are] ready to protect our Homes and do service in the County." The line between his time and ours had never been more transparent.

To the litany of African Americans killed by people of my race desperate to maintain a caste system predicated on hate and fear, add the name of Ahmaud Arbery, who was himself a descendant of the Gullah-Geechee people shipped from West Africa to the Georgia coast and forced into slavery. Thomas Spalding, the man who "owned" Arbery's nineteenth-century ancestors on nearby Sapelo Island, moved in the same circles as the Scarletts. Two of Arbery's assailants, Gregory and Travis McMichael, were the descendants of an enslaver in neighboring Charlton and Camden Counties, where Francis Muir Scarlett first found work as an overseer. Gregory McMichael was employed by the same Brunswick Police Department that employed Stanton Scarlett. Through another branch of my family, it even seems I share a very distant common ancestor with all three of the men charged in Arbery's murder—as if a blood tie were needed to prove we're connected.

All along, my research into the past kept butting up against contemporary events. In 2015, two weeks after I spent the night in a slave cabin at the Hofwyl-Broadfield Plantation, a gunman murdered nine parishioners inside the Mother Emanuel Church in Charleston, South Carolina. A year later Donald Trump took the White House, vowing to "make America great again" ("it's code," Black friends said). A year after that, white supremacist violence erupted in Charlottesville, Virginia. In May 2020, as the truth about Ahmaud Arbery's death was finally emerging, forty-six-year-old George Floyd died in Minneapolis after a police officer jammed his knee into Floyd's neck and held it there for nearly nine minutes. "I can't breathe," Floyd begged.

"I simply wanted to have them stop," Fricie Griffin said.

Nor was George Floyd the last African American man or woman to die at the hands of cops in the United States in the summer of 2020. "Because white men can't / police their imagination," Rankine writes, "Black men are dying."

I had told myself we were making progress. Obama, the National Museum of African American History and Culture in DC, groups like Coming to the Table, the Slave Dwelling Project, Black Lives Matter. Growing talk of reparations. In early 2019 I was in Brunswick when the Georgia Historical Society unveiled a historical marker on Butler Island honoring the thousands of people Pierce Butler had enslaved on his plantations—including the 436 whom he had auctioned off in Savannah in 1859 to pay down debts. The new marker stood near the original 1957 markers extolling Pierce Butler and Fanny Kemble and the Dutch engineers who had reportedly designed the rice plantation's intricate system of dikes and canals. During the unveiling ceremony, a trio of African American women in traditional African dress poured libations of rice and called out the names of ancestors. Bubba Hodge, the white mayor of nearby Darien (where Mason Scarlett hunted "lawless" Blacks in 1899), spoke of the cruelty Pierce Butler's enslaved workers had endured. "This place tears my heart when I think back to all that those people had to go through. What we have to answer for is what we do from now on."

But I was in a bubble. In 2021 I attended a talk in Ann Arbor by Nikole Hannah-Jones, creator of the 1619 Project. Someone asked if she thought we'd made progress.

"No," she answered.

Afterward, outside the lecture hall, I fell into a conversation with a young Black woman from Detroit. I told her I had been disheartened by Hannah-Jones's answer. "I feel like in the past few years we *have* made progress," I said. The woman, a diversity coordinator at a school in the Detroit suburbs, looked me in the eye and said, "She's right." Her eight-year-old son, she said, had come home from school earlier that year crying because the other kids refused to play with him. "He's the only Black kid in his class," she continued. "*You* may feel you've made progress in the past five years. I don't."

Born nearly two centuries apart, Ahmaud Arbery and Fricie Griffin died in the same Georgia town where the federal building is named after Frank M. Scarlett, a man who kept the public schools in Savannah segregated for a full ten years after *Brown v. Board of Education*, thanks to Judge Scarlett's insistence that white and Black children had "distinguishable educability capabilities."

The more I read and heard about Ahmaud Arbery's death and life, the more his story and Griffin's merged—each young man with his wide grin and gregarious personality, his particular gifts. "People around our coastal community say that seeing Ahmaud run through their neighborhood was a highlight of their day," a white resident of Glynn County wrote in the aftermath of Arbery's murder. "That he smiled and waved at them, and that they looked forward to it because it made them feel better."

I had sensed the same kind of grace in Fricie Griffin.

Ahmaud Arbery lived on Fancy Bluff Road, across the highway from Satilla Shores. Another tract of old Scarlett land. The house he shared with his mother—the house Wanda Cooper put up for sale the week her son's attackers were arrested, because she could not bear to live there anymore—stands less than a mile from the cemetery at Oak Grove where my Scarlett ancestors are buried and where, in 1856, they interred their "*Old nurse* Maum CHARLOTTE." Another half mile is the graveyard where people of African descent enslaved by the Scarletts buried their loved ones in unmarked plots under a stand of live oaks.

William Bartram, who visited what is now Glynn County in 1773 while colonists were battling for their freedom from England, wrote of the singular beauty of this place—its pine forests and magnolia groves, fox squirrels and tortoises. "A glorious apartment of the boundless palace of the sovereign Creator," he called it, in prose that inspired both Wordsworth and Coleridge.

By the time Bartram visited, European settlers had begun converting this pristine wilderness into a "mental and moral prison," as Fanny Kemble termed it, for people of African descent. Bartram himself, a Pennsylvania Quaker, dabbled in slavery before ultimately renouncing the business.

Where does it come from, the impulse to buy and sell and torture our own kind? I have reached this point in my search and still have no answer—only that I know I, too, am capable of doing it. "We are just as good and bad as the oldest and youngest or any," Whitman admonished. "What the best and worst did we could do."

Knowing my grandmother wanted to be buried in Georgia soil, my mother procured a vial of it some months before Mamie's death and, without telling any of us, had it shipped north to Virginia in time for her funeral. Mary King Hilsman Pettigrew died on December 15, 1994. I drove out from Michigan for the service. Mamie had been cremated, and her ashes sat in a plain box on a pedestal beside an open rectangle of earth next to my grandfather's grave in a cemetery in downtown Tappahannock. There weren't many of us—my mother and father, Uncle

Bob and his wife, a handful of cousins, a few caregivers. We huddled together under a canopy in the brisk winter air. The priest spoke briefly, then began emptying the container of Georgia soil into Mamie's grave. I glanced at my mother. "That's not *her*," my mother whispered fiercely. "That's *dirt* from Georgia."

Near the end of the service, an African American nurse we had hired to care for my grandmother in her last years, a woman named Eliza who had tended Mamie with tireless devotion, asked if she could speak. We had not thought to include her.

"Of course," the priest said.

Eliza stood and with difficulty made her way to the front of the gathering. She was a large woman, and the space was small. I have no memory of what she said—nor does anyone else from my family who was there (I asked). I jotted an account of the funeral in my journal that night but made no mention of Eliza, whose last name I have also forgotten. I dwelled instead on the confusion over what, exactly, was being poured into Mamie's grave that day. I left Eliza out of the record as surely as we had left her out of the burial service. She has her say nevertheless, because the story is incomplete without her.

NOTES ON SOURCES

BEFORE

Ahmaud Arbery, a twenty-five-year-old African American, was killed by two white men while jogging through the Satilla Shores neighborhood of Brunswick, Georgia, on February 23, 2020. On William Bartram, see Van Doren, *Travels*; and Magee, *Art and Science*. The Wesley quote comes from his *Thoughts on Slavery* and is reprinted in Scott, "Editor's Introduction." FMS published his ad in the *Brunswick Advocate* on June 15, 1837, 3.

1. MIDNIGHT

I spent the night at Hofwyl-Broadfield Plantation with Joseph McGill, founder of the Slave Dwelling Project, and Prinny Anderson on May 22, 2015.

2. THE FAMILY ALBUM

The Scarlett homestead in Brunswick was destroyed by fire sometime shortly before February 2, 1897. One member of the Scarlett family said of the fire, "I have often wondered and said that I could not understand why it was that the Lord would send such terrable disasters on good Christian people but it seems to me that the good people are punished a great deal more than the wicked" (Mason Scarlett to VTS, February 2, 1897, Scarlett-Tison Family Collection, GHS). Margaret Mitchell's letter to Frances Scarlett Beach is reproduced in Harwell, *Letters*, 78. For decades after the release of *Gone with the Wind*, only a handful of critics questioned its treatment of Blacks and exaltation of plantation life, and Mitchell dismissed them as "Left Wingers." See also Faust, "Clutching the Chains." On Mitchell's Gerald O'Hara, see Mitchell, *Gone with the Wind*, 68.

3. FANNY KEMBLE

For background on Frances Anne (Fanny) Kemble, see Clinton, *Fanny Kemble's Civil Wars*; Clinton, *Fanny Kemble's Journals*; Kemble, *Journal of a Residence*; Scott, "Foreword"; Scott, "Editor's Introduction"; and Wister, "Butler Place." "Shot at": Clinton, *Fanny Kemble's Civil Wars*, 112. "Hail, strange land": Clinton, *Fanny Kemble's Journals*, 40. "Consequently": Clinton, *Fanny Kemble's Journals*, 52. "Honor and obey": Clinton, *Fanny Kemble's Civil Wars*, 77–78. "As an Englishwoman": Clinton, *Fanny Kemble's Journals*, 2. "Disgracefully": Clinton, *Fanny Kemble's Journals*, 92. "Long and vehement" and "tear our house": Clinton, *Fanny Kemble's Journals*, 85. "I am about . . . I have alas!": Clinton, *Fanny Kemble's Journals*, 96–97. On FK's arrival at Butler Island on December 30, 1838, see Clinton, *Fanny Kemble's Civil Wars*, 119. On the history of Pierce Butler and his ancestors, see Bell, *Major Butler's Legacy*. "Wild waves": Clinton, *Fanny Kemble's Journals*, 156. For Mitchell's story about Frances Anne (Fanny) Kemble and Pierce Butler, see Mitchell, "Georgia Romances"; and Pyron, *Southern Daughter*, 170.

4. LETTERS

Born on March 14, 1785, in London, FMS would have been twenty-seven in 1812 when he went to work as an overseer at Crawford's Dyke; his parents were William Scarlett, a "victualler," and Elizabeth Scarlett, residents of Chiswell Street (Scarlett-Tison Family Collection, GHS). Copies of Richard M. Stites's letters to FMS (1812–13) are in SA. For more on Stites, see the J. Randolph Anderson Collection on Wayne, Stites, and Anderson Family, MS 0846, GHS; and the Scarlett files in the Bryan-Lang Historical Archives, Woodbine GA. My thanks to director Judy Buchanan for her help when I visited Bryan-Lang in 2014. The number of enslaved people in Georgia in 1812—one hundred thousand—was nearly fourfold what it had been twenty years earlier (Cobb, *Georgia Odyssey*, 10–13). "Excess of births over deaths": Albanese, *Plantation as a School*, 139, citing Phillips, *Plantation and Frontier Documents*, 1:121–22. I discovered the ad for a "sober, industrious and active MAN" in the June 4, 1807, edition of the Savannah *Public Intelligencer*, directly beneath a notice of an estate sale for which FMS was administrator. On overseers in general, see Albanese, *Plantation as a School*; Baptist, *Half Has Never*

Been Told; Douglass, *Narrative of the Life*; Stampp, *Peculiar Institution*; and Rawick, *American Slave*, 3:76. On drivers see Albanese, *Plantation as a School*, 139–40; Stampp, *Peculiar Institution*, 40–41; and Wilkerson, *Caste*, 156. "Slave driver": Kinsey, *Georgia Narratives*, 3:76. "Disgusting swagger": Douglass, *Narrative of the Life*, 210–11. "They are to be responsible": Phillips, *Plantation and Frontier Documents*, 1:120; also quoted in Stampp, *Peculiar Institution*, 40–41. Information on FMS and the Glynn County militia comes from "Scarlett, Francis Muir, 1785–1869," SA; and Huxford, *Pioneers of Wiregrass Georgia*, 2:249. A record of the September 26, 1811, wedding of FMS and Nancy Ann Crum Scarlett is inscribed in the "Family Record" inside the Scarlett family Bible in GHS. "And to them": Clinton, *Fanny Kemble's Journals*, 141. Richard Steckel gave his presentation at the University of Michigan School of Public Health on March 19, 2013. "There was no family": Mitchell, *Gone with the Wind*, 81. "The prejudice . . . imprisonment": Clinton, *Fanny Kemble's Journals*, 47–48, 56–57; Clinton, *Fanny Kemble's Civil Wars*, 106. Historian Peter H. Wood first suggested calling plantations "slave labor camps" (Wood, "Slave Labor Camps"); my thanks to Peter H. Wood for alerting me to this source. In a presentation at the 2016 Slave Dwelling Conference, a staff member from Preservation Virginia asked how many visitors would clamor to visit Monticello if it were renamed Thomas Jefferson's Slave Labor Camp.

5. PROPERTY

On intergenerational trauma, see Schützenberger, *Ancestor Syndrome*. "Unspeakable grief . . . from one generation to another": Schützenberger, *Ancestor Syndrome*, 45–47. On the lives of southern women, Black and white, in the plantation household, see especially Faust, *Mothers of Invention*; Fox-Genovese, *Within the Plantation Household*; Glymph, *House of Bondage*; and Jones-Rogers, *They Were Her Property*. Ann Crum Scarlett's parents, devout Methodists, would have insisted she know her scripture. Birth records for FMS and Ann Crum Scarlett's children come from the Scarlett family Bible "Family Record" (Scarlett-Tison Family Collection, GHS) and the Scarlett cemetery in Brunswick GA. "Wretched hole": Clinton, *Fanny Kemble's Journals*, 90–91. The story of Mary Ann Scarlett's betrothal appears in a letter from Judge Frank M. Scarlett to my grandmother's sister Virginia Blanton, June 2, 1969, SA. For general information on FMS's acquisition of Oak Grove, see "Completion of Highway Opens Section," *Brunswick Pilot*, July 13, 1928; Linda Barr, "The Scarletts: A Family Well-Known in Coastal Legends," *Brunswick News*, September 30, 1982; and Scarlett family correspondence, SA. It's impossible to verify the precise date and circumstances of FMS's acquisition of Oak Grove because the Glynn County record books containing the deed for Oak Grove were destroyed by fire (Amy Hedrick, email to author, March 18, 2015). On FMS's career in government, see "Scarlett, Francis Muir," Scarlett-Tison Family Collection, GHS; and Cate, *Our Todays and Yesterdays*, 232–33. In 1819 William Piles borrowed $4,000 from FMS and James Powell, with ten enslaved persons as collateral (Glynn County Deed Book G, 407–8, March 1, 1819, Deeds and Land Records, Glynn County Courthouse, Brunswick GA). "Slavery is the great and foul": Baptist, *Half Has Never*, 156–57. On typical planters' homes in coastal Georgia, see Fox-Genovese, *Within the Plantation Household*, 105–6, 119; and Clinton, *Fanny Kemble's Journals*, 139. "Please leave Tara": Edwards, *Road to Tara*. For FMS's activity in the Georgia state legislature, see *Journal of the House of Representatives of the State of Georgia*, 1859–65; and *Journal of the Senate of the State of Georgia*, 1859–65; volumes are available at GA. Information on Glynn County demographics, circa 1830, comes from Klibanoff, "Ahmaud Arbery." "[Slavery] may be": Bullard, *Robert Stafford*, 114–15. On FMS's support for Andrew Jackson, see "Anti Tariff Meeting in Glynn County, Georgia," *Savannah Georgian*, August 15, 1828, 2. For the number of people enslaved by FMS in 1830, see U.S. census, 1830, Glynn County GA. "RUNAWAY": *Brunswick Advocate*, June 8, 1837, 3. "WANTED TO PURCHASE": *Brunswick Advocate*, June 15, 1837, 3. "One of the strongest": *Savannah Georgian*, July 13, 1837, 2.

6. DAUGHTERS' WORK

"Finest wedding": F. Scarlett to Blanton, June 2, 1969, SA. Background on JP comes from Hedrick, "Parland"; Gresham and Brooke, *Descendant Identification*, 3; Rock and Philips, *Data Recovery Excavations*; Singleton, "Report," 79–80; Amy Horton, "Old Grave Must Be Moved," *Brunswick News*, January 12, 2000; anonymous obituary for John Parland in *Georgian* (Savannah), September 15, 1836; and copy of a 1918 letter from Mrs. William Wadsworth King to the *Brunswick Pilot*, Scarlett-Tison Family Collection, GHS. "I pity them . . . wives and daughters": Clinton, *Fanny*

Kemble's Journals, 121; Kemble, *Journal of a Residence*, 192. "Slightly intoxicated": F. Scarlett to Blanton, June 2, 1969, Scarlett-Tison Family Collection, GHS. Judge Scarlett's source is a "Mr. A. R. Berrie," who claimed Parland "was thrown from his horse which he had just purchased and was trying him out to see if the horse was worth what he paid for him. He had just received the horse from Arabia." An account of JP's death in the Scarlett family Bible notes that he fractured his skull "in a shocking manner," Scarlett-Tison Family Collection, GHS. For more on Parland's burial, see Gresham and Brooke, *Descendant Identification*. The precise number of enslaved people "owned" by JP in 1836 seems to have been 168 (Parland, "Inventories and Appraisements," D:320–21, 352–53). "Better securing": "Inventories and Appraisements," E:113; Jean and FAP appear to have attended Montpelier Institute in Monroe County, Georgia, sometime around 1847. In addition to the 1836 inventory of JP's estate, the name "Charlotte" turns up among a lot of enslaved people JP acquired when he purchased Colonel's Island in 1832 from fellow planter Joseph Demere. The name "Charlotte" also turns up on inventories of other property that ultimately found its way to JP and from him to the Scarletts. The name morphs from Charlotte to Sharlotte to Sharlott, depending on the document. A "Charlotte" turns up on a list of enslaved people JP purchased shortly after his marriage to Mary Ann in 1833. The sale, witnessed by FMS in his capacity as justice of the inferior court of Glynn County, saw the transfer of this Charlotte from an enslaver named Cooper to Parland. She and seven others, including Charlotte's child, a girl whose name appears to be Sofie, sold for a collective $2,000 (Glynn County Deed Book H, 329, Deeds and Land Records; Parland, "Inventories and Appraisements," vol. D; Singleton, "Archaeology," 291–307.) On the removal of JP's grave in 2000, see Gresham and Brooke, *Descendant Identification*, 4–6; and Rock and Philips, *Data Recovery Excavations*, 34. In 2015 I spoke by phone with two sisters, Cordilia and Shonda Parland, who believed they were descended from JP. "And you will see trouble": Baptist, *Half Has Never*, 241. "In which the grandchildren": quoted in Gorra, *Saddest Words*, 255. "Striking resemblance . . . relationships" and "I have written down": Clinton, *Fanny Kemble's Journals*, 147, 158–59. "Dingy mulatto": Clinton, *Fanny Kemble's Journals*, 128. "Right-handed power": Baptist, *Half Has Never*, 287. On FAP's commitment to state asylum, see Rock and Philips, *Data Recovery Excavations*, 22, citing Glynn County

Probate Court, Parland, Guardian Bond for Frances A. Parland, lunatic, March 23, 1874; and Letter of Guardianship for Frances A. Parland, December 7, 1897, both in Glynn County Probate Court, Glynn County Courthouse, Brunswick GA. I am grateful to Carolyn Rock for allowing me to accompany her to the excavation site on Colonel's Island on May 18, 2015, and for so generously sharing her team's findings with me then and subsequently.

7. SECRETS

On use of padlocks by the enslaved, see Penningroth, *Claims of Kinfolk*, 91; and Rock and Philips, *Data Recovery Excavations*, 85, 160, 460; Olmsted, *Cotton Kingdom*, 184–85."Hovels," "little counteracted," "filthy, pestilential" and "In the North": Clinton, *Fanny Kemble's Journals*, 102, 120–21. "At the first gray streak": Reiss, *Wild Nights*, 122, 126; "Oh, master": Douglass, *Narrative of the Life*, 11; Reiss, *Wild Nights*, 124. Many planters (Thomas Jefferson among them) believed African Americans required less sleep than whites. "The citizen": Albanese, *Plantation as a School*, 96, citing Tocqueville, *Democracy in America*, 1:507–8. "An indescribable sensation": Clinton, *Fanny Kemble's Journals*, 137–38. "My great great grandfather's": Ed Wood, email to author, December 1, 2010. I am profoundly grateful to Ed Wood for his kindness, generosity, and willingness to share his family's stories with me. "Rather unpleasant": Clinton, *Fanny Kemble's Journals*, 147. "Yellow babies": Mitchell, *Gone with the Wind*, 426–27. "The mulattoes": Chesnut, *Mary Chesnut's Diary*, 100; Pierpont, "Critic at Large," 92. "Somehow special": Berry, *Hidden Wound*, 2–5. I am grateful to Wendell Berry for permission to quote throughout *Scarlett* from his urgent reflection on slavery's impact on both white and Black Americans in *Hidden Wound*. On slavery as a curse to whites as well as Blacks, see also Harriet Jacobs, who said, "I can testify, from my own experience and observation, that slavery is a curse to the whites as well as to the blacks. It makes the white fathers cruel and sensual; the sons violent and licentious; it contaminates the daughters, and makes the wives wretched" (Jacobs, *Incidents*, quoted in Morrison, *Origin of Others*, 28–29). "Beyond the considerable": Berry, *Hidden Wound*, 104–5. "The black claws": quoted in Pierpont, "Critic at Large." "Jes a small girl": Glymph, *House of Bondage*, 55, citing Kinsey, *Georgia Narratives*, 373. Copies of Fanny Scarlett's correspondence from

1850 to 1863 are in SA. "Immediately the vicinity": *Atlanta Constitution*, August 19, 1884, 2, quoting from "Georgia Gossip: Short Talks with the Scribes of the Country Press; A Negro Man Tied to the Tracks of a Railroad," *Atlanta Constitution*, August 19, 1884, 2. Information on Madison Scarlett comes from Ed Wood, conversation with the author, December 1, 2010; "Madison Scarlet [*sic*]"; *Brunswick Advertiser and Appeal*, July 4, 1877 http://www.glynngen.com/newspapers/glynn/advertiser.htm; U.S. census, 1910; Madison Scarlett Death Certificate, #26411, in Death Certificates, Vital Records, Public Health, RG 26-5-95, GA and Georgia's Virtual Vault, accessed June 30, 2017, http://vault.georgiaarchives.org/cdm/singleitem/collection/gadeaths/id/188929/rec/41. Background on Ann Scarlett Cochran comes from Wood and Allen, *Black America Series*. For background on Judge Frank M. Scarlett, see Farrant, *Julian Scarlett*; "Death Takes Popular U.S. Judge Frank Muir Scarlett Thursday," *Southeast Georgian*, November 25, 1971; and Emanuel, *Elbert Parr Tuttle*, 271–73.

8. LOST

"That is when": Green, *Negro Motorist Green Book*. The Scarletts were founding members of the Emanuel United Methodist Church in Brunswick, Georgia. "When in their presence": Berry, *Hidden Wound*, 19. My understanding of African American burial customs comes from Clinton, *Fanny Kemble's Journals*, 137–38; Berlin, *Many Thousands Gone*, 104–7; Cate, *Our Todays and Yesterdays*, 156; Parrish, *Slave Songs*, 29–31; Young, *Rituals of Resistance*; and a conversation with Gregory Grant of the Geechee Kunda Cultural Arts Center and Museum in Riceboro, Georgia, on May 16, 2015. On Gullah-Geechee culture, see P. Morgan, *African American Life*. My thanks to Jason Young for his clarification of the term "Gullah-Geechee" and his insights into Gullah-Geechee culture, history, and religion. "When a slave died": Katie Darling, vol. 16, "Texas Narratives," quoted in the 2003 documentary film *Unchained Memories*. Edda Fields-Black spoke on June 10, 2016, at a national gathering of Coming to the Table in Harrisonburg, Virginia. All quotes from Frances (Fanny) McDonald Scarlett's correspondence are from copies of her letters (1850–63) in Scarlett-Tison Family Collection, GHS. "Unstable": Campbell, "Reminiscences"; my thanks to Michael McDonald for sharing this document with me. Background on Fanny's father, Alexander, also comes from Redfearn, *Alexander McDonald*. "Americans reconciled the gap": Jon Meacham, "Hard Times," *New York Times Book Review*, January 22, 2023. "The slave auctioneer's": Frederick Douglass, quoted in Charles M. Blow, "A Rancher's Romantic Revisionism," *New York Times*, April 26, 2014; for more on Christian hypocrisy among slaveholders, see Douglass, *Narrative of the Life*, 57, 78–79, 120–23; and Meacham, "Hard Times." On FDS status at the time of his marriage to Fanny McDonald, June 29, 1852, see U.S. census 1850, Glynn County GA; Appointments of U.S. Postmasters, 1832–1971, M841, National Archives, Washington DC; Georgia Military Affairs, vol. 6, 1830–35, 129; *Charleston Courier*, January 27, 1852, 1; *Savannah Georgian*, September 2, 1842; *Macon Weekly Telegraph*, June 28, 1853, 2. For FDS activity on behalf of Parland estate, see PP. "ONE HUNDRED AND FIFTY": *Charleston Courier*, August 24, 1844, 3; the notice appears in the same paper on August 10, 14, 16, 17, 19, 20, 21, 22, and 23. "Committed": *Charleston Mercury*, August 27, 1844, 3. Details of FDS payments to South Carolina jailers and law firms are found in PP, August 30–31, 1844. On the capture of Dick and Eliza, and FDS and David Scarlett in Savannah, see PP, November 1844 and December 18–19, 1844; and "Inward Coastwise Slave Manifests." Information on slave patrols and their link to rural southern police departments comes from Klibanoff, "Ahmaud Arbery." For the shipping of Lucinda, see "Inward Coastwise Slave Manifests." For FDS's sale of the enslaved man Jacob on December 17, 1842, see Heather M. Pierce, "Slavery in Florida: 1840s–1850s," an educational module based on primary sources available at the Florida Historical Society's Library of Florida History, Cocoa FL, n.d. (PDF in SA). My information on the work of enslaved women, especially midwives, comes primarily from Cooper, "Midwives of Invention." My thanks to Abby for calling my attention to this paper and for all her many insights and suggestions. On the work of enslaved women in plantation households, see Fox-Genovese, *Within the Plantation Household*; Glymph, *House of Bondage*; and Jones-Rogers, *They Were Her Property*. "Negro woollens" and "osnaburg": PP; Singleton, "Report," 87; and Wilkerson, *Caste*, 144. "Powerless embers": Clinton, *Fanny Kemble's Journals*, 104–5. "You are loosed": Douglass, *Narrative of the Life*, 66–67. On JP's advertisement for freedom seekers, see "One Hundred Dollars Reward," *Savannah Georgian*, December 9, 1829, 2. Between the official end of the slave trade in 1808 and the outbreak of war in 1861, roughly a quarter-million enslaved people were smuggled from Africa, Cuba, and elsewhere into the United States. Details on *The Wanderer* come from Calonius, *Wanderer*; Jordan, *Slave-Trader's Letter-Book*; and author conversations with Andrea Marroquin of the Jekyll Island Visitors Center, 2010 and 2011. When I shared the story of FMS and *The Wanderer* with Eric Calonius and asked if he thought the story was plausible, he answered, "The story certainly could be true. Charles Lamar and the other conspirators were well connected with the New York slave dealers, as I mentioned in the book. So the information is entirely plausible" (Eric Calonius email to author, April 26, 2010). On the Weeping Time, see Bell, *Major Butler's Legacy*; Bailey, *Weeping Time*; Link, "Review"; Kristopher Monroe, "The Weeping Time," *The Atlantic*, July 10, 2014; and Clinton, *Fanny Kemble's Civil Wars*, 162. Under the byline "Q. K. Philander Doesticks," reporter Mortimer Thomson—Horace Greeley's star correspondent at the *New York Tribune*—wrote a sensational six-column article about the Butler auction that ran in the *Tribune* on March 9, 1859, and was reprinted on March 11 by popular demand. "Cancer": Baptist, *Half Has Never*, 381–83. "All things must come": Fanny McDonald Scarlett correspondence, Scarlett-Tison Family Collection, GHS.

9. TROUBLE

"Well knowing the uncertainty": Glynn County GA. My thanks to the late Dave Pettee, who found FMS's will online for me. On Scarlett slaveholding figures in 1850, see U.S. census, Glynn County GA. In the early 2000s, Tom Blake set out to compile a list of the nation's largest slaveholders, using data from the 1860 census. He tallied 11,020 individual enslavers in ten different states, representing a total of 792,219 enslaved people—or 20 percent of all U.S. slaves. My Scarlett ancestors made the list (Blake, "Large Slaveholder Project"). My thanks to Carolyn Rock for checking the 1860 U.S. census and confirming that James Hamilton Couper's wealth exceeded that of the Parland sisters. Before gambling debts ruined him, Pierce Butler had once rivaled Couper for wealth. On storage of property by the enslaved, see Penningroth, *Claims of Kinfolk*, 92–101. "Our little sunbeam": JFMS to JAPK and FAP, March 19, 1862, SA. "Paterrollers": Mitchell, *Gone with the Wind*, 41; the story of the Clayton Wild Cats appears on page 38. "We have uniformed ourselves": Governor's Incoming Correspondence, Civil War, Governor Joseph

E. Brown of Georgia, Morrow, Georgia State Archives; my thanks to Carolyn Rock for finding this document. "Every Southern woman": Clinton, *Fanny Kemble's Journals*, 161. "Saturnalia" and "war of extermination": Baptist, *Half Has Never*, 390–91; Cobb, *Georgia Odyssey*, 21–22. "White man's Republic": *Daily Telegraph* (Macon), January 19, 1861, 1, quoted in Mohr, *Threshold of Freedom*, 49. Information on FDS possessions, circa 1861, comes from PP; on June 14, 1849, the Parland Estate paid twenty-five dollars for a "Newfoundland dog." "A certain lot . . . said negro slaves": Glynn County Deed Book N, 252–53, Glynn County Courthouse, Brunswick GA. "Unmaking": Glymph, *House of Bondage*, 95–96. On Franklin Holcomb's debt, see Glynn County Deed Book N, 252–57, Glynn County Courthouse, Brunswick GA. "Hopeless lunatic": Guardianship Agreement, Glynn County GA, PP, December 7, 1897. Some family members theorize that FAP's condition was the result of a devastating childhood illness, contracted in 1849 (JFMS to Carrie Hull, December 28, 1849, SA; Debi Schneider, email to author, April 11, 2011). Andrew Delbanco notes that to nineteenth-century Americans, the term "insanity" was synonymous with "depression" (*War before the War*, 241). "Oh Jeannie": JFMS to JAPK and FAP, August 7, 1862, Scarlett-Tison Family Collection, GHS. "Blue-eyed": Fannie Webb Holt to JFMS, correspondence, Typescript, 1946, Scarlett-Tison Family Collection, GHS. "I hope you receive": JFMS to JAPK and FAP, April 1, 1862, Scarlett-Tison Family Collection, GHS. On conditions in Brunswick in 1861, see Cate, *Our Todays and Yesterdays*, 214; Myers, *Children of Pride*, 772; and Rock and Philips, *Data Recovery Excavations*, 10. "He became a soldier": author visit to Christchurch Cemetery, Saint Simons Island GA, May 17, 2015; "Capt Hamilton Couper." "Oh Puss, I realize," "I have committed," "bare walls," and "miserable": JFMS to FAP, November 13, 1861, Scarlett-Tison Family Collection, GHS. "Reduce to subjection": Excerpts from O. J. Hickox Jr., "A Test of Character," regarding Major Jesse Campbell McDonald, Operations Officer, Clinch's Regiment, Fourth Georgia Volunteer Cavalry, Provisional Army of the Confederate States, sent from Michael McDonald, email to author, December 22, 2011. "The gunboats just": JFMS to JAPK and FAP, March 19, 1862, Scarlett-Tison Family Collection, GHS. On events in and around Brunswick in 1862, see "The Occupation of Brunswick," *New York Times*, April 9, 1862, http://www.glynngen.com/military/civilwar/glynn/occofbwk.htm; and unidentified clipping, Historic Civil War Misc., Bryan-Lang Historical Archives, Woodbine GA. "Broken open . . . many a pang": JFMS to JAPK and FAP, March 19, 1862, Scarlett-Tison Family Collection, GHS. On the contraband colony on Saint Simons Island, see Albanese, *Plantation as a School*; Clinton, *Fanny Kemble's Civil Wars*; Higginson, *Army Life*; and Mohr, *Threshold of Freedom*. "Sallie's little Dave . . . for that reason": JFMS to JAPK and FAP, March 19, 1862, SA. "We needed this discipline": JFMS to JAPK and FAP, August 7, 1862, Scarlett-Tison Family Collection, GHS. "Slavery has to go": Chesnut, *Mary Chesnut's Diary*, 66; Fox-Genovese, *Within the Plantation Household*, 358. "Meta wrote . . . and comes back" and "It was the most quiet": JFMS to JAPK and FAP, March 19, 1862, Scarlett-Tison Family Collection, GHS. "I am having homespun": JFMS to JAPK and FAP, September 10, 1862, Scarlett-Tison Family Collection, GHS. "Now that we have proven": JFMS to JAPK and FAP, March 19, 1862, Scarlett-Tison Family Collection, GHS. "I try to teach": JFMS to JAPK and FAP, October 17, 1862, Scarlett-Tison Family Collection, GHS. "It was so much nearer": this quote and the rest of Fanny Scarlett's account of Matilda's actions at Glencoe (her "treachery") comes from JFMS to JAPK and FAP, August 7, 1862, Scarlett-Tison Family Collection, GHS.

10. REVOLT

"The transformation . . . old terms": Glymph, *House of Bondage*, 95, 132. "Psalm-singing": Frederick Douglass, *My Bondage and My Freedom*, 1866, 149–50, quoted in Glymph, *House of Bondage*, 35. On the violence of slaveholding women, see also Faust, *Mothers of Invention*; Fox-Genovese, *Within the Plantation Household*; Glymph, *House of Bondage*; and Jones-Rogers, *They Were Her Property*. "So high strung": JFMS to JAPK and FAP, March 19, 1862, Scarlett-Tison Family Collection, GHS. The Coming to the Table session, "Staying at the Table—No Matter What," took place in May 2014 and was led by Pat Russell and Ann Holmes Redding, to whom I remain grateful. "I think we know": JFMS to JAPK and FAP, March 19, 1862, Scarlett-Tison Family Collection, GHS. "Betrayed trust": JFMS to JAPK and FAP, April 1, 1862, Scarlett-Tison Family Collection, GHS. On the treatment of formerly enslaved people regarded as "contrabands," see Delbanco *War before the War*, 379–80. "Terrible corporal": Myers, *Children of Pride*, 935. Fanny Scarlett's account of the escape of Matilda, King, and the others appears in JFMS to JAPK and

FAP, March 19, 1862, Scarlett-Tison Family Collection, GHS. My thanks to Jaime Bracewell and Tim Cole for helping me retrace King and Matilda's escape route by boat on September 17, 2016. "Contrabands . . . shell or two": S. W. Godon to Gideon Welles, March 30, 1862, Scarlett-Tison Family Collection, GHS. "I have also placed . . . those people": Mohr, *Threshold of Freedom*, 80; *New York Daily Tribune*, August 9, 1862, 3. At one point Union commander S. W. Godon informed his superiors: "My supplies have been mostly from Pierce Butler's place" (Clinton, *Fanny Kemble's Civil Wars*, 181–82; Bell, *Major Butler's Legacy*). For accounts of the contraband colony on Saint Simons Island, see Albanese, *Plantation as a School*; Bullard, *Robert Stafford*, 229–31; Clinton, *Fanny Kemble's Civil Wars*, 181–82; Higginson, *Army Life*; Mohr, *Threshold of Freedom*; Taylor, *Reminiscences of My Life*; and "Occupation of Brunswick." "I little thought": Bell, *Major Butler's Legacy*, 373. "Coats, 75 cents": Bell, *Major Butler's Legacy*, 363. "All of them so eager": Taylor, *Reminiscences of My Life*, 11. "Their love" and "Never had I seen": Higginson, *Army Life*, 19, 129–30. "But they all seemed": Higginson, *Army Life*, 55. "I feel lighter": Stampp, *Peculiar Institution*, 382. On the Brunswick Harbor and Land Company, see Rock and Philips, *Data Recovery Excavations*, 36; Singleton, "Report," 81; and Burnette Vanstory, "Future of Colonel's Island Now Has Industrial Tinge," *Atlanta Journal-Constitution*, n.d., Scarlett-Tison Family Collection, GHS. On the disappearance of the home of FDS and JFMS at Fancy Bluff, see Barr, "Scarletts"; and "Completion of Highway." On Glencoe's use as a training field for blimp pilots, see Holt to JFMS, Scarlett-Tison Family Collection, GHS. "Shining black": Mitchell, *Gone with the Wind*, 42–43. "Central to its unmaking": Glymph, *House of Bondage*, 95–96. "An aged colored man": *Brunswick Advertiser and Appeal*, April 4, 1885, https://gahistoricnewspapers.galileo.usg.edu/lccn/sn89053386/1885-04-04/ed-1/seq-6/.

11. LET THEM FLOW

"God grant": JFMS to JAPK and FAP, January 19, 1863, Scarlett-Tison Family Collection, GHS. "One evening . . . sparing him to me": JFMS to JAPK and FAP, October 17, 1862, Scarlett-Tison Family Collection, GHS. "She and Mother": JFMS to JAPK and FAP, December 3, 1862, Scarlett-Tison Family Collection, GHS. "Far back . . . the Yankies" and "so much troubled": FDS to JAPK and FAP, September 10, 1862, Scarlett-Tison

Family Collection, GHS. "Irascible, violent": Albanese, *Plantation as a School*, 96, 113, quoting Tocqueville, *Democracy in America*, 1:507–8. "If Southern writers": Haskell, *Frankly, My Dear*, 207–8. "These are our dark": FDS to JAPK and FAP, September 10, 1862, Scarlett-Tison Family Collection, GHS. "It is possible": JFMS to JAPK and FAP, January 19, 1863, Scarlett-Tison Family Collection, GHS. "Has proven himself": JFMS to JAPK and FAP, September 10, 1862, Scarlett-Tison Family Collection, GHS. "Big fat smart spoiled": JFMS to JAPK and FAP, October 17, 1862, Scarlett-Tison Family Collection, GHS. "Sad and sorrowful": Chesnut, *Mary Chesnut's Diary*, 155–56. For Higginson's visit to an abandoned house on Saint Simons Island, see Higginson, *Army Life*, xiv; in the summer of 1865, the Freedmen's Bureau noted "abandoned lands" totaling one thousand acres on Pierce Butler's former Saint Simons plantation (C. Morgan, "Unfortunate Propensity," 217). "So much devilment": Glymph, *House of Bondage*, 106. Governor Joseph Brown's response to Emancipation is described in Mohr, *Threshold of Freedom*, 217. "A direct bid": Myers, *Children of Pride*, 967. "He won't look": Chesnut, *Mary Chesnut's Diary*, 195. "Imperative duty": Clinton, *Fanny Kemble's Journals*, 164. "The slaves in whom": Kemble, *Journal of a Residence*, frontispiece. "Inflexible impartiality" and "immense amount": Kemble, *Journal of a Residence*. On the reaction to Kemble's *Journal of a Residence*, see Clinton, *Fanny Kemble's Civil Wars*; and Scott, "Editor's Introduction." "The first ample, lucid": quoted in Clinton, *Fanny Kemble's Civil Wars*, 179. "Almost every": Clinton, *Fanny Kemble's Journals*, 15. "Forced her, flogged her" and "severely flogged": Clinton, *Fanny Kemble's Journals*, 156–59. On Margaret Davis Cate's campaign to discredit Kemble, see Cate, *Our Todays and Yesterdays*, 142; Cate, "Mistakes in Fanny Kemble's Georgia Journal," *Georgia Historical Quarterly*, March 1960; Clinton, *Fanny Kemble's Journals*, 16; Davis, *Island Time*, 107. The story of Judge Frank M. Scarlett querying a citizenship applicant in 1947 comes from a transcript in Scarlett-Tison Family Collection, GHS of an undated article in the Brunswick press. "Scanty clothing . . . female frame": Kemble, *Journal of a Residence*, 67. "To prevent chills . . . indolence": "Slave Life in the South: A Southern Marton from Louisiana," *Cincinnati Daily Enquirer*, July 27, 1863. "I hear them shouting": JFMS to Carrie Hull, March 28, 1850, Scarlett-Tison Family Collection, GHS. On Fanny Scarlett's illness, see Holt to JFMS, Scarlett-Tison Family Collection, GHS. Holt surmised that

Fanny died of cancer. "What you are": Faust, *This Republic of Suffering*, 6, 9–10. Fanny Scarlett's obituary appeared two weeks before Lincoln memorialized the dead at Gettysburg ("Died, at Waynesville," *Savannah Republican*, November 3, 1863, 3). "All will be right": FDS to JAPK and FAP, September 10, 1862, Scarlett-Tison Family Collection, GHS. FDS's death date: "Family Record," Scarlett family Bible, GHS; Scarlett-Tison Family Collection, GHS; and Scarlett cemetery, Brunswick GA. On Major Jesse Campbell McDonald's capture and imprisonment, see Redfearn, *Alexander McDonald*, 34. "God may be changing": Mohr, *Threshold of Freedom*, 268–69, quoting from *Southern Christian Advocate*, September 29, 1864, 2. "I will not bear arms": "Compiled Service Records of Confederate Soldiers Who Served in Organizations from the State of Georgia," National Archives, Catalogue 586957, National Archives; according to this document, a preprinted surrender form, GSS was a private of the Fourth Ga. C. Regiment of the Georgia Cavalry. "Compelled to yield": quoted in Gorra, *Saddest Words*, 228. On FDS's sale of Glencoe and mortgage of Fancy Bluff—both to his brother David Scarlett—see Glynn County Deed Book N, 326–27, Deeds and Land Records. In 1868 FDS and others were officially incorporated as the Turtle River and Screven Railroad Company (General Assembly of the State of Georgia, 1868, 1:114). On FDS as an attorney, see Glynn County Courthouse Property Records, N-466, Glynn County Courthouse. "The choicest plums": *Brunswick Advertiser and Appeal*, June 13, 1877, http://www.glynngen.com/newspapers/glynn/advertiser.htm. "*Suis stat viribus*": Errol Lea-Scarlett address to Scarlett Family Reunion, Jackson Hole, Wyoming, July 11, 1996, in *Scarlett Letter*, November 2000, 274 (family history compiled by William Scarlett). "For his soul's sake": Clinton, *Fanny Kemble's Journals*, 132. "She is like a straight deep": Clinton, *Fanny Kemble's Civil Wars*, 246. After their first encounter, James told his mother that Kemble's "splendid handsomeness of eye, nostril and mouth were the best things in the room" (Clinton, *Fanny Kemble's Civil Wars*, 220–21). "We are too apt to see": James, "Fanny Kemble," 107. Many residents of Saint Simons Island are so spooked by Ebo Landing they refuse to fish there (author conversation with Amy Lotson Roberts of the Saint Simons African American Heritage Coalition, May 19, 2015). "What became . . . had never been": Q. K. Philander Doesticks [Mortimer Thomson], *New York Tribune*, March 9 and 11, 1859, reprinted as "What Became of the

Slaves on a Georgia Plantation? Great Auction Sale of Slaves at Savannah, Georgia, March 2d & 3rd, 1859: A Sequel to Mrs. Kemble's Journal," in Kemble, *Journal of a Residence*. While some of those Pierce Butler sold in Savannah eventually found their way back to Butler Island and Saint Simons, many did not. On the postwar search by newly freed people for missing loved ones, see Williams, *Help Me*.

12. NEW ORDER

"Miserable *War*": [India Royall?] to VTS, April 24, 1867, Scarlett-Tison Family Collection, GHS. "Dear Sister Jinny": [FDS] to VTS, n.d., Scarlett-Tison Family Collection, GHS. The wedding date for VTS and GSS appears in "Family Record," Scarlett family Bible, GHS; Scarlett-Tison Family Collection, GHS. "Bountiful hospitality": Lucian Lamar Knight, *Georgia's Landmarks, Memorials and Legends*, vol. 1, 1913, typescript in SA. "Champion sweet potato": *Macon Weekly Telegraph*, January 29, 1878, 3. "Little babe," "Sweet little pet," and "Darling Annie Belle": quotes are from correspondence to VTS, 1867, Scarlett-Tison Family Collection, GHS. On African Americans living on Colonel's Island and Fancy Bluff after the war, see Rock and Philips, *Data Recovery Excavations*, 29; Singleton, "Archaeology," 303; and Amy Hedrick, email to author, May 20, 2016. All quotations from Henry Louis Gates come from Gates, "Truth Behind." "Within a few years . . . surroundings": Du Bois, "Negro Landholder of Georgia," 647–48. "All subjects relating": O'Donovan, *Becoming Free*, 115. "Over a century ago": Eric Foner, *Reconstruction*. "Thoroughgoing white supremacist": Blight, *Race and Reunion*, 45. "Forever war": Gorra, *Saddest Words*, 272. "It was made impossible": Gorra, *Saddest Words*, 276. The Ku Klux Klan was founded the year the war ended. Because the chief aim of the Freedmen's Bureau was to establish labor systems to keep Black people working to produce cotton, rice, sugarcane and other crops that drove the economies of both the South and the North, many agents focused on creating and enforcing labor contracts to keep African Americans tied to the land. While Douglas Risley, the agent in charge of the bureau around Brunswick, seems genuinely to have cared about African Americans, many Freedmen's Bureau agents brought "a condescending arrogance as well as racism to the job," says Heather Andrea Williams (*Help Me*, 145). "Calm, peaceful" and Ann Crum Scarlett death: "Scarlett, Francis Muir," Scarlett-Tison Family Collection,

GHS; unidentified FMS obituary, Scarlett-Tison Family Collection, GHS; "Scarlett, Francis Muir, 1785–1869," in Huxford, *Pioneers of Wiregrass Georgia*, 2:249. In February 1875 Glynn County surveyor W. T. Penniman resurveyed and divided the late FMS's property at Oak Grove into six equal lots, each containing 412 acres; copies of that survey, rendered by MKHP's sister Virginia Hilsman Blanton, are in Scarlett-Tison Family Collection, GHS. On the distribution of Scarlett land at Oak Grove in the nineteenth century, see Rock and Philips, *Data Recovery Excavations*, 36; Singleton, "Report," 81; and Joyce Jackson, "New Town of South Brunswick Was Started on Island in 1888," *Brunswick News*, undated clipping in Scarlett-Tison Family Collection, GHS. "Little old retainers": MKHP to author, June 22, 1983. "Biscuit": Barr, "Scarletts"; MKHP to author, October 22, 1981. "This faithful old": Scarlett-Tison Family Collection, GHS. Information on Daniel Parland comes from Rock and Philips, *Data Recovery Excavations*, 29; and an author conversation with Cordilia Parland Parrish and Shonda Parland, August 1, 2015. "Tells us more": Blight, *Race and Reunion*, 286. Most formerly enslaved African Americans who returned to the Georgia coast after the war had worked the same land during slavery, notes Karen Cook-Bell (*Claiming Freedom*, 42). On exploitative contracts, typical was the Georgian who proposed replacing slavery with a "system of serfdom" (Levine, *Fall of the House*, 296). On Georgia politics in 1867–68 and subsequent years, see Clinton, *Fanny Kemble's Civil Wars*, 210, 215; Cobb, *Georgia Odyssey*, 28–29; Duncan, *Freedom's Shore*, 52–54; and O'Donovan, *Becoming Free*, 251–63. "Scourge of Reconstruction," "many of them," and "It was the large . . . into being": Mitchell, *Gone with the Wind*, 491, 612–13. When it came to the Klan, Mitchell, otherwise a scrupulous researcher, made no effort to substantiate her claims: "As I had not written anything about the Klan which is not common knowledge to every Southerner," she said, "I had done no research upon it" (quoted in Pierpont, "Critic at Large," 97). All the more interesting, then, that Mitchell later told David Selznick she wanted to eliminate any mention of the Klan from the movie version of her book (Haskell, *Frankly, My Dear*, 139). "Fantasy of interethnic rape": Fiedler, *What Was Literature?*, quoted in Haskell, *Frankly, My Dear*, 27–28. "Mulattoes," "yellow babies," and "black fools": Mitchell, *Gone with the Wind*, 426–27. "Southern gentlemen . . . ineffaceable blood": Du Bois, *Souls of Black Folk*, 72–73. On Dixon and Mitchell's mutual admiration society, see Edwards, *Road to Tara*; Haskell, *Frankly, My Dear*, xi; Pierpont, "Critic at Large," 96–97; and Storace, "Look Away," 276–77, 289–90. "Having to testify" and "he was uppity": Mitchell, *Gone with the Wind*, 695, 583. On the number of lynchings in Georgia during MKHP's first year, see Cobb, *Georgia Odyssey*, 41; Brundage, *Lynching*, 16. Donald Mathews notes that from 1889 to 1899, approximately 188 people a year were lynched in the South (Mathews, *Altar of Lynching*, 49). For a more detailed account of lynchings in the South, see Stevenson, "Equal Justice Initiative"; Stevenson and EJI speak repeatedly of the "era of racial terror" rather than the "Jim Crow era." "Epidemic of rape": Pierpont, "Critic at Large," 96; Haskell, *Frankly, My Dear*, 103; Storace, "Look Away," 271, citing Pyron, *Southern Daughter*, 31. On Georgia General Assembly's disenfranchisement of Black voters in 1907, see Duncan, *Freedom's Shore*, 116. "Soft rays": "Hilsman-Pettigrew Wedding Yesterday," undated clipping in Scarlett-Tison Family Collection, GHS. On annual KKK parades in Brunswick, see Brundage, *Lynching*, 22–23; and *Brunswick News*, October 29, 1926, http://www.glynngen.com/newspapers/glynn/bwknews.htm. "I always felt": MKHP to author, January 22, 1983, Scarlett-Tison Family Collection, GHS.

13. INDUSTRY

"They are men": Mitchell, *Gone with the Wind*, 742. In addition to GSS, the 1868 freeholders agreement was signed by J. M. Tison and R. M. Tison; absentee signatories were FDS and John Scarlett (brother to GSS and FDS). Agreement of the Freeholders of the Twenty-Seventh District, Glynn, Ga., in regard to regulating labor for the ensuing year, December 14, 1868, photocopy in SA. On widespread white terror at the prospect of armed Black insurrections, see C. Morgan, "Unfortunate Propensity," 219. "Most comprehensive effort": quoted in Cobb, *Georgia Odyssey*, 30–31. "The fact of their . . . Mr. Blue": James Houston to GSS, January 5, 1871, SA; a James Houston was mayor of Brunswick in the 1830s. "The most comprehensive": quoted in Cobb, *Georgia Odyssey*, 30–31. "A citizen": *Brunswick Advertiser and Appeal*, September 6, 1876, http://www.glynngen.com/newspapers/glynn/advertiser.htm; "For the instruction . . . same school": Act and Resolutions of the General Assembly of the State of Georgia, 1873, 1:256; the Georgia General Assembly appointed FDS to the Glynn County Board of Education in early 1873.

FDS was appointed postmaster of Fancy Bluff in October 1880; prior to the war he had also served as postmaster for Fancy Bluff, stepping down in 1851 ("Appointments of U.S. Postmasters"). On postmaster Isaiah H. Lofton, see Lowe, "That Hogansville Affair." On GSS's involvement with the South Brunswick Terminal Railroad Company, see Rock and Philips, *Data Recovery Excavations*, 36; Glynn Co. Deed Book EE, 520–21, Deeds and Land Records, Glynn County Courthouse; Jackson, "New Town"; and Joyce Jackson, "Old Railroad on Colonel's Island Was Delight to Local Residents," *Brunswick News*, undated clippings in SA. On peonage, see Blackmon, *Slavery by Another Name*. "You didn't have . . . look about her": Mitchell, *Gone with the Wind*, 708. "We used to tie" and "She never could talk": MKHP to author, August 21, 1976. "Horrified": unidentified typescript, presumably by MKHP, Scarlett-Tison Family Collection, GHS. "I sometimes wonder": MKHP to RLP Jr., December 5, 1967, Scarlett-Tison Family Collection, GHS. On Tony's wartime arrest and subsequent pardon, see Holt to JFMS, Scarlett-Tison Family Collection, GHS. The information about Alec marrying a *Wanderer* survivor appears in the unsigned caption to a photograph of Alec Massie in Scarlett-Tison Family Collection, GHS. "Jahnee! . . . mashie barrow was coon": undated typescript in Scarlett-Tison Family Collection, GHS. "They were burdened": Berry, *Hidden Wound*, 8–9. "Door's enough to watch": Parrish, *Slave Songs*, 33–34. "She never wore . . . pot of them": MKHP to author, August 6, 1982, and June 22, 1983. "Once you begin": Berry, *Hidden Wound*, 5. "We all have roots . . . powerful things": MKHP to author, February 19, 1978. On Stribling's *The Forge*, see Storace, "Look Away," 293–94. "An encyclopedia": Quoted in Pierpont, "Critic at Large," 87–88; and Haskell, *Frankly, My Dear*, 23–24. "No story takes": Pierpont, "Critic at Large," 88. I am grateful to Kathleen Marcaccio and her fellow Windies for allowing me to spend a weekend with them in and around Atlanta in the summer of 2016. "Love, Identification . . . so thoroughly captivated": Haskell, *Frankly, My Dear*, xiii, 17. On Margaret Mitchell's relationship with Benjamin Mays and her contributions to Morehouse College and Fulton DeKalb Hospital, see Nix and Bohan, "Color Line"; and Dahleen Glanton, "Of Race and a Southern Novel," *Chicago Tribune*, March 31, 2002. "No black man or woman": Pat Conroy, preface to Mitchell, *Gone with the Wind*, 17. In 2010 former Atlanta mayor Andrew Young produced a documentary film, *Change in the Wind*, about Margaret Mitchell's secret relationship with Morehouse College President Benjamin Mays; see also "Andrew Young Presents." On David Scarlett's involvement with the Freedmen's school and church, see Freedmen Act Agent Records, National Archives, including the letter from David C. Scarlett to Lieutenant [Douglas] Risley, October 29, 1868; my gratitude to Michael McDonald for emailing me these documents on September 28, 2011. David Scarlett seems to have donated the school to the Black community in Camden County (Spring Bluff) on November 1, 1868, "to hold and to have this same unto said trustees and their successors in trust for the full term of ninety-nine (99) years" (Freedmen Act Agent Records, National Archives). The John Parland Estate papers note that David C. Scarlett went with his brother FDS to Savannah in November 1844 to retrieve "2 runaway negroes" (PP). Evidence that David C. Scarlett attended Georgia's 1865 Constitutional Convention comes from *Journal of the Proceedings*, in GA. A record of David C. Scarlett's activity with the Emanuel Methodist Church in Brunswick appears in Rev. J. D. Snyder, "History of Emanuel Methodist Church," circa 1920, Emanual Church Archive, Brunswick GA. "Love and affection": Fields, "Camden County."

14. MATILDA

"Land poor": Barr, "Scarletts." Information on the century-long dissolution of Scarlett land in Glynn County comes from this Barr article as well as "Completion of Highway"; B. N. Nightingale, Affidavit, May 6, 1981 (a copy of which is in Scarlett-Tison Family Collection, GHS); Clarke Adickes, Memoranda to Scarlett Cousins, September 20 and 28, 2000, SA; Thomas E. Dennard Jr. to heirs of the Pauline Scarlett Estate, May 13, 1983, SA; and MKHP to Scarlett Stainton, January 8, 1984, Scarlett-Tison Family Collection, GHS. When Colonel's Island was returned to the Scarletts (as heirs of John Parland) in 1867, the family quickly sold seventy-six acres to a pair of Brunswick businessmen on the condition they establish a business on the island within three years; it seems the two men, Carl Epping and Henry A. Wayne, were lumbermen (Singleton, "Report," 298, citing Glynn County Records 1859–69, 516–18, and Glynn County Records 1875–89, 173, 192, 234, 261; see also Rock and Philips, *Data Recovery Excavations*, 429; and Jackson, "Old Railroad." "Hopeless": Guardianship Agreement, Glynn County GA, PP, December 7, 1897). Both FAP and JAPK attended Georgia's elite Montpelier Institute, south of Atlanta, one of the first schools in the state to admit girls (PP, ca. 1847). "It's crucial" and "For however": Neiman, *Learning from the Germans*, 129, 34. For her more recent views on Germany's relationship to the past, see Susan Neiman, "Historical Reckoning Gone Haywire," *New York Review of Books*, October 19, 2023; and Neiman, "Germany on Edge," *New York Review of Books*, November 3, 2023. My profound thanks to Susan Neiman for alerting me to these essays and to her evolving views. On the Central State Hospital in Milledgeville, see Doug Monroe, "Asylum: Inside Central State Hospital, Once the World's Largest Mental Institution," *Atlanta*, February 18, 2015. For JP's wealth at the time of his death, 1836, see Rock and Philips, *Data Recovery Excavations*, 19, citing Glynn County Wills, Inventory and Appraisements Books D, 352. Background on Matilda and King Hippard comes from the 1880 U.S. census, image 0122, roll 149, Family History Film 11254148, Brunswick, Glynn County GA, 60C. Information on Matilda and King's offspring comes from U.S. census records, Georgia, Glynn, Brunswick, 057. On King Hippard opening a Freedmen's Bank account for his daughter Mary Maxwell, see "U.S. Freedmen's Bank Records." Information on King Hippard's holdings in 1880 comes from "Selected U.S. Federal Census." Background on Columbus Hippard comes from Amy Hedrick's glynngen.com, with links to "Coastal Families 2"; Amy Hedrick, emails to author, February 27, 2011, and March 3, 2011; author conversation with Amy Hedrick, May 20, 2015. For information on African Americans in the U.S. military during and after the Civil War, see Cook-Bell, *Claiming Freedom*, 30; and Reidy, "Black Men." On Madison Scarlett's military service, see "Madison Scarlet [*sic*]." Madison Scarlett joined the navy in 1863, at age twenty, and helped patrol the waters around Brunswick as a "3rd Class Boy" on the USS *Fernandina*. On the contraband "Robert," who fled FMS's property at Oak Grove during the war, see *Daily Chronicle and Sentinel*, July 7, 1862, http://www.glynngen.com/~afam/articles.htm. According to his death certificate, Madison Scarlett died on September 9, 1923; he was seventy-three years old, which would mean he was born circa 1849 or 1850. (Madison Scarlett death certificate, Georgia State Board of Health, Bureau of Vital Statistics, Glynn County, sent to me by Ed Wood, December 1, 2010). Information on Madison and Julia Tison Scarlett comes from Ed Wood, emails to author, December 1 and 7, 2010, and January 26, 2011; and author conversation with Ed Wood, November 19, 2014. My description of Bethel plantation comes from "Garden at Bethel, Tison Plantation about 1870, as Described by Annie Belle Scarlett Hilsman," Scarlett-Tison Family Collection, GHS. The story of Alec Massie saving Bethel from destruction by fire comes from an unidentified typescript on Alec Massie in Scarlett-Tison Family Collection, GHS. "Refused to quit": Knight, *Georgia's Landmarks*, Scarlett-Tison Family Collection, GHS. Background on Lucian Lamar Knight comes from Knight, "Lucian Lamar Knight." John Mason Berrien Tison's bequests are found in his will, dated May 20, 1882 ("Will Book G").

15. SONGS

"Unusually strong": "Hilsman-Pettigrew Wedding Yesterday," undated clipping in SA. Background on RLP's military service and business activities in Haiti comes from Pettigrew, *Story of Fort Liberty*; and Robert Leslie Pettigrew Jr., "Chronology of RLP Jr. Life," unpublished manuscript, ca. 2006, Scarlett-Tison Family Collection, GHS. "Vicious industry," "of magnetic personality," "iron heel," "to a backward world," "The feat has," and "second independent nation": Pettigrew, *Story of Fort Liberty*, 19, 60, 82–83, 65, 58. Background on the U.S. occupation of Haiti (from 1915 to 1934) comes from Laurence Dubois and Deborah Jenson, "Haiti Can Be Rich Again," *New York Times*, January 8, 2021. The RLP scrapbook is part of Scarlett-Tison Family Collection, GHS. My grandparents also hired Lydia and Maxfield Parrish's daughter Jean to teach my mother and her siblings in Haiti. "These primitive songs . . . its beauty" and "the opportunity": Parrish, *Slave Songs*, x, 9, vi. "Juba dis": RLP Jr. to author, October 17, 2016. "I seem to have . . . an infant": MKHP to author, January 23, 1982. "For good measure" and "a letter from Dauphin": Parrish, *Slave Songs*, 32–33. Parrish's sings eventually gave rise to the Georgia Sea Island Singers, whom Alan Lomax would record; the group still exists. "The resources": Morrison, *Origin of Others*, 35–36. "We ole 'uns": Glymph, *House of Bondage*, 13, quoting Ann Parker, *North Carolina Narratives*, vol. 15, pt. 2, p. 157. From 1936 to 1938, the federal government conducted a massive program to collect the histories of formerly enslaved African Americans. Undertaken by the Federal Writers' Project of the Works Progress Administration, the program is commonly known as the WPA Slave Narrative Collection. It took place in seventeen states and resulted in more than two thousand pages of testimony notable for their vividness of detail, despite a deeply flawed approach to the program, with interviewers being almost exclusively whites under directions to produce supposedly phonetic transcriptions. "That it is unwise" and "were barbarians": Parrish, *Slave Songs*, 20–22. "I don't know of any": Lester Monts, email to author, December 30, 2019. Parrish writes with admiration of Kemble on page 23 of *Slave Songs*. Information on the Great Migration is taken primarily from Wilkerson, *Warmth of Other Suns*. On annual KKK parades in Brunswick, see Brundage, *Lynching*, 22–23; and *Brunswick News*, October 29, 1926, http://www.glynngen.com/newspapers/glynn/bwknews.htm. "Prohibit even the most casual" and "Not unlike European": Wilkerson, *Warmth of Other Suns*, 40, 38. The story of the woman who boiled flour sacks is from Wilkerson, *Warmth of Other Suns*, 100. "The Negro farm hand": Wilkerson, *Warmth of Other Suns*, 54. "The master's grand-nephew": W. E. B. Du Bois, quoted in Blight, *Race and Reunion*, 251–53. "The fact that . . . saying it": Cone, *Spirituals and the Blues*, 129–30. Photographs of MKHP with nurses are in Scarlett-Tison Family Collection, GHS.

16. JUSTICE

"Doomed by my," "It was one of those," and "racial contrivances": Berry, *Hidden Wound*, 63, 45–47. "They loved us . . . never a snake": MKHP to author, June 22, 1983. "Your grandmother . . . spoke her mind": RLP Jr. to author, September 19, 2016. "Negro burned" and "Lake City": *Brunswick Times-Call*, November 17, 1900, 1, https://chroniclingamerica.loc.gov/lccn/sn90052411/1900-11-17/ed-1/seq-1/; and November 28, 1900, 1, https://chroniclingamerica.loc.gov/lccn/sn90052411/1900-11-28/ed-1/seq-1/. On the implication of African American criminality, see Mathews, *Altar of Lynching*, 48. "Let the good work": quoted in Brundage, *Lynching*, 198. "The Same Old": *Brunswick Times-Call*, November 17, 1900, 1, https://chroniclingamerica.loc.gov/lccn/sn90052411/1900-11-17/ed-1/seq-1/. "My son can't learn": Wilkerson, *Warmth of Other Suns*, 39. On Coleman Blease, see "Coleman Livingston Blease"; and "Blease, Coleman Livingston." As governor, Blease pledged to pardon any lyncher convicted by a jury. On Margaret Mitchell's response to 1906 Atlanta violence, see Pierpont, "Critic at Large," 96; Haskell, *Frankly, My Dear*, 103; and Storace, "Look Away," 271–72, citing Pyron, *Southern Daughter*, 31. "Concerted uprising": Mitchell, *Gone with the Wind*, 695. On the relative calm in postwar coastal Georgia, see Armstrong, "Task Labor"; Brundage, *Lynching*; and Duncan, *Freedom's Shore*. "Racial terror lynchings": "Lynching in America." In both Glynn and McIntosh Counties, Blacks owned around 5 percent of all land—more than they did in other parts of Georgia (C. Morgan, "Unfortunate Propensity," 210). "Agitation on the race question": *Savannah Morning News*, [1906?], quoted in Brundage, *Lynching*, 131. "Cultivate the best": *Savannah Morning News*, December 1889, quoted in Brundage, *Lynching*, 192. "I'm just so proud": author to MKHP, September 5, 1987. "Georgia Blood . . . but it is there": MKHP to author, September 15, 1987. On Mason Scarlett's expedition to Darien and the so-called Darien Insurrection involving the case of Henry Delegale, see Brundage, *Lynching*; Mathews, *Altar of Lynching*, 241–43; and *Atlanta Constitution*, August 30, 1899, 3; September 3, 1899, 4; September 6, 1899, 3; September 16, 1899, 3. "He was the drinker": MKHP to RLP Jr., March 3, 1984, Scarlett-Tison Family Collection, GHS. "I know that you and Papa": Mason Scarlett to VTS, February 1, 1897, Scarlett-Tison Family Collection, GHS. "In his early life": *Brunswick News*, October 16, 1932, 8, http://www.glynngen.com/newspapers/obits/S.htm. "The things that influenced": Wright, *Black Boy*, 190, quoted in Brundage, *Lynching*, 139. "Officers Lamb and Scarlett": "ATTEMPTED MURDER—Dangerous Negro's Rash Act Yesterday," *Brunswick Times-Call*, March 5, 1899, 1, http://www.glynngen.com/afam/articles.htm. "The most penetrating eyes": MKHP to RLP Jr., March 3, 1984, Scarlett-Tison Family Collection, GHS. "The drop was sprung": This and other details about Griffin's execution come from *Atlanta Constitution*, June 15, 1901, 5, http://www.glynngen.com/~afam/articles.htm. I've been unable to verify whether Griffin's execution was, in fact, the first legal hanging in Brunswick in seventy years. Donald Mathews notes that, although Georgia outlawed public executions in 1893, it did not stop large crowds from attending extralegal lynchings (Mathews, *Altar of Lynching*, 120; Trotti, "Scaffold's Revival," 202).

17. *STATE V. FRICIE GRIFFIN*

Note: the name "Fricie" appears interchangeably with "Tricy" in the press, but because "Fricie" is the name cited in the official trial transcripts, I have primarily used that name in my account of Griffin's ordeal. "Tricy Griffin Confession": *Savannah Morning News*, June 13, 1901; all quotes from Griffin's statement come from this source. The online run of the *Brunswick Times-Call* for 1900 and 1901 is available at https://chroniclingamerica.loc.gov. "If you searched": author conversation with Karen Branan, February 11, 2020. My thanks go to Karen Branan for her own excellent book, *Family Tree*; for sharing her many insights into Fricie Griffin's story; and for advising me to get the transcripts of the trial and the Georgia Supreme Court appeal. Details from the transcript of Fricie Griffin's trial in the Glynn County Superior Court come from "The State vs. Fricie Griffin. Brief of Evidence, Recorded in Vol. 1 Testimony Felony Cases, Page 72," in Glynn County Courthouse (Griffin Trial). Details from Griffin's appeal to the Georgia Supreme Court come from *Fricie Griffin v. State*, Georgia Supreme Court Case File A-24559.pdf (Griffin Appeal); my thanks to Don Evans for procuring the latter for me from GA. "Jury Was Out . . . Penalty": *Brunswick Times-Call*, December 15, 1900, 1. "Tricy Griffin has been identified": *Brunswick Times-Call*, November 1, 1900. Press accounts alternately spell Marion Lattimore's surname "Latimer." As with Fricie Griffin's name, I am using the spelling (Lattimore) that appears in the trial transcripts. "Popular," "well known and universally liked," and "defenseless": *Brunswick Times-Call*, October 9, 1900, 1. An African American woman who saw the posse head off in pursuit of Lattimore's killer on the night of October 7, 1900, would recall, "I said there must be something happened when all those white folks are riding so" (Griffin Trial). "Nothing could be done" : *Brunswick Times-Call*, October 9, 1900, 1. "The murderer's trail . . . great odds against him": *Brunswick Times-Call*, October 30, 1900, 1. On Griffin's first night in jail, the sheriff slept in the building to prevent a lynching. "Fat reward": *Brunswick Times-Call*, October 10, 1900, 2. "Is proven": *Brunswick Times-Call*, October 30, 1900, 1. "Handsome": Holt to JFMS, Scarlett-Tison Family Collection, GHS. Griffin's portrait appeared on the front page of the June 15, 1901, edition of the *Brunswick Times-Call*. Informed that Griffin had asked to have his picture taken, the *Brunswick Times-Call* had earlier taunted, "Wants His Picture 'Took.' / Anxious to Have His Beauty Struck Before He Dies" (*Brunswick Times-Call*, May 29, 1901, 1); this same article contains the quote from Jailer Rudolph about Griffin's being "the best prisoner he ever had." The death row interview with Griffin appears in the *Brunswick Times-Call*, June 13, 1901, 1. "Very kindly called": this and subsequent quotations from the prosecution come from Griffin Trial. "Theater of the gallows": Trotti, "Scaffold's Revival," 199. On the execution of Black Americans as "crucifixions," see Du Bois, *Souls of Black Folk*; and Mathews, *Altar of Lynching*. "Cut off in the twinkling," "Fricie, God has forgiven . . . beyond the skies," and "Though I walk . . . ready to die": *Brunswick Times-Call*, June 15, 1901, 1. "You don't contend": Griffin Appeal. Harry Ward's Minstrels played Brunswick's Grand Opera House on December 14, 1901, the day before the verdict was rendered in Griffin's superior court trial; the *Times-Call* published a glowing review of the minstrel show in the same edition that announced Griffin's guilty verdict (*Brunswick Times-Call*, December 15, 1900, 1, 4). "Griffin was then led" and "Had Griffin been caught": *Brunswick Times-Call*, June 15, 1901, 1, 2. "Stare them in the face": *Brunswick Times-Call*, December 15, 1900, 4. Citing a study on death penalty cases, legal justice advocate and EJI founder Bryan Stevenson notes that "the race of the victim is the greatest predictor of who gets the death penalty in the United States" (Stevenson, *Just Mercy*, 142).

18. MR. SCARLETT

Accusations against Stanton Scarlett from Asbell and Dart appear in Griffin Trial. Bella Law's testimony is documented in both Griffin Trial and Griffin Appeal. In the Griffin trial transcript that went to the Supreme Court—which for the most part replicates the Superior Court transcript—I found two words tellingly X-ed out: "bosom" and "fucked" (Griffin Appeal). "I of course knew": Harwell, *Letters*, 78. Throughout much of American history, Isabel Wilkerson writes in *Caste*, "upper-caste men, the people who wrote the laws, kept full and flagrant access to lower-caste women, whatever their age or marital status" (112). "With our grandmother": MKHP to Mrs. Bailey, Bryan-Lang Historical Library, Woodbine GA, November 27, 1980. "What a wonderful combination": Annie Lee Tison Wright to Meta Scarlett, October 2, 1921, SA. On Stanton Scarlett's death, see "George Stanton Scarlett Jr." Donald Mathews notes that it was typical for men en route to the gallows to speak "on themes appropriate to the day," including clichés such as "bad women and whiskey," in what was effectively a Christian morality play (*Altar of Lynching*, 121–22). "I killed Conductor Latimer . . . at once": *Savannah Morning News*, June 13, 1901.

AFTER

Among multiple sources on Ahmaud Arbery's murder, see especially Rick Rojas, Richard Fausset, and Serge F. Kovaleski, "Georgia Killing Puts Spotlight on a Police Force's Troubled History," *New York Times*, May 9, 2020; George Yancy, "Ahmaud Arbery and the Ghosts of Lynchings Past," *New York Times*, May 12, 2020; and Klibanoff, "Ahmaud Arbery." "Meditation": Jim Barger, "Ahmaud Arbery Holds Us Accountable," *Bitter Southerner*, May 14, 2020. "Each time it begins" and "Because white men can't": Rankine, *Citizen*, 107, 135. My deep thanks to Claudia Rankine for allowing me to quote from *Citizen* in the final chapter of *Scarlett*; © 2014 by Claudia Rankine. Reprinted with the permission of the author. All rights reserved. "We have uniformed": Governor's Incoming Correspondence, Civil War, Governor Joseph E. Brown of Georgia, Morrow: Georgia State Archives. Ahmaud Arbery was a descendant of the extraordinary Geechee leader Bilali Muhammed, born in Africa circa 1770 and brought to Georgia on a slave ship circa 1802 (Klibanoff, "Ahmaud Arbery"). The unveiling of the new marker on Butler Island took place on March 3, 2019; during the ceremony one of the African American women called out as she poured libations, "Fanny Kemble, our white Harriet Tubman." "Distinguishable educability capabilities": quoted in Emanuel, *Elbert Parr Tuttle*, 269–70. "People around . . . made them feel better": Barger, "Ahmaud Arbery." "Mental and moral prison": Clinton, *Fanny Kemble's Journals*, 91–92. "A glorious apartment": Van Doren, *Travels*. "We are just as good and bad": Whitman, *Leaves of Grass*, 156.

BIBLIOGRAPHY

Albanese, Anthony Gerald. *The Plantation as a School: The Sea-Islands of Georgia and South Carolina, a Test Case, 1800–1860*. PhD diss., Rutgers University, 1970.

"Andrew Young Presents." Andrew Young. Accessed October 3, 2019. http://andrewyoungpresents.blogspot.com/.

"Appointments of U.S. Postmasters, 1832–1971." Ancestry.com. Accessed June 5, 2019. https://search.ancestry.com/cgi-bin/sse.dll?indiv=1&dbid=1932&h=1744092&tid=&pid=&usepub=true&_phsrc=Tgv28&_phstart=successSource.

Armstrong, Thomas F. "From Task Labor to Free Labor: The Transition along Georgia's Rice Coast, 1820–1880." *Georgia Historical Quarterly* 64, no. 4 (Winter 1980): 432–47.

Bailey, Anne C. *The Weeping Time: Memory and the Largest Slave Auction in American History*. New York: Cambridge University Press, 2017.

Baptist, Edward E. *The Half Has Never Been Told: Slavery and the Making of American Capitalism*. New York: Basic Books, 2014.

Bell, Malcolm, Jr. *Major Butler's Legacy: Five Generations of a Slaveholding Family*. Athens: University of Georgia Press, 1987.

Berlin, Ira. *Many Thousands Gone: The First Two Centuries of Slavery in North America*. Cambridge ma: Belknap, 1998.

Berry, Wendell. *The Hidden Wound*. Boston: Houghton Mifflin, 1970.

Blackmon, Douglas A. *Slavery by Another Name: The Re-enslavement of Black Americans from the Civil War to World War II*. New York: Anchor Books, 2008.

Blake, Tom. "Large Slaveholder Project of 1860 and African American Surname Matches from 1870." RootsWeb. Accessed March 20, 2015. http://freepages.genealogy.rootsweb.ancestry.com/~ajac/.

"Blease, Coleman Livingston." *South Carolina Encyclopedia*. Accessed January 25, 2020. https://www.scencyclopedia.org/sce/entries/blease-coleman-livingston/.

Blight, David W. *Race and Reunion: The Civil War in American Memory*. Cambridge MA: Belknap, 2002.

Branan, Karen. *The Family Tree: A Lynching in Georgia, a Legacy of Secrets, and My Search for the Truth*. New York: Atria Books, 2017.

Brundage, W. Fitzhugh. *Lynching in the New South: Georgia and Virginia, 1880–1930*. Urbana: University of Illinois Press, 1993.

Bullard, Mary Ricketson. *Robert Stafford of Cumberland Island: Growth of a Planter*. Athens: University of Georgia Press, 1995.

Calonius, Eric. *The Wanderer: The Last American Slave Ship and the Conspiracy That Set Its Sails*. New York: St. Martin's Griffin, 2008.

Campbell, J. H. "Reminiscences of the McDonald and Campbell Families." Unpublished manuscript, 1932.

"Capt Hamilton Couper." Find a Grave. Accessed December 20, 2018. https://www.findagrave.com/memorial/28379425/hamilton-couper.

Cate, Margaret Davis. *Our Todays and Yesterdays: A Story of Brunswick and the Coastal Islands*. Brunswick GA: Glover Brothers, 1926.

Change in the Wind. Mays House Museum. Accessed June 20, 2016. http://www.mayshousemuseum.org/Page3.htm.

Chesnut, Mary Boykin. *Mary Chesnut's Diary*. 1905. Reprint, New York: Penguin, 2011.

Clinton, Catherine. *Fanny Kemble's Civil Wars: The Story of America's Most Unlikely Abolitionist*. New York: Simon and Schuster, 2000.

———, ed. *Fanny Kemble's Journals*. Cambridge MA: Harvard University Press, 2000.

"Coastal Families 2." RootsWeb. Accessed September 4, 2011. http://wc.rootsweb.ancestry.com/cgi-bin/igm.cgi?op=show&db=glynn2&recno=1591.

Cobb, James C. *Georgia Odyssey: A Short History of the State*. 2nd ed. Athens: University of Georgia Press, 2008.

"Coleman Livingston Blease." *Wikipedia*. Accessed November 23, 2020. https://en.wikipedia.org/wiki/Coleman_Livingston_Blease.

Cone, James H. *The Spirituals and the Blues: An Interpretation*. 1972. Reprint, Maryknoll NY: Orbis Books, 1991.

Cook-Bell, Karen. *Claiming Freedom: Race, Kinship and Land in Nineteenth-Century Georgia*. Columbia: University of South Carolina Press, 2018.

Cooper, Abigail. "Midwives of Invention: Black Healers and Spiritual Rebirth in Civil War Refugee Camps." Paper presented at the American Historical Association, Atlanta, 2016.

Darling, Katie. "Texas Narratives." *Unchained Memories: Readings from the Slave Narratives*. Vol. 16. New York: HBO Video. 2003.

Davis, Jingle. *Island Time: An Illustrated History of St. Simons Island, Georgia*. Athens: University of Georgia Press, 2013.

Delbanco, Andrew. *The War before the War: Fugitive Slaves and the Struggle for America's Soul from the Revolution to the Civil War*. New York: Penguin, 2018.

Douglass, Frederick. *My Bondage and My Freedom*. 1866. Reprint, New York: Penguin, 2003.

———. *Narrative of the Life of Frederick Douglass, an American Slave*. 1845. Reprint, New York: Vintage, 2018.

Du Bois, W. E. B. "The Negro Landholder of Georgia." *Bulletin of the United States Department of Labor* 6, no. 35 (1901): 647–48.

———. *The Souls of Black Folk*. 1903. Reprint, New York: Skyhorse, 2019.

Duncan, Russell. *Freedom's Shore: Tunis Campbell and the Georgia Freedmen*. Athens: University of Georgia Press, 1986.

Edwards, Anne. *Road to Tara: The Life of Margaret Mitchell*. Lanham MD: Taylor Trade, 1983.

Emanuel, Anne. *Elbert Parr Tuttle: Chief Jurist of the Civil Rights Revolution*. Athens: University of Georgia Press, 2011.

Farrant, Don. *Julian Scarlett: Strange Disappearance of Cyclops*. Brunswick GA: Harbor Sound, 1996.

Faust, Drew Gilpin. "Clutching the Chains That Bind." *Southern Culture* 5, no. 1 (Spring 1999) 6–20.

———. *Mothers of Invention: Women of the Slaveholding South in the American Civil War*. Chapel Hill: University of North Carolina Press, 2004.

———. *This Republic of Suffering: Death and the American Civil War*. New York: Knopf, 2008.

Fiedler, Leslie. *What Was Literature? Class, Culture, and Mass Society*. New York: Simon and Schuster, 1982.

Fields, Tara D. "Camden County, Georgia: Slave Deed Abstracts, 2004–2008." Bryan-Lang Archives and Foundation. Accessed May 27, 2012. https://sites.google.com/view/bryan-lang-foundation/research-tools/camden-county-ga-slave-abstracts.

Foner, Eric. *Reconstruction: America's Unfinished Revolution, 1836–1877*. New York: HarperCollins, 1988.

Fox-Genovese, Elizabeth. *Within the Plantation Household: Black and White Women of the Old South*. Chapel Hill: University of North Carolina Press, 1988.

Gates, Henry Louis, Jr. "The Truth behind '40 Acres and a Mule,'" *The African Americans: Many Rivers to Cross*. Accessed August 7, 2015. http://www.pbs.org/wnet/african-americans-many-rivers-to-cross/history/the-truth-behind-40-acres-and-a-mule/.

"George Stanton Scarlett Jr." Find a Grave. Accessed November 23, 2020. https://www.findagrave.com/memorial/62583006/george-stanton-scarlett.

Glymph, Thavolia. *Out of the House of Bondage*. Cambridge: Cambridge University Press: 2008.

"Glynn County Ga Archives Wills." Glynn County Archives. Accessed November 14, 2010. http://files.usgwarchives.net/ga/glynn/wills/scarlett297gwl.txt.

Gorra, Michael. *The Saddest Words: William Faulkner's Civil War*. New York: Liveright, 2020.

Green, Victor H. *The Negro Motorist Green Book*. New York: Green, 1949.

Gresham, Thomas H., and Ted O. Brooke. *Descendant Identification and Notification Plan for the John Parland Gravesite, Colonels Island, Glynn County, Georgia*. Athens GA: Southeastern Archeological Services, 2000.

Hannah-Jones, Nikole. Speech at the University of Michigan, Ann Arbor, September 22, 2021.

Haskell, Molly. *Frankly, My Dear: "Gone with the Wind" Revisited*. New Haven CT: Yale University Press, 2009.

Hartman, Saidiya. *Lose Your Mother: A Journey along the Atlantic Slave Route*. New York: Farrar, Straus and Giroux, 2008.

Harwell, Richard, ed. *Margaret Mitchell's "Gone with the Wind" Letters, 1936–1949*. New York: Macmillan, 1976.

Hedrick, Amy. "Parland." Accessed September 10, 2016. www.glynngen.com/cemetery/glynn/parland.htm.

Higginson, Thomas Wentworth. *Army Life in a Black Regiment*. East Lansing MI: Michigan State University Press, 1960.

Huxford, Folks. *Pioneers of Wiregrass Georgia: Sketch List*. Huxford Genealogical Society. Vol. 2. 2002. https://huxford.com/?page_id=382.

Jacobs, Harriet. *Incidents in the Life of a Slave Girl: Written by Herself*. Edited by Jean Fagan Yellin. Cambridge MA: Harvard University Press, 1987.

James, Henry. "Fanny Kemble." In *Essays in London and Elsewhere*. New York: Harper, 1893.

Jones-Rogers, Stephanie E. *They Were Her Property: White Women as Slave Owners in the American South*. New Haven CT: Yale University Press, 2019.

Jordan, Jim. *The Slave-Trader's Letter-Book: Charles Lamar, the Wanderer, and Other Tales of the African Slave Trade*. Athens: University of Georgia Press, 2018.

Journal of the Proceedings of the Convention of the People of Georgia, Held in Milledgeville in October and November 1865: Together with the Ordinances and Resolutions Adopted. Milledgeville GA: Orme and Son, 1865.

Kemble, Frances Anne. *Journal of a Residence on a Georgian Plantation in 1838–1839*. Edited by John A. Scott. Athens: University of Georgia Press, 1984.

Kinsey, Mollie. *Georgia Narratives*. Federal Writers' Project. Vol. 4. www.loc.gov/resource/mesn.042/?st=gallery.

Klibanoff, Hank. "Ahmaud Arbery." *Buried Truths*. Podcast. 2020. www.wabe.org/shows/buried-truths/.

Knight, Lydia F. "Lucian Lamar Knight, 1868–1933." *New Georgia Encyclopedia*. Accessed November 23, 2020. https://www.georgiaencyclopedia.org/articles/arts-culture/lucian-lamar-knight-1868-1933.

Levine, Bruce. *The Fall of the House of Dixie: The Civil War and the Social Revolution That Transformed the South*. New York: Random House, 2013.

Link, William A. "Review of *The Weeping Time*." *Georgia Historical Quarterly* 102, no. 2 (2018): 186.

Lowe, Tony B. "'That Hogansville Affair': The Failed Assassination of the African American Postmaster Isaiah H. Lofton." *Georgia Historical Quarterly* 103, no. 1 (2019): 31–56.

"Lynching in America." Equal Justice Initiative. Accessed January 29, 2020. https://lynchinginamerica.eji.org/explore/georgia.

"Madison Scarlet [*sic*]." *Sailor Detail*. National Park Service. Accessed November 12, 2019. www.nps.gov/civilwar/search-sailors-detail.htm?sailorId=sca0005.

Magee, Judith. *The Art and Science of William Bartram*. University Park: Pennsylvania State University Press; London: Natural History Museum, 2007.

Mathews, Donald G. *At the Altar of Lynching: Burning Sam Hose in the American South*. New York: Cambridge University Press, 2018.

Mitchell, Margaret. "Georgia Romances That Live in History." *Atlanta Journal*, May 13, 1923.

———. *Gone with the Wind*. 1936. Reprint, New York: Scribner, 2011.

Mohr, Clarence L. *On the Threshold of Freedom: Masters and Slaves in Civil War Georgia*. Baton Rouge: Louisiana State University Press, 2001.

Morgan, Chad. "'An Unfortunate Propensity for Attempting to Manage Business': The Butler Family of Georgia and the Origins of the Lost Cause." *Georgia Historical Quarterly* 104, no. 3 (2020): 206–43.

Morgan, Philip, ed. *African American Life in the Georgia Low Country: The Atlantic World and the Gullah Geechee*. Athens: University of Georgia Press, 2010.

Morrison, Toni. *The Origin of Others*. Cambridge MA: Harvard University Press, 2017.

Myers, Robert Manson, ed. *The Children of Pride: A True Story of Georgia and the Civil War*. New Haven CT: Yale University Press, 1972.

Neiman, Susan. *Learning from the Germans: Race and the Memory of Evil*. New York: Farrar, Straus and Giroux, 2019.

Nix, Jearl, and Chara Haeussler Bohan. "Reaching across the Color Line: Margaret Mitchell and Benjamin Mays, an Uncommon Friendship." *Social Education* 77, no. 3 (2013): 127–31.

Northrup, Solomon. *Twelve Years a Slave*. 1853. Reprint, Mineola NY: Dover, 1970.

O'Donovan, Susan Eva. *Becoming Free in the Cotton South*. Cambridge MA: Harvard University Press, 2010.

Olmsted, Frederick Law. *The Cotton Kingdom: A Traveller's Observations on Cotton and Slavery in the American Slave States*. Edited by Arthur M. Schlesinger. New York: Knopf, 1953.

Parker, Ann. *North Carolina Narratives*. In Glymph, *House of Bondage*, 15:13.

Parland, John. "Inventories and Appraisements." Glynn County Probate Court. 1836. http://www.glynngen.com/slaverec/parland_jno.htm.

Parrish, Lydia. *Slave Songs of the Georgia Sea Islands*. New York: Creative Age, 1942.

Penningroth, Dylan. *The Claims of Kinfolk: African American Property and Community in the Nineteenth-Century South*. Chapel Hill: University of North Carolina Press, 2004.

Pettigrew, Robert Leslie. *The Story of Fort Liberty and the Dauphin Plantation*. Richmond VA: Cavalier, 1958

Phillips, Ulrich B., ed. *Plantation and Frontier Documents: 1649–1862*. Cleveland: Clark, 1909.

Pierpont, Claudia Roth. "A Critic at Large: A Study in Scarlett." *New Yorker*, August 31, 1992, 87–103.

Pyron, Darden Asbury. *Southern Daughter: The Life of Margaret Mitchell*. Oxford: Oxford University Press, 1991.

Rankine, Claudia. *Citizen: An American Lyric*. Minneapolis: Graywolf, 2014.

Rawick, George P., ed. *The American Slave: A Composite Autobiography*. 19 vols. Westport CT: Greenwood, 1972.

Redfearn, Daniel Huntley. *Alexander McDonald of New Inverness, Georgia, and His Descendants*. Miami: Literary Licensing, 1954.

Reidy, Joseph P. "Black Men in Navy Blue during the Civil War." *Prologue Magazine* 33, no. 3 (Fall 2001). https://www.archives.gov/publications/prologue/2001/fall/black-sailors-1.html.

Reiss, Benjamin. *Wild Nights: How Taming Sleep Created Our Restless World*. New York: Basic Books, 2017.

Rock, Carolyn, and Charles L. Philips Jr. *Phase III Data Recovery Excavations at the Colonel's Island Slave Settlement (9GN173)*. Charleston SC: Brockington Associates, 2016.

"Savannah, Georgia Inward Coastwise Slave Manifests, 1811–60." Digital Library of Georgia Accessed April 9, 2011. http://search.ancestry.com

/Browse/view.aspx?dbid=1714&iid=31888_1120704930_0005-00048&pid=11591&email.

Schützenberger, Anne Ancelin. *The Ancestor Syndrome: Transgenerational Psychotherapy and the Hidden Links in the Family Tree*. Translated by Anne Trager. New York: Routledge, 1998.

Scott, John A. "Editor's Introduction." In Kemble, *Journal of a Residence*, ix–lxi.

———. "Foreword to the Brown Thrasher Edition." In Kemble, *Journal of a Residence*, xi–viii.

"Selected U.S. Federal Census Non-population Schedules, 1850–80." Ancestry.com. Accessed April 11, 2016. http://search.ancestry.com/iexec?htx=View&r=an&dbid=1276&iid=32668_236693-00196&fn=F+D&ln=Scarlett&st=r&ssrc=&pid=5430100.

Singleton, Theresa. "The Archaeology of Afro-American Slavery in Coastal Georgia: A Regional Perception of Slave Household and Community Patterns." PhD diss., University of Florida, 1980.

———. "Report on the Historic Excavations, Colonel's Island, Glynn County, Georgia." In Steinen, *Cultural Evolution and Environment*, 69–133.

Stampp, Kenneth. *The Peculiar Institution: Slavery in the Antebellum South*. 1956. Reprint, New York: Vintage, 1989.

Steinen, Karl T., ed. *The Cultural Evolution and Environment of Colonels Island, Georgia*. Carrollton GA: West Georgia College, 1978.

Stevenson, Bryan. "Equal Justice Initiative." Accessed March 2, 2025. www.eji.org.

———. *Just Mercy: A Story of Justice and Redemption*. New York: Spiegel and Grau, 2014.

Storace, Patricia. "Look Away, Dixie Land." In *Best American Essays, 1992*, edited by Susan Sontag, 268–96. New York: Ticknor and Fields, 1992.

Taylor, Susie King. *Reminiscences of My Life in Camp*. Boston: published by the author, 1902.

Tocqueville, Alexis de. *Democracy in America*. New York: Appleton, 1898.

Trotti, Michael A. "The Scaffold's Revival: Race and Public Execution in the South." *Journal of Social History* 45, no. 1 (2011): 195–224.

"U.S. Freedmen's Bank Records, 1865–74." Family Search. Accessed April 9, 2016, https://familysearch.org/ark:/61903/3:1:s3sw-nw89-w1?mode=g&i=481&wc=3mdr-bz4%3a1551794203%2c1551794201%3fcc%3d1417695&cc=1417695.

Van Doren, Mark, ed. *Travels through North and South Carolina, Georgia, East and West Florida, the Cherokee Country, the Extensive Territories of the Muscogulges, or Creek Confederacy, and the Country of the Chactaws*. By William Bartram. 1791. Reprint, New York: Dover, 1955.

Wesley, John. *Thoughts upon Slavery*. London, 1774.

Whitman, Walt. *Leaves of Grass*. 150th anniversary ed. New York: Penguin, 2005.

Wilkerson, Isabel. *Caste: The Origins of Our Discontents*. New York: Random House, 2020.

———. *The Warmth of Other Suns: The Epic Story of America's Great Migration*. New York: Random House, 2010.

"Will Book G." Glynn County Probate Court. Accessed June 28, 2019. www.glynngen.com/court/glynn/will/abstracts1.htm.

Williams, Heather Andrea. *Help Me to Find My People: The African American Search for Family Lost in Slavery*. Johns Hopkins Series in African American History and Culture. Chapel Hill: University of North Carolina Press, 2012.

Wister, Frances Anne. "Butler Place and Fanny Kemble." *Old York Road Historical Society Bulletin* 14 (1950): 10–11.

Wood, Ed, and Benjamin Allen. *Black America Series: Glynn County Georgia*. Charleston SC: Arcadia, 2003.

Wood, Peter H. "Slave Labor Camps in Early America: Overcoming Denial and Discovering the Gulag." In *Inequality in Early America*, edited by Carla Gardina Pestana and Sharon V. Shalinger, 222–38. Hanover NH: University Press of New England, 1999.

Wright, Richard. *Black Boy: A Record of Childhood and Youth*. New York: Harper and Row, 1966.

Young, Jason. *Rituals of Resistance: African Atlantic Religion in Kongo and the Lowcountry Region of Georgia and South Carolina in the Era of Slavery*. Baton Rouge: Louisiana University Press, 2007.

INDEX

Illustrations are indicated by F *with a numeral; all appear following pages 76 and 124*